THE GREY COAT HOSPITAL
WESTMINSTER

Nobody Said It Would Be Easy
by Dr Lisl Klein

Dr Lisl Klein 1928-2015

Student of The Grey Coat Hospital

January 1939 – July 1946

NOBODY SAID IT WOULD BE EASY

By the same author

Multiproducts Ltd. A case study on the social effects of rationalised production (HMSO, 1964).

A Social Scientist in Industry (Gower Press, 1976).

New Forms of Work Organisation (Cambridge University Press, 1976).

Working with Organisations: papers to celebrate the 80th birthday of Harold Bridger. Editor and author of paper titled 'Inside and outside; a struggle for integration' (Tavistock Institute of Human Relations, 1989).

Putting Social Science to Work: the ground between theory and use explored through case studies in organisations, with Ken Eason (Cambridge University Press, 1991).

Working Across the Gap: the practice of social science in organizations (Karnac Publications, 2005).

The Meaning of Work: papers on work organization and the design of jobs (Karnac Publications, 2008).

NOBODY SAID IT WOULD BE EASY

Lisl Klein

Book Guild Publishing

Sussex, England

First published in Great Britain in 2012 by
The Book Guild Ltd
Pavilion View
19 New Road
Brighton, BN1 1UF

Typesetting in Garamond by
YHT Ltd, London

Printed and bound in Great Britain by
CPI Group (UK) Ltd, Croydon, CR0 4YY

A catalogue record for this book is available from
The British Library.

ISBN 978 1 84624 777 4

Contents

Acknowledgements and an Apology   vii
Map of Czechoslovakia showing the Sudeten-German region   viii
Prologue   ix

BOOK ONE   1

Karlsbad   2
Roots   9
A Family   20
    Udritsch   21
    Neusattl   26
Fanni Blatny   30
The Thirties   38
    Juan-les-Pins   38
    Karlsbad   41
Leaving   47
    Prague   47
    The American connection   51
England   57
Evacuation   66
London   75

BOOK TWO   83

Transitions   84
The Transition to Work   92
Industry   96
    On the fringes of politics   101
Moving into Research   103

CONTENTS

Research on Work Organisation 109
  Widening horizons 115
Research on Industrial Organisation 122
Social Science Adviser in Industry – The Esso Years 126
  The job 130
  Outside the job 132
  The professional environment 136
  More about the job 138

BOOK THREE 143

The Tavistock Years 144
The Work 155
  On making use of the social sciences 155
  On organisation 155
  On how work is organised 161
  On working with groups 171
  More about the use of the social sciences 173
  More about the fringes of politics 174
  Changes 180
  Getting sacked 182

BOOK FOUR 189

The Bayswater Institute 190
The Czech Republic 195
Karlovy Vary 201
  A weekend in Karlovy Vary 210
  A double life 216

APPENDIX 1 From a box of letters 225
APPENDIX 2 Grandfather Wilhelm's notebook 229
APPENDIX 3 Extract from *My Life in Industry* by George Clift 239

Acknowledgements and an Apology

I am grateful to a number of friends and colleagues who have read and commented on drafts of this book: John Adler, Harold Bridger, Celia Davies, Glyn England, Marie Jahoda, Michelle Kass, Carol O'Brien, Stephen Overell, Derek Raffaelli, Sandra Schruijer, Brian Shackel, Sylvia Shimmin, Richard Trehair. Sadly, I can't thank all of them personally – the book has been so long in the making that several of them have in the meantime died.

Some of these friends and readers have pointed out that there is some disjuncture between the 'life' and the 'work' aspects of the book ('. . . as if we have two books under the same cover'). They are right, and I am acutely aware that I haven't managed to deal with this adequately. I can only ask them for their tolerance and to regard this as work-in-progress. But at the age of eighty-four I really do have to let it go.

I am also grateful to my colleagues in the Bayswater Institute, who have put up with the inordinate amount of time I have taken out to do this job. Chris Chism, its administrator, has given innumerable kinds of help, not least that of her friendship. Thank you.

CZECHOSLOVAKIA FROM 1918 TO 1938, SHOWING THE SUDETEN-GERMAN REGION

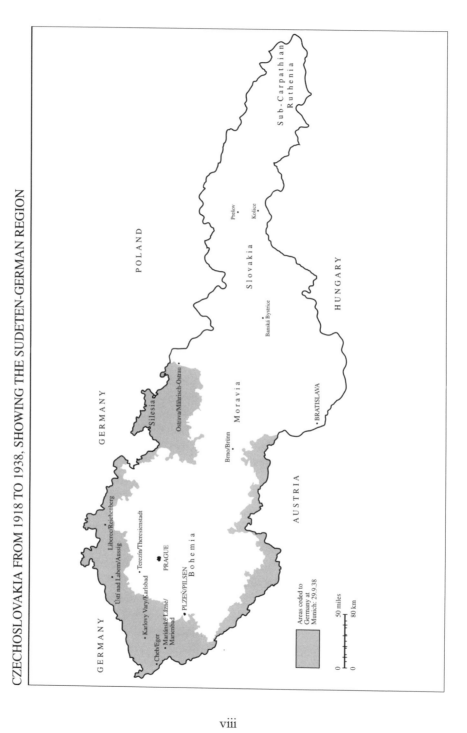

Prologue

Recently I travelled to Prague to give a lecture on the use of the social sciences in industry. I travelled by train, which meant arriving at the Wilson railway station from which my mother and I had left Czechoslovakia some seventy years earlier. I can still see the cluster of relatives seeing us off standing in the dim light of the platform as the train pulled out at nine in the evening. The Pilsen relatives had come to Prague, and even ten-year-old Peter had been allowed to stay up. Now they were still there, ghosts in old-fashioned clothes. Puzzled by what I have been up to in the meantime, and sad that I don't have children. But loving me unconditionally anyway.

BOOK ONE

This memoir has been a long time in the making. It started about fifteen years ago when I discovered a box of family papers with records going back to 1746. Since then the project has been picked up and put down many times. First, on a whim I translated the papers, which were collected by my grandfather around 1910, from their original German; then that merged into putting down some more recent family history; then that, in turn, merged into autobiography, which now takes up most of this volume.

Karlsbad

When I began to write this book, Karlsbaders in England were meeting at each other's funerals. They were drawn there as much by the common experience of Karlsbad – the sense of being part of a privileged club and at the same time sharing an irrecoverable loss – as by thoughts and feelings for the dead. The dead person had been a member of the club; at least now he or she was free from homesickness. In Germany the other exiles, the Sudeten Germans who were expelled by the Czechs after the war, were also homesick and passed this homesickness on to their children. They had reunions, maintained a newspaper, the *Karlsbader Zeitung* (published in Nuremberg), exchanged news of birthdays, anniversaries and deaths, and recalled the joy with which they had welcomed Hitler in 1938. Walking through the foyer of a hotel on his way out to the balcony to address the crowd, Hitler had absent-mindedly shaken someone's hand. The young man swore he would never wash that hand again. 'We wonder if he managed to keep his resolution?' wrote the author coyly – fifty years later! But their homesickness was palpable, and I shared it.

The hot spring at the base of a high rock in a lovely wooded valley at the foot of the Ore Mountains in Bohemia was discovered, it is said, in 1347, when King Charles IV was out hunting. A stag was cornered by the hounds and jumped from the rock, some of the hounds jumped after it, and when the king and his huntsmen rode back to the base of the mountain they found the stag and the hounds in agony in near-boiling water. Gradually a bathing-place was established, and a town developed along the valley of the little river Tepl, to where it joins the Eger.

The river Eger – Ohre in Czech – runs parallel to the north-west border of Czechoslovakia and gives its name to a part of the Sudeten-German region, the Egerland. Egerländer humour is robust and earthy, the language rooted in peasant life. The powerful Egerländer dialect, shared by Jews and gentiles and across all classes, and the oft-repeated songs and stories served to keep people's feet on the ground in the face of cosmopolitan glitz; for in the nineteenth and early twentieth centuries taking the waters was fashionable among the cultured and wealthy. Edward VII, I am sorry to say, frequented Marienbad, the competition twenty miles up the road. But we claimed Goethe, Schiller, Beethoven, Peter the Great and many others, famous and not so famous. Some of them left moving tributes to how a stay in Karlsbad had benefited them, among them one Dr Phil. Karl Th. Hoesst from Hamburg, who in 1915 had this poem carved on a marble tablet next to one by Goethe at the side of a wooded walk:

Mein Karlsbad

Wohlbefinden bietet manche Quelle
Aus der Erde triefend Urgestein
Aber nur an dieser heiligen Stelle
Fand ich Heilung meiner Gallenpein

A bad poem deserves a bad translation:

Many a spring may offer healing
Pouring from earth's ancient rocky ground.
But only in this holy place
Relief from gallstones' pain I found ...

In nineteenth-century England spas such as Bath and Tunbridge Wells still had this function of providing pleasant settings for the pursuit of health and recreation. Bath, with its rituals like the musical evenings in the Pump Rooms – the 'Rooms' – provides the background against which Jane Austen's characters visit each other, plan their entertainments, experience love and rejection. By the twentieth century this lifestyle had waned in England but on the Continent it continued, with industrialists and film producers now mingling with the leisured aristocracy. When I was about six a visiting American film producer asked my mother to let me do a screen test. She said no, and I have never forgiven her. The fact that Shirley Temple got to be ambassador to Czechoslovakia as well just rubs salt in the wound.

The 1920s produced, here as elsewhere, their own brand of frivolity: Egerländer earthiness and the cultured atmosphere of spa life sometimes mingled happily and sometimes not. They also produced a sharper and less sympathetic observer than Jane Austen. Here is the satirist Egon Adler, in 1922, on Karlsbad cultural life, especially as lived by the female of the species:

Relations to art, literature, theatre and music are maintained through journals like 'The Lady', 'World of Elegance' and 'The Housewife's Journal'... If a citizen has climbed to the dizzy height of being able to distinguish between Picasso and Boccaccio, the rest unanimously and without envy appoint him expert in questions of art.

The favourite branch of the arts is music, because listening even to a boring concert not only requires very little effort, but also offers a favourable opportunity to let one's newest toilette be seen. Since the concerts at the Kurhaus are not enough to fulfil this need, a chamber music society has been established. But to put an end to the style offences of the past, I would like to offer some advice to unmusically dressed ladies: Bach and Haydn demand black crêpe de chine, buttoned high at the neck, with a serious expression; Bruckner and Mahler require livelier colours and a little rouge, Mozart and Schönberg low décolleté, jewellery, and raised eyebrows. Boycott Beethoven, the swine would have boycotted you. Some, though not all, would be well advised to bring scores and look into them earnestly. But please don't forget to turn the page now and then – about every three minutes where it says adagio, one-and-a-half minutes for presto ...

The theatre, too, would undoubtedly be frequented occasionally by one or the other nonentity, were it not for the fact that performances take place at the time allocated to bridge...[1]

I was born in Karlsbad in 1928, into a gap between disasters: the First World War had ended with the dismantling of the Austro-Hungarian Empire and the creation, in 1918, of the state of Czechoslovakia. Its first President was Tomáš Masaryk, who had campaigned for restoration of an ancient independence. The country included the Sudetenland, near the western and north-western borders with Germany, inhabited by people whose culture and language were more Austrian/German than Czech. After Hitler came to power he claimed this area as being German. Tension between the Sudeten-German minority and the Czechs was to resonate down the decades and generations, and is not resolved yet. It was to climax with Hitler's occupation in 1938.

During my first ten years life followed a number of threads. One of them was the family: meals, births, quarrels and jealousies, school, a bout of diphtheria, grownups worrying about money, uncles and aunts who lived in Karlsbad, other uncles and aunts who visited. My father was among the youngest in a family of ten and had married late, so my cousins were largely

---

[1] Egon Adler, *Die Entdeckung Karlsbads*. Privately printed, 1922.

4

grown up and I was the only child for many uncles and aunts to dote on. There was swimming in summer, skiing and skating in winter – about November one began to throw stones at the ice to see if it would hold, and the tinny sound of the Skaters' Waltz coming from a loudspeaker among the trees still rings in my ears – walking in the forest to look for fungi and blueberries, excursions to nearby lakes. There was the market where farmers' wives from round about brought butter, each farm's butter slightly different so that the prudent housewife tasted several before buying, and where carp swam in tanks. And always there were family stories and reminiscences, jokes that acquired a patina from re-telling, cakes that were a triumph or a disaster.

Another thread was the town itself and its life as a spa. This took place during the strictly defined 'saison' (Egerländer pronunciation 'sayesong') between May and September. This was a town of wide, sanded paths under luxuriant chestnut trees, open-air terraces on which to take breakfast, fashionably dressed visitors taking the waters, afternoon concerts at the bandstand and Tanztee (tea dances). The 'Kurgäste' – guests who had come for the cure – were not tourists in the modern sense. To take the cure you settled in for several weeks. You found a hotel or pension or rented rooms (local people often withdrew to the darker rear rooms of their houses to accommodate paying guests). You registered with a doctor, who prescribed a regime. Then you settled into a pattern of drinking at least six glasses of the repulsive hot water a day, starting with one before breakfast, taking walks, playing cards or dancing in the afternoon, listening to music, gossiping and flirting. No wonder people felt better.

Set all this in a landscape of meadows, forests and mountains, and the result adds some objective justification to the sense of loss. It is no wonder we are all homesick. To my shame, I felt a little glad to hear of the damage being done to this landscape by the ecological neglect of the decades after the war. It made it less painful not to be there.

For hovering over it all at a third level, edging its way into most conversations on the sunny terraces over coffee or at the skating-rink at Klein-Versailles (a pretentious name for a little pond, but it was beautiful), was anxiety and speculation about Germany and Hitler. There was a young girl who came to take me out for walks in the afternoon. Her name was Resi – to call her a nanny would be overdoing it. I have a very clear memory of sitting in a meadow talking with her about how worried I was about Hitler and what he might be going to do. Since Resi was only with us before we went to France when I was five, I must have been younger than that. One of the stranger things about coming to England later was to find that people there did not discuss politics with children, as if they were a different species.

5

At the end of the 'saison' many people who were involved with the spa business – waiters, cooks, hotel managers, and indeed some of the guests – upped sticks en masse and removed to the French Riviera, where it all started over again. My father said that you could be sitting in a café in Nice telling Karlsbad stories and if you got one wrong or forgot a punch-line, the waiter serving your coffee would finish it for you. These stories improved with repetition. Like the one about the triumphant headline in a local paper during the First World War: *'Přemysl wieder in unserem Besitz!'* ('Přemysl once more in our possession!'), when no one knew it had been lost. Or the proud Karlsbad mother: *'Meine Gusti hat Schenkel! Und an Bekanntenkreis!!'* ('My Augusta has thighs! And a social circle!!')

Karlsbad had a fairly large Jewish population. By that time they were not very religious and on the whole not very consciously Jewish, maintaining contact only with the major festivals, if that. Their children had Christmas trees as well as Chanukah candles and in their cooking Jewish, Czech, Austrian and Hungarian elements were effortlessly fused.

During the 1970s I ran some seminars in Israel. One or two people there tried to make me 'rediscover my Jewish roots', particularly the wife of the director of the Jerusalem Institute of Management. I finally managed to stop her proselytising with this illustration of how assimilated we had been: Karlsbad was in a mainly Catholic region, and sometimes there were processions. There was one at the beginning of the 'saison', when the bishop processed through the town blessing the springs (as well he might; my father, agnostic like most Jews, held me up to be blessed, just in case). The *Fronleichnam* or Corpus Christi procession, in particular, was an important occasion. The bishop was preceded by little girls in white dresses scattering flower petals. And little Jewish girls were also put into white dresses to scatter flower petals, on the general principle that if there was something going on you took part in it. At the age of four I too was put into a white dress and given a basket of flower heads – my mother had gone early to the market – to scatter in front of the bishop. But there were limits: the procession led to the church where a mass was to be held, and at the door of the church my mother appeared from the crowd and plucked me out of the procession. That far she would not go.

I was once taken into the church by Resi, though. When the priest appeared at the altar I called out, 'Oh, look! That man looks like daddy in his nightshirt!' There was a strange noise behind us, and I looked round. A whole row of old ladies in shawls were kneeling at prayer and trying to stifle their laughter.

As my uncle Luis wrote in a letter, 'It was Hitler who made us into Jews.'

This uncle – Alois, or Luis – was one of my father's older brothers. As a young man he had built up a linen store in which he employed my father and my cousin Hans, and then branched out into the hotel business. In 1926 he bought a piece of land with an old café on it, and on this land he built what was to become a world-famous Park Hotel, which he called the 'Richmond'. I honestly thought, and told my friends, that there was a place in England that was named after it. I have a newspaper cutting about its opening in 1933, dripping with admiration for its splendour and for the splendour of the international clientele present for the occasion.

The terraces of the Richmond Park Hotel were crowded in summer. The keynote was elegance. There were elegant two-toned men's shoes, which are in England called 'co-respondents'. Well, yes, probably. And elegant strappy women's sandals. And painted toenails! That was a marvel to me, the first time I saw it. They belonged to the wife of a maharajah, and I just stood in front of her and stared down. I also stood and stared up at the half-dozen gambling machines in one of the ground-floor rooms, willing people to win and rushing to help pick up the coins if they did. But most of all I stared at the band and the dancing.

Tanztee was from three to six in the afternoon in summer on the main terrace, or indoors in the ballroom if it rained. The bandleader was R.A. Dvorsky, and from the age of six till we left home when I was ten I was in love with him. Posters showing his stylised face with its pencil moustache flanked the driveway that led from the road, across the little river, to the hotel. There were three broad parallel drives: one for cars and horse-drawn cabs driving in, one for cars and cabs driving out, and the central one for people walking. This was lined with chestnut trees, and under every second chestnut tree stood his portrait.

Mr Dvorsky didn't conduct the band, he led from the piano, and every Sunday afternoon I stood devotedly glued to the piano, watching. The drummer pretended to be jealous, and the conductor teased in a slightly nasty way, but Mr Dvorsky was kind. When we were leaving to go to England I wrote to tell him about it, and he sent me some sheet music of his repertoire, which I still have. The band combined the international influences of jazz, swing and rhythm with some Czech musical traditions, and played two-steps, quick-steps, foxtrots, tangos. Although as a small child I did not take part in the dancing, it may be through this regular watching and listening that a love of and even skill at dancing entered my bones. I find it hard to sit still when there is dance music, and surprise people by being a good dancer.

I was also in love with a glamorous Greek dancer called La Bella Smaru, who danced a solo twice during the afternoon. She was the cause of my first major disenchantment. One afternoon she invited me back to her dressing room. I was thrilled, but then I saw the row of different-coloured satin dancing shoes lined up to go with her different costumes. Where there had been a tear in the satin it was cobbled together, not very well, with black cotton. It came as a real shock. In her case I know what the influence on my own dancing was, because I used to go home and practise her routines in my bedroom.

At six, when people had left to go home if they were Karlsbaders or to prepare themselves for the evening if they were visitors, the waiters would rake the yellow sand on the paths and under the tables to make it look fresh and ready again. That was when they also had time to relax a bit and stand and chat with me, for they were my friends. Even when the Hitler time came and many of the waiters and waitresses joined the Nazi Party, it wasn't personal. 'You see, Mrs Klein,' one of the waitresses explained to my mother, 'the Social Democrats promised us a lot of things, but we're no better off. Now the Nazis are promising us a lot of things. It's worth a try.'

Roots

When my aunt Fanni went into exile she took with her some papers relating to family history. She never explained to me what these were. She did, however, say that she was making some notes towards a family history. What she wanted to do, I know, was to trace how political and historical events had impacted on one family. When she died in 1950 I inherited this small box of papers. On the top were her pencilled notes. But they were very disappointing: her shaky handwriting meant that there was very little on a page, much of that was illegible, and there were, in any case, very few pages. So I left it, and it was not until many years later that I really investigated the rest of the box.

The first document is a small black notebook with beautiful copperplate handwriting, which begins: 'Our family history, as far as it can be documented, starts in 1746, the year in which my great-grandfather Veit or Feisch Klein was born in Udritsch.' This is the small village near Karlsbad where my father was born. Who wrote this? Considerable detective work leads me to think that it must have been my grandfather, Wilhelm Klein. But he died in 1918. Did Fanni keep this little notebook all these years and take it into exile with her? Hard as it is to grasp, I cannot make sense of the names and dates in any other way. I will therefore assume that my grandfather is the author:

Our family history, as far as it can be documented, starts in 1746, the year in which my great-grandfather Veit or Feisch Klein was born in Udritsch. However, we could go even further back, since the names of my great-great-grandparents, the parents of Veit's wife Sara, appear in the Jewish register in Udritsch. They were called Maier, but there is no further information about them except that they lived in Böhmisch Neustadt, district Kralowitz, in the first decades of the eighteenth century. However, since Jews only began to be allowed to take surnames in the reign of Joseph II, that is from the year 1780, we can be certain that the name Maier at that time, that is before Joseph, was not a surname but a forename. One may assume with equal certainty that

9

of my ancestors my great-grandfather Veit or Feischl, who lived under Joseph II, would have been the first to take the surname Klein.

Oh, but it is definitely Wilhelm's story, for here is the letter addressed to him on which it is based, dated 1911. There are in fact two versions of this letter, and they are not quite identical. Someone has made a copy and in the process made a few changes, and I cannot be sure which is the original and which the copy. It seems that around 1910 my grandfather in Karlsbad started to work on a family history, and that he wrote to a friend in Udritsch asking him to look up parish records. In a small village the church recorded all the inhabitants, Jews as well as Christians. Then he supplemented his friend's account from his own knowledge. I will merge the two versions, as best I can, adding my grandfather's amendments; the thought that I am collaborating with my grandfather in this work across eighty-five years literally makes the hair on the back of my neck tingle:

30.1.11

My dear friend!

As you requested, I obtained access to the Jewish records from the priest Joseph Schmidt. The priest even entrusted me with the records for a few days to copy out extracts, for which I am indebted to him. I enclose an extract of the most important items from the record book. The oldest Jewish record only begins with the year 1804, therefore these records do not show when the first Jewish families came to Udritsch.

But it seems that, according to the numbering of houses which took place in 1788 and which was done in sequence, there were either no Jews living in Udritsch yet at that time, or the Jews' houses were deliberately left out of this numbering, and were afterwards marked with Roman numerals. So the old Jewish Malach house has number I, and after 1848 number 64, the old brandy house number II and after 1848 number 63; this last one, incidentally, had alterations made by the landowner in the [eighteen-]twenties. Thus the Jews were brought to Udritsch by the landowner as 'Schutzjuden', i.e. protected Jews.[2] Since

---

[2] *Schutz* = protection. According to a newspaper cutting featuring a series on local history, undated but probably from around 1910, the position of Jews in the social order had been that they could not take up residence in a place or seek employment without being explicitly and formally included in the protection of the *Obrigkeit* – literally those above, masters, probably the landowner. For this protection they had to pay of course. A decree addressed in 1763 to one Moyses Isac, *Schutzjude* in Staub, lists as normal protection tax 29 fl. (presumably florins) as well as 10 pounds of Insslet (?) and two Strich (?) of sheeps' feet in addition to the annual meat dues of 3 fl; but he 'is in no way permitted to let his cousin Wolff Joachim or any other foreign Jewish riffraff live there; the first-named must either pay the annual fifty fl. protection money which has been demanded of him or remove himself immediately'.

brewing of beer and brandy manufacture were formerly the trades in [can't read] and [can't read], it may be assumed that the first Jews were simply employed to make brandy by the officials who needed experienced tradesmen for brandy manufacture. Thus the Jews were brought in by the landowners, and the first-born of a family enjoyed the right as protected Jew to the tenancy of the brandy house which belonged to the landowner.

By chance I succeeded in obtaining from the merchant Josef Potzauer the loan of a tenancy protocol said to be from the year 1815, which tells a lot about the situation in Udritsch at that time. Through the goodwill of Mr Potzauer I will send you the original, you can have it copied, but then be sure to send it back, I have taken responsibility for its return. According to this the brother of your grandfather, Abraham Klein, obtained the tenancy of the old brandy-house, no. II, from 1815 to 1822 and the right to manufacture brandy for 206 fl. per year. Before that, your great-grandfather Veit Klein was already the tenant of the same house, because he is described in the parish record as the Brandy-Jew. It is also important to note that in the old brandy-house, which as a Jews' house has the Roman numeral II, there were two other Jewish families which were, however, excluded from the tenancy arrangements.

It may certainly be assumed that your [great-] grandfather Veit Klein was the first to take this surname; before that they were only allowed to have forenames beside the name of the father, not until the time of Emperor Joseph II did they have to choose surnames. One could imagine, therefore, that the first Klein was small of stature and that this was noted by the official who was registering names. In the same way the owner of the oldest Jewish house, no. I, may have got his name Kandler as a practical joke of the officials against the village poet of the day, Kandler. (What could the poor poet do against this and how could he object? He just had to accept it.)[3] But this can no longer be researched from documents, the important archive was unfortunately entrusted to some merchants by Julius Rindl for [can't read], whereby much was destroyed. A few items were saved by chance, such as the enclosed [*Lizitationsprotokoll*]. I also found a bill from the teacher Josef Zörner in the Schoolteacher's Diary of 1835, which his daughter Anna Geingl lent me and which I have copied for you.

---

[3] What was the joke? Was it perhaps that his name was being used for a Jew?

From these extracts from the records, I believe you will be able to begin a family history quite well with the birth, in 1746, of your great-grandfather, the tenant of the brandy house in Udritsch, Veit Klein. More than that I could not find out for you.

With heartfelt greetings to you and your family,

Your old friend

Leopold Maier

The next document must be one of the enclosures. This too exists in two versions with minor variations, and I will again merge them:

Your father Moses Klein is the first recorded person in the oldest record, 1805. He was born in number 56, the extension of the inn no. 56 owned at that time by [can't read]. Your grandfather Jakob was tenant there. Your father's brothers David, 1807, Benjamin, 1809, Veit, 1812, were born in no. 19, Esther, born 1813, in no. 60, Wolf, 1817, also in no. 60, also Elisa, born 1822 in no. 60 (a Christian house). Jakob Klein was still living there in 1837 and 1839. Under the notice of death of the one-and-a half-year-old child Elisabeth there is a note: 'Jakob Klein is at the moment in Kresch'. I suppose he was only there on a visit.

Your grandfather died 13.6.1857 in no. 33. According to an older parish record, this little house, number 33, was owned in 1781 by a shoemaker Kuhlmann, who died that year aged seventy-one. I could not find out when your father acquired this house and rebuilt it. Your great-uncle Isaak was married on 6.8.1817 to Rachel Kornstein, still lived at that time in number 16. In 1842 Isaak Klein lived in the brandy-house, no. 63, probably in the so-called Itzig-room to the right of the entrance which, if I remember, was built of wood and was probably the remaining part of the old wooden brandy-house.

Grandfather Wilhelm supplements this:

At the beginning of the eighteen-thirties, my father Moses Klein bought the little house no. 33 in Udritsch from the descendant of the shoemaker Killmann who died in 1781. He re-built it to the condition in which it still stands today. But since in his day Jews were not allowed to own either houses or land, my father registered the house in the name of his friend Viten, and only got formal possession of it in the year 1848. Both I and my siblings were born in that house. Now the house is owned by a certain Mr Buxbaum from Luk.

I will shorten the rest of the writing of Leopold Maier and will only report the most important points.

Aha! It is indeed grandfather Wilhelm who made this copy, and who added to it from his own knowledge. This, then, is his summary of the story:

From the records my great-grandfather Veit was born in 1746, died 1811. Great-grandmother Sara, daughter of Maier from Neustadt was born 1748 and died 1813. Veit was a protected- and brandy-Jew, as was his first-born son Abraham. On the other hand his other sons Isak and Jakob, of whom Jakob was my grandfather, did not have the same rights from the landowner, and are only recorded as trading-Jews. They also did not enjoy the landowner's protection and were therefore very much at a disadvantage vis-à-vis their older brother. With their limited opportunity of trading they could not come to anything, while Abraham, who was at the same time a so-called Court Jew, became wealthy.

This Abraham, who had no children, adopted his nephew Moses Hirsch, and Moses Hirsch was the father of Schmuel and ... Hirsch ... Jews in the country mostly lived in Jew-houses, several families to-gether in one house. Jew-houses were houses which, since olden times, were only in the possession of Jews. If Jews wanted to live in a Christian-house this required the special permission of the higher authority, and in the country this was only the landowner who ruled over a large number of villages and whose officials had authority both in economic and judicial matters, in which they could pronounce judgement over the landowner's subjects.

The house no. 14, in which you later lived with your family and in which your children were born, was also owned in 1787 by a shoe-maker Franz Anton Kuhlmann, who died there aged seventy. ...

The custom of identifying people by the houses they live in has persisted. All houses in Karlsbad have names, and when Karlsbaders meet they identify themselves to each other in this way. In the 1970s my mother and her youngest sister Trude were living in London. They did not get on particularly well, but they could always find the way back to common ground by imagining a walk-through of their own village, Neusattl, in terms of who lived where: did the butcher's shop come next or was it farther along, and what happened to that frightfully ugly daughter?

13

Grandfather Wilhelm's notebook goes on to record a family tree, interspersed with comments; and he then goes on to do the same for the family of his wife Karoline (both are in Appendix 2). The information about my grandmother's family is less systematic, but there is more detail about some of the people. Her brother Natan went to America in 1851; her brother Sigmund joined him there in 1856 and her brother Rudolf in 1865. Sigmund studied at the University of Philadelphia. When the Civil War broke out he volunteered for the Army of the Northern States, but was killed in the second year of the war at the age of twenty-one.

In the generation before that, an uncle of my grandmother's, who had also landed in America, arrived back home mysteriously after having disappeared for some years. The romantic story of this part of my grandmother's family appears in the Prague Jewish weekly *Selbstwehr*, dated 15.11.1915, in an article which is itself a translation of a twenty-five-year-old essay by the 'excellent English journalist and politician Lucien Wolf'. I have shortened and paraphrased the somewhat flowery prose of the German article:

In the remote village of Hareth, in a hut at the edge of the forest, lived a widow called Kohn, who brought up her three sons and one daughter with great difficulty and in great poverty. The oldest son, Simon, made a bare living going from house to house selling English cotton cloths which he bought in Prague, while the second son, Samuel, was known in the district as a good-hearted but wild good-for-nothing who liked the inn and the girls better than working, and the card game best of all. Then there was another son, Joachim, and finally the little girl, Resi, who was known for her sharp tongue and whom all the boys in the village courted.[4]

One day, Samuel Kohn disappeared. He had last been seen drinking and playing cards in the inn in the company of unknown men, and after angry words had wandered off in the direction of Saaz, a picture of misery. Weeks and months passed without news of him. The months turned into years, and the widow sadly accepted that her son had been the victim of a crime. Lives, especially the life of a Jew, did not count for much in the Ore Mountains in those days.

Gradually, however, the rumour spread that Samuel Kohn was alive and well. Letters with a foreign postmark arrived in the hut at the edge

---

[4] This list is not quite consistent with the family tree that my grandfather compiled.

of the forest, and it began to appear more comfortable. One morning in the eighteen-thirties all Hareth was brought into high excitement by a story which a farmer brought into the village: he had been passing the widow Kohn's hut late at night when a large carriage, drawn by six horses and with four black servants in elegant livery, had drawn up at the door. According to this farmer, a very impressive-looking gentleman had descended from the carriage and entered the hut, followed by the black servants with the luggage, among which was a mysterious-looking piece. The farmer had looked through the window and swore by all the saints that, when this piece was opened in the presence of the widow, it was filled to the brim with newly-minted gold pieces.

Soon a dozen acquaintances were knocking on Mrs Kohn's door with one excuse or another. They found her beaming with happiness. The story was in essence true: her lost son Samuel had really returned home. She did not, however, satisfy their curiosity about the trunk full of money.

It seems that, on the day he disappeared, Samuel Kohn had been cheated of everything he had by a troop of card-sharps. As he left the inn with empty pockets, he felt unable to go back and admit to his mother how foolish he had been. He wandered off to the nearby county town and then begged his way through to Hamburg. He worked his passage on a sailing-boat to New Orleans, became a merchant there and earned a large fortune. When he returned to Europe, he paid a brief visit to his mother and saw her comfortably settled in Tüppelsgrün near Karlsbad. Then he moved on to Paris, where he took a post in a bank and then founded a banking house. He did not marry, but adopted his nephew Eduard, a son of his brother Simon, had him thoroughly trained and employed him in his Paris business. His brother Joachim he sent to New Orleans to look after his interests there; for his sister Resi he provided a generous dowry.

Later Samuel Kohn handed the Paris banking house over to his nephew Eduard, who took a Mr Reinach of Frankfurt as partner and founded the firm Kohn, Reinach and Company.

Exceptionally fortunate though it is, Samuel Kohn's story is overshadowed by that of his younger brother Joachim, who followed in his footsteps. He made a fortune in New Orleans, which at that time was the home of a number of enterprising Jews. Among them were the brothers Armand and Michael Heine, cousins of the poet Heinrich Heine. The two families intermarried. Eduard Kohn and his partner

Reinach took wives from one branch of the Heine family, and Joachim's only daughter Emilie married Michael Heine. She bore him a daughter on 10th November 1858, and seventeen years later this daughter, Marie Alice Heine, great-granddaughter of the old widow Kohn from Hareth, married Armand de Chapelle, duc de Richelieu, and her son is currently [1890?] head of this mighty house.

Marie Alice's first husband died in 1880, and nine years later she married as her second husband Albrecht I, sovereign prince of Monaco. The story of the Princess of Monaco's descent from the old Hyman Heine of Buckeburg, the 'little Jew with the thick long beard', of whom his grandson Heinrich made such fun in his memoirs, has been much repeated in recent times. People interested in family history may like to enjoy as a pendant to this the no less romantic story of her descent on her mother's side.

As I said, I only discovered these documents in 1992. I had heard several elements of the story before, as word-of-mouth family history handed down by my father and aunt Fanni. One was that we were somehow related to Heinrich Heine. Another was that we were somehow related to Prince Rainier of Monaco. A third was that Kohn, Reinach and Co was the banking house that sold the Suez Canal shares to Benjamin Disraeli. A fourth concerns, I think, my grandmother's father and her brother Rudolf. My father told that when he was a boy this grandfather, usually referred to as the Steebner grandfather, often used to walk along with his hand on my father's shoulder. The grandfather was stiff with arthritis and used the boy as a support. My father came to know that hand very well. Years later he went to America and was to meet his uncle Rudolf, whom he had never seen. Waiting among the crowds in the lobby of a New York hotel, he suddenly saw a hand that he recognised. It did indeed belong to his uncle.

Of this same Steebner grandfather – the one with the distinctive hand – my father told the story that as a young man he had wanted to visit his brother in Paris, and had walked all the way. When he got there he settled into some lodgings and then wanted to explore the city. To make sure that he would find the way back to his lodgings he looked around carefully, noted that next door was a shop with the sign *Modes, Robes* over it, and wrote this down. He duly got lost and showed a policeman his note, asking where to find *Modes, Robes*. Well, Paris has a lot of dress shops. Eventually he had to go into a post office where he sent a telegram home, which said, *'Wo wohn' ich in Paris?'* ('Where am I staying in Paris?')

This became common coinage in the family as a way of groping in the dark when one is lost or muddled. Even now, if I am thoroughly muddled about something, or when I am sitting in front of a pile of research data wondering how I am going to make sense of it, I ask myself, '*Wo wohn' ich in Paris?*'

There are some other papers in this box. There are newspaper cuttings from the 1880s, when someone on the local paper must have done some historical research. They have been pieced together to make a history of Udritsch. Other cuttings give bits of the history of the other villages and townships in the area. There is a letter, dated December 1912, from a distant American relative called Sophie Davidson, giving answers to enquiries my grandfather had made about her branch of the family.

And there is the bill from the village teacher, which grandfather's friend Leopold Maier had copied. Isaak Klein (1784–1854), the son of that first traceable ancestor Veit, was a butcher. It seems that he and his brother Jakob traded meat for schooling for their children, for in December 1835 the schoolmaster Josef Zörner notes:

Meat received from Isaak Klein	
3 lbs mutton @ 13 Kr[5]	39 kr
9 lbs beef @ 13 kr	1 f 57 kr
4½ lbs ditto @ 13 kr for the funeral	58 kr
2 lbs fish less 5…[?]	40 kr
7 lbs beef	1 f 31 kr
2 lbs ordered by the sisters	36 kr
3 lbs for the funeral, 2nd day	39 kr
Still ordered for 5 …[?]	15 kr
3 lbs delivered to the house	39 kr
	7 f 44 kr
Schooling from March 1834 to last February 1836 1 f 32 kr	
March, makes	3 f 50
I am still owed	3 f 54 kr

Isaak Klein from March 1836 till the end of August 23 kr schooling to pay, has provided 5 lbs mutton @ 15 fl, amounts to 1 f 15 kr, I still have to pay 20 kr.

[5] Kr stands for Kreuzer; 60 Kreuzer made one Gulden or Florin, that is why 9 lbs beef @ 13 kr cost 117 kr, i.e. 1 florin 57 kr. I am indebted to my cousin Michael Klein and his friend Dr Roland Irmer for researching this.

Jakob Klein has 22 kr schoolfees, has provided 1 1/2 lbs beef.
With Isaak Klein the school fees have been cleared up to end of
October 1837, does not owe anything.

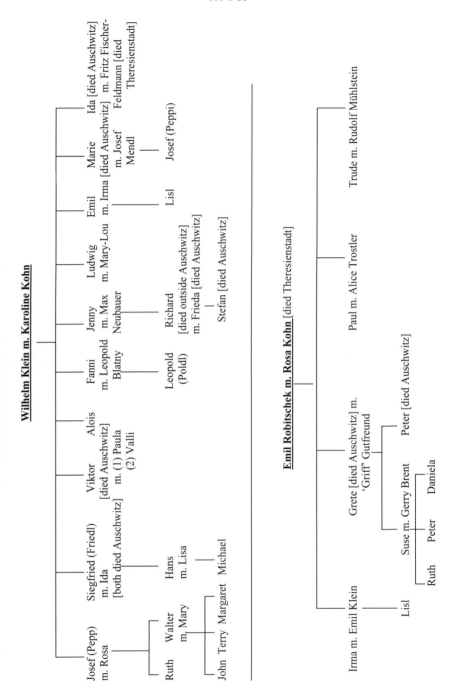

Wilhelm Klein m. Karoline Kohn

Josef (Pepp) m. Rosa — Siegfried (Friedl) m. Ida [both died Auschwitz] — Viktor [died Auschwitz] m. (1) Paula (2) Valli — Alois — Fanni m. Leopold Blatny — Jenny m. Max Neubauer — Ludwig m. Mary-Lou — Emil — Marie [died Auschwitz] m. Josef Mendl — Ida [died Auschwitz] m. Fritz Fischer-Feldmann [died Theresienstadt]

Hans m. Lisa

Ruth — Walter m. Mary

John Terry Margaret Michael

Leopold (Poldl) — Richard [died outside Auschwitz] m. Frieda [died Auschwitz] — Stefan [died Auschwitz]

Lisl — Irma — Josef (Peppi)

Emil Robitschek m. Rosa Kohn [died Theresienstadt]

Irma m. Emil Klein — Grete [died Auschwitz] m. 'Griff' Gutfreund — Paul m. Alice Trostler — Trude m. Rudolf Mühlstein

Lisl — Suse m. Gerry Brent — Peter [died Auschwitz]

Ruth Peter Daniela

19

A Family

The terraces of the Richmond were for Sunday afternoons, and that only during the summer season. For the rest of the year Karlsbad belonged to its inhabitants going about their normal lives. We lived at the workaday end of the town, the other end from the Richmond. Before we went to France in 1934 my father worked in his brother's linen shop and his free time he, or sometimes both my parents, spent convivially with relatives and friends, often in one or other coffee house. He was also a considerable sportsman. He was an excellent skater, taught me to ski and skate and swim, and as a young man had ridden and fenced. Skiing, I felt, was not what it was cracked up to be. This wasn't resort-type skiing, there were no lifts or cars. You struggled uphill for two hours in order to have perhaps ten minutes going down. But I loved skating, and when I see on television the amazing quality of skating that has now been achieved, I want to share it with him.

My mother I see, perhaps in an oversimplified way, as the archetypal housewife: hot soup when my father and I came home from skating or skiing on a cold winter's day, meals for the extended family on special occasions, and prudent and skilful housekeeping. Much of social life took the form of visiting hither and thither. Visiting was a serious pastime; ladies in particular visited, and the more sensitive of them kept score of who had visited whom more often. The very few quarrels between my parents that I can recall were about money. He was rather casual about it, and she worried. Even now, as I contemplate a jumble of half-worn shoes, I can hear my mother's voice saying 'there's wear left in those', and find it impossible to throw them away. One small bonus from all the things that happened later is that I have never worried about money. I reasoned that my parents worried about money and were careful to save it, and they lost everything – so what was the point? Money as such has not been a problem for me: at times when I have been very poor I have adapted and made whatever I had stretch, and lately, when there has been enough or even more, it has not bothered me.

Both my mother and my father came from villages near Karlsbad. They were very different in temperament, my father placid and calm, my mother volatile and generally referred to as *nervös*. That does not mean nervous, it means highly strung, sensitive. When she held my hand as we walked along, her little finger twitched, and when I asked why, she said it was because she was *nervös*. My parents shared a sense of humour and both had a great deal of wit, and they were both rooted in the practicalities of village life. It may have been this that helped kindle an affinity when they met at a dance in Karlsbad; it was certainly this that linked two otherwise very different families. He was twenty-one years older. In fact he was four months older than his mother-in-law and had already, by the time he met my mother, led a quite adventurous life.

Udritsch

My grandfather Wilhelm Klein and his wife Karoline (my second name) had ten children, all but the first three born in Udritsch. Many generations of his family had lived there before him. In 1885 Karoline died in childbirth at the age of thirty-eight; the twins who caused her death and who also died would have made twelve. My father, the youngest of the boys, was six at the time; the youngest girl, Ida, was only two. The eldest daughter, my aunt Fanni, was eleven. She once told me that she had no memories of her mother except as either pregnant or nursing a baby. They were very poor but were not aware of it, since everyone else in the village was poor too.

Soon after his wife's death my grandfather Wilhelm moved his family to Karlsbad. Fanni, together with their grandmother, largely took care of them, plunged into this responsibility as a young girl who could have done with some mothering herself. She told me once that no one had explained to her about menstruation. For a long time she was terrified every month that her insides were falling out.

This early responsibility must be how her passionate, mothering love of the whole family took root. During the anxious and desperate period from 1938 one can see in the letters of the by now middle-aged brothers and sisters how they turned to her for guidance with major decisions. Her commitment to family – brothers, sisters, their children, the extended family in America – was central to her life; together with her commitment to socialism, it lasted through the devastation of learning what eventually happened to most of them, until her death.

Six of my grandfather's ten children, including my father, settled in Karlsbad. First there were the three 'girls', Fanni, Marie and Ida. Fanni was involved in politics all her life. She married an Austrian trade unionist,

Leopold Blatny, but he died only four years later. After the state of Czecho-slovakia was created in 1918, she became a Member of Parliament. By the time I knew her she was widowed, and it may be because her only son died while a student, just two months before I was born, that she was to take such great and loving interest in my own development. Whenever she came back to Karlsbad from a parliamentary session in Prague there would be a present for me. Fanni had some neurological problem, which caused her hands to tremble, and there were things she could not do for herself. In particular, anybody who visited was hijacked to write letters for her, and letters from her are all in different handwriting. People vied to do things for her, because their own gain from the contact was so great.

One of my most secure and rich memories is of listening to her talk while I was darning her stockings. I had trouble with thin areas in the stockings, and ladders that merged into holes without clear-cut edges were a problem, but proper holes, with definite edges, were a real pleasure to fill in. From my childhood on, until her death when I was twenty-one, I loved to listen to her talk, of her ideas and ideals, her life and the family's. I only wish that I remembered more and that more of the story was written down. The bits one remembers are just that – bits. History in the village school, for instance – under Austrian rule, of course – meant learning chapters of the history book by heart: the teacher would stand in front of the class and ask, 'What had Maria Theresa hardly?' And the class would answer in chorus, 'Hardly had Maria Theresa ascended the throne ...'

Marie was the second of the 'girls'. She had married a Czech civil servant who had died fairly young, leaving her with a son to bring up and dependent on her older brothers. Her son Peppi later emigrated to the United States, but I don't know what happened to him.

Ida was the youngest of the 'girls' – in fact, the youngest of all the children. She married Fritz Fischer-Feldmann, who had employed a match-maker to find him a wife because he was too shy to go courting. They were very happy but had no children, so here was yet another source of love for me. A custom developed – I no longer know how – of giving me lunch once a week, with special treats. They lived on the other side of the valley and Ida would hang a white towel out of the window (we had no phone) when I was to set off to come over. She also had a doll's complete wardrobe made for me one Christmas – real dresses made by a real dressmaker, and hats and coats and underwear. It was a wonderful source of playing and I tried hard not to let it be soured by the fact that, to achieve it, my mother had lent her my favourite doll without asking. From the beginning of my life to the end of hers my need for some boundaries and space was something my mother either could not understand or could not concede. When the milkman came and she was short of change, I would have loved to give her some from my piggy bank. But she just helped herself to it, and could not understand why I was upset.

Fritz was a lovely man – intelligent, funny and loving. He was a doctor, but what he really loved was to go hunting. With his pipe, dogs, gun and a large feather in his hat he features in a book of cartoons and satiric verses about Karlsbad 'characters' published by the same Egon Adler.[6] In a photograph of him taken on the steps of the Richmond in 1933 he has the pipe and is clearly holding me the way a huntsman holds a gun. There is another photo, taken in his home. He put me on a sofa and put one of his dogs next to me. I was afraid of the dog and started to edge away. Fritz shouted at me to sit still, and the child in the photograph is clearly not sure which to be more afraid of, the dog or the photographer. But I loved him very much.

Alois (Luis) left school at fourteen when his mother died. He started work as an apprentice in a draper's shop in Luditz, and in 1898 started his own linen and drapery shop in Karlsbad. My father worked there and until I was five I was sometimes taken to visit the shop for my morning walk, to be taken by my father to the *Konditorei* over the road for a biscuit, and to be petted by the staff. They saved the ends of rolls of ribbon for me; I had a whole drawer full of shining, coloured ribbons of every width and texture. It was by then a very luxurious store. American heiresses ordered their trousseaux there, probably embroidered by the same seamstresses in the villages around Karlsbad about whose working conditions Fanni was campaigning. In 1934 Luis made this company over to its employees, and from then on all his attention was absorbed by his hotels. He owned two: the Atlantic Palais, where he made money, and the Richmond, where he spent it. The family tut-tutted over his luxurious taste and wondered whether it was connected with his homosexuality. He hadn't realised that he was homosexual until he married – a marriage that lasted less than a week and ended in the fastest divorce in history.

It has always fascinated me how a passionate commitment to socialism and some rather successful entrepreneurial business ventures seemed to go along side-by-side quite happily in the one family. Fanni was forever tapping Luis for contributions to one or other of her good causes; he probably wrote cheques just to get her out of his office.

Years later, in London, Luis and Fanni lived in a tiny flat off Holland Park Avenue lent to them by an English friend. They were very poor and I had

[6] Egon Adler, *Das entdeckte Karlsbad.* Privately printed, 1925.

enormous admiration for the way in which Luis coped with his new circumstances. This elegant hotelier, who had had mimosa flown in from Nice for some special occasion at the Richmond, now went with his shopping bag to buy potatoes in Shepherd's Bush market, because they were cheaper there than at the local greengrocer's. Such resilience was not, of course, any corny 'adaptation to change' nowadays so beloved of management textbooks, but the surfacing of an old and solid contact with reality.

Siegfried (Friedl) was described by Fanni as the kindest and nicest of the brothers and sisters. When Fanni had to catch a bus at six in the morning to go to Prague, he would meet her at the bus stop with a flask of tea. He married his cousin Ida Goldmann, and their son Hans also worked in Luis's shop. Hans married a German girl whose family did not want her to marry a Jew and, when the difficult times came, tried to persuade her to divorce him. But she wouldn't. When their son Michael was born in 1935 my mother used the occasion to tell me about the facts of life. Well, most of them.

My father Emil was the youngest of the boys, only six when his mother died. He was a tough little boy, tending to get into fights. For that matter, he got into fights as a grown man. One of my family's claims to fame is that my father got into a fight with Enrico Caruso over a woman on board ship on the way to America.

My father told how he and his friends used to follow the lamp-lighter along a street and throw their caps at the gas lamps, to put them out again. Or they would hide behind a wall with their catapults and flick pebbles at the horses, to make them bolt. Different technologies create different opportunities for mischief among young boys.

Two of my uncles, Joseph and Viktor, had moved away from Karlsbad, but came back on visits. Joseph (Pepp) was grandfather's eldest son. He emigrated to America as a young man in 1882, worked his way up in the way required by the American Dream, and became a successful industrialist, chairman of a sizeable corporation. Like many first-generation immigrants, he felt responsible for the large family of young brothers and sisters back home, especially the sisters, and sent money home regularly. During the Second World War he again sent a monthly sum to his sister Fanni, who had escaped to London.

When I was fourteen Pepp wrote to my parents, telling them to take me out of school and apprentice me to a dressmaker. I thought the idea hilarious; my parents were hurt and offended. It was not until many years later, when I got to know his son Walter, that I understood what this was about: the poor chap must have been terrified that here was going to be yet another female relative who would become dependent on him. But at some level I must have understood, nevertheless. After Fanni and Luis, the last of the uncles and aunts, died, there was no contact with the New York Kleins, and although in my isolation I longed to have some contact with family, I did nothing to make myself known to them. I didn't contact them, even when I visited the United States, until I was over fifty, by which time there was no doubt that my fare home was taken care of and that I would not be asking for anything. In this way I missed out on knowing some very nice people. Immodestly, I think they missed out on some fun too. I don't know what kind of a dressmaker I would have made.

Pepp's move to the United States was part of the great movement of central and eastern European peoples westwards, some to escape pogroms and some to seek their fortunes. The shipping companies knew how to exploit this. Walter told how his father, as a boy of sixteen, arrived at the dock in Hamburg to be presented with a tin plate, a tin mug and a sack. There was a heap of straw on the ground, and the passengers were told to fill their sacks with straw. Either Pepp didn't understand what this was about, or perhaps he was a bit lazy – in any event he didn't put much straw into his sack. But this was to be his bed, and for the next five weeks he slept on this excruciatingly uncomfortable mattress on the floor, herded together and fed like an animal with hundreds of others.

Walter told me this story when I was visiting New York in 1993. The following day I flew back to England, by Concorde. The contrast was mind-boggling: stewardesses who had carefully learned the names of the passengers ('Would you like a drink, Dr Klein?'), smoked salmon and fillet of beef at 58,000 feet while listening to Beethoven on the stereo, and home in three-and-a-half hours. The gap may have been more than a hundred years, but it was, after all, only one generation.

Viktor was an outdoor person and a sportsman; there are photos of him riding and fencing. After a fairly adventurous youth he settled down to fruit farming in Austria with his second wife, Valli. They had no children, though my father said that Viktor had probably provided me with a few illegitimate cousins in the villages around Karlsbad.

The last two of my aunts and uncles, Ludwig and Jenny, had died as young adults: Ludwig, my father's great hero, emigrated to the United States as a young man but died there in the 1920s. He had married an Irish-American girl and there are some charming, homespun letters in a child-like hand-writing, from an unknown Mary-Lou Klein. Jenny also died young. She had married a distant relative who, I was told, ill-treated her. Her son, Richard Neubauer, became a very handsome young man who studied law. He married the rabbi's daughter, Frieda, and their little boy Stefan was born when I was eight. They lived near us and I was often allowed to look after and play with the baby, and helped prepare for his first birthday party. I still use one of the recipes Frieda showed me, a 'cake' consisting of layers of rye bread sandwiched together with different – and different-coloured – savoury fillings.

So, of my grandfather's ten children, two had died and two had left Karlsbad. The others had stayed in Karlsbad and it seemed to me sometimes that the whole town was peopled with uncles and aunts. Their own few children were grown up by the time I was born, so that, even though as a child I missed having brothers and sisters of my own, I had this warm, busy family life around me.

Neusattl

Whereas Udritsch was a source of memories and stories for my father's family, my mother's parents were still living in Neusattl when I was small, and we went there on visits. It was an open-cast mining village – you knew you were getting near it when you could see from the train window the rows of little wagons swinging on overhead cables. Train journeys meant putting on old clothes, because the smuts from the coal-fired engine flew in at the windows and settled on everything. When my mother and her sisters were young, on the other hand, an outing to Karlsbad – nowadays about twenty minutes by car – was an occasion for taking the train and putting on one's best clothes and a hat.

My mother's father was the village doctor, and was also medical officer for the local district of the railway. This meant that he had travel concessions, and my grandmother did much of the family's travelling, taking children to relatives for holidays, and other errands. This grandfather, Emil Robitschek, was an autocrat who would not allow his daughters to be educated or find a profession. My grandmother was famous for her cooking, and for getting the punch-lines of jokes wrong.

My mother was the eldest of four children. She was highly intelligent, but the only work she was allowed to do was to assist her father with nursing duties in his surgery. This evolved into nursing wounded soldiers who were accommodated in a local hospital during the First World War. Rolling cigarettes for these soldiers at the age of sixteen, and of course trying out the cigarettes, turned her into a life-long heavy smoker. When she became ill in England at the age of seventy-five, medical myopia was so firmly entrenched that her doctor looked only for lung problems and missed her bowel cancer.

26

The second child was her sister Grete, and then came the twins, Paul and Trude. Even the youngest daughter Trude who, in contrast to my mother's rather serious nature, was flighty and frivolous as well as being very pretty, resented all her life that she had not been allowed to learn to be a milliner and work in a hat shop.

Grete married first and had two children: Suse, who was four years older than I, and Peter, who was almost the same age. Her husband had a great gift of humour, and for my parents' wedding wrote a poem with a scurrilous verse for each member of the large family into which she was marrying. He also wrote poems to his wife on various occasions, of which this New Year's greeting is an example:

Hier 'ne Rechung, da 'ne Rechnung,
Mahnung dort mit kurzer Frist.
Kind, Du hast ja keine Ahnung
Wie das Neujahr fröhlich ist

(Here an invoice, there a bill,
Last reminder, briefest notice.
Kid, you don't have an idea
Just how happy the New Year.)

Peter and I did not exactly grow up together, but we were only four months apart in age and were together a great deal. He was funny, charming and friends with everyone. He was frequently in trouble, but was generally forgiven as soon as people saw his mischievous grin inviting them to share the adventure. Once we were able to read, we swapped detective stories: there was a twopenny-blood kind of series with many tales in which the detective hero escapes at the last moment from some dire trap, to nail the culprits. These one read with a torch under the bedclothes, but that way one got through them too quickly. Peter seemed to have a better supply than I, and visits to the Gutfreunds had the added incentive of swapping and replenishing my stock.

Sometimes we fought. One fight developed when we were about six because Peter said you had to be married before you could have babies, and I said you didn't. Neither of us knew the mechanics of it, but our cook Julie had a baby who lived out in the country with Julie's mother and sometimes visited. And she wasn't married, so there!

Trude and her husband Rudolf (Rudl) lived in Prague. As a young man Paul had gone to Singapore, first working there for the Bata shoe company and later starting an import–export business of his own. I think he first got shipped off there by his father because of some trouble in his job, but I am not sure. In the mid-1930s he came home to look for a wife, got engaged to Alice Trostler, and returned to Singapore where his bride was to follow him. His sister Trude wrote to congratulate him, and at the same time wrote to a friend saying what a dreadful girl he had got involved with. But she put the letters in the wrong envelopes. Once a thing like that has happened you can't forget it, and it hung between the three of them for the rest of their lives.

Grete's husband died when Suse and Peter were only ten and six. Grete and the children moved to Pilsen together with my grandmother, who by then was also widowed. In 1939 Trude and her husband left for Singapore to join Paul. I have a box of letters from both sides of the family from that time, and one of the saddest is from my grandmother describing their departure and saying, 'Now three of my children are far away, and I am supposed to be happy about it.' Suse, aged fourteen, was sent to Palestine with a children's transport. Growing up there during the war years she became a passionate Zionist, which caused problems for us when we came into contact after the war. For her, for a time, it involved hatred of all things British, while I had become very British indeed. Her mother and Peter died in Auschwitz.

When the Japanese captured Singapore, Paul and Alice escaped to Australia where his firm had a branch. Trude and Rudl caught the last boat leaving Singapore to wherever it was going. This turned out to be Bombay. Rudl eventually obtained a job with the Indian subsidiary of the British Oxygen Company and they settled in Calcutta, where they seemed to take on some of the habits of the British Raj. There are photographs of them playing golf, at the swimming club, at cocktail parties. It was such a different world from the one my mother and I were then living in, as well as being so far removed from village life in Neusattl, that it is hard to find points of contact. In the 1960s they retired to England, where Rudl died and Trude lived to survive my mother. The two sisters had little in common, but their sense of family was strong and they met regularly, each of them telephoning me after every meeting to complain about the other.

After the war Paul and Alice took Suse from Palestine to live with them in Australia. They showered her with clothes and presents and parties in a mistaken attempt to make up for the difficult years and the loss of her mother and brother. It would have been better to provide her with some kind of solid base and an education. She accepted their largesse in spite of a lingering longing for the idealistic life in Israel, and in her more serious moments said that she would have loved to study medicine. She married, produced three young Australians with accents you can cut with a knife, and divorced. Her son she called Peter.

I first met these three young people when I visited Australia in 1970. Not being experienced with adolescents, I felt my way very cautiously. Once I took Peter, who was fifteen, out to dinner to try to get to know him. Very circumspectly I asked, 'Do you smoke?' With deep scorn for my naïveté and in the fiercest of Australian accents he said, 'Gave it up when I was eleven!' His uncle would have been proud of him.

It amazes me how this fairly small – for those days – family, from an ordinary small village, got scattered: my grandfather's four children ended up in London, Sydney, Calcutta and Auschwitz.

Fanni Blatny

The single greatest influence on my own life was my father's sister Fanni. She transmitted to me the values that shaped her own life, although the expression of those values would eventually take me more into professional than political activity. She was a social democratic member of the Czech Parliament from its beginning, soon after the new state of Czechoslovakia was created in 1918. Her story is best told by herself: I have here an article published in 1931, when she was fifty-eight, entitled 'My first speech', about how it all began for her. There is nowadays so much unthinking gloating at the supposed defeat of the 'Left' in Europe; it is too convenient to forget its human and compassionate base:

> The small West Bohemian village of Udritsch, where I was born and lived till my twelfth year, is not exactly designed to educate one to socialism.
>
> It is far from any larger town, and far from the busy main road, so that the events of history hardly ever touch it; and it is so small that all its houses fit along one short street. When a procession passes through on its way to the nearby place of pilgrimage, it has barely intoned the words 'Mother of God, Mother of God' before the houses of Udritsch have been left behind.
>
> At the same time, spending my childhood in this little village lost to the world was not without benefit for me. Because of it I understood from childhood the thinking and feeling of simple people. I did not have to find my way back to them, I belonged to them.
>
> My mother died young, aged thirty-eight, giving birth to twins, after she had already brought ten children into the world. I was only eleven, and don't have many memories of her: pregnant, nursing, pregnant, nursing – a monotonous cycle, almost pitiful. One has to be as good a person as my mother was to cope with this deadening women's lot. And she was good: like a broody hen she rounded us up if a thunderstorm threatened or there were gypsies in the neighbourhood. Year

in, year out, early and late, she gave protection and care, and this extended to others as well. When smallpox broke out in one family, she took them food and left it by the door, even though she might be endangering her own children. And when two children died in a fire which they had caused themselves while playing, and which had burned down several huts, my mother was the only person who walked behind the coffin.

With my father, goodness almost merged into weakness, the smallest of us could twist him round our fingers. For instance my brothers sometimes took their mischief so far – this was already after our move to Karlsbad – that the police occasionally asked to see my father and advised him to warn the boys and 'deal with' them. By this they meant a beating, but my father was just as likely to 'deal with' the boys by treating them to sausages on the way home from the police station.

This weakness is all the more surprising as my father's mother had a quite unusual strength of will. When duty called her, she could rise to extraordinary heights. She was seventy and on her deathbed, quite ready to die after a life filled with work, when she heard that my mother's end was nearing. And her sheer strength of will got the better of the death agony that was already taking hold. She knew that the house-full of children needed her, she must not die now. Every quarter of an hour a mouthful of wine, until her heart was beating properly again, and then she went back to living and working.

And what awaited her was not easy. She had been used to an orderly life and had to start managing a household which was economically shattered. She was rooted with all her being in village life, and was now expected to move with us into the town. It was asking a lot of an old woman to force herself to go on living and to take on such changes, but grandmother did it and for several more years cared for us under difficult and for her strange conditions.

It was the 'village poor man' who first made me aware of social need and injustice. He never did anything to harm us village children, yet we were as afraid of him as of fire. Only from a great distance did we dare to watch as he searched for fleas among his clothes. If he came near, we ran away in terror. One time we were so engrossed in our games that we did not notice his approach in time, and turned too late to run away. He said, 'Children, what are you running away for? Better to take an axe and just kill me.' These words pursued me for a long time and still resonate in me. The suffering of a man marked out by society can rarely have found a more moving and simple expression.

31

It was only years later that I came across articles about socialism written by Franz Mehring in the journal 'Gartenlaube'. They began to provide some clarity and a basis of ideas for my social feelings and painful compassion. I was introduced further into this way of thinking by a relative who had learned about theoretical socialism at the University and who is still now a socialist University teacher in Vienna. In those days, incidentally, he felt he had to demonstrate his convictions by wearing a large hat, which he had bought jointly with a friend of similar views – their money would not stretch to two hats. Childish dressing up? Maybe. But the new ideas did not burn themselves into my heart and my brain with any less heat or any less honesty because of it, they filled my whole thinking.

From then on I went to every social democratic meeting, the only woman among the handful of men who formed the party in Karlsbad in those days. I was unspeakably shy, spoke with nobody, never opened my mouth. But I was there, I belonged to the fighters, and I was filled with fire. The amusements of other young people of my age meant nothing to me, had nothing to offer, I belonged to a different world.

One day, some years later: general meeting of the party and election of officials. The Chairman asks me whether I am willing to be elected. I stand up and say, 'no'. The Chairman asks me to explain why. At that moment I hate him, who was later to be my dear friend Oswald Hillebrand, with all my heart. He has forced me to stand up again, to stand there while others are sitting down, to have them all looking at me, and to say something. It was the first 'speech' I ever made, a whole sentence with a proper beginning and end. The sentence was 'because I'm going away.' It wasn't true, I had no intention of going away, I had no greater wish than to be allowed to carry out some function. But the words 'because I'm going away' formed a rounded whole, and in my dreadful situation that was the most important thing, I felt saved by them. They were, incidentally, not taken seriously, I got elected.

In 1912 I got engaged to a former worker in the china factory, to the great astonishment of the woman who used to come hawking goods from door to door. She came to see us one day and unpacked her message right away: 'Just imagine how wicked people are, Miss! They're saying you're engaged to a worker'. 'I am'. A short, embarrassed pause, then: 'You're quite right! They're usually more intelligent than anyone else!'

After the wedding we moved to Vienna, but my husband died after only four years of the most harmonious marriage. Like me he was completely given up to socialism, and it had educated him to be a wonderful human being. He worked ceaselessly to develop his own learning and that of others. The liberating power of knowledge and joy of the arts fulfilled him. Nothing gave him greater pleasure than to study the treasures of our museums.

When I returned home after his death, I found everything changed and in disorder. The men were at war, women and children were doing war-work, partly just to be able to eat and partly because of compulsory orders. Organisations were thus robbed of members and of their best representatives. If this weapon of the proletariat was not to be lost by the time the men came back from war, we women would have to move in and take on campaigning for the socialist idea, we would have to go out and become speakers. Speakers! Dear God! So four or five of us, it wasn't more than that, each learned a few sentences by heart. I, for instance, learned a piece from a brochure by Therese Schlesinger about direct and indirect taxation. And then the whole group of 'speakers' toured the nearby villages. We stayed together, because we wouldn't have had the courage to do this fearsome work on our own, and on an agreed cue one would always stop and the next in line take over.

So we painfully brought our poor little lectures to the people, and what lectures they were. How we tortured ourselves and how much more we tortured our listeners. And yet, they understood us and liked us. For a thread of common need, of common anger and despair was spun from them to us. From our stammering, stumbling, clumsy words they could feel what we were trying to say, they heard the call for which they had been longing for such a long time. Women's organisation after women's organisation emerged, in spite of our lectures. They shot from the earth like springs that are only waiting for the touch of the searching [divining] rod to start flowing. We were that rod, no more than a simple tool. Nevertheless that was when the ground was laid for the strong socialist women's organisation of Karlsbad which today stands with its four thousand members beside the equally strong organisation of the men.

Time rushed away with us. Austria collapsed, there was revolution and a new order. In the course of a very few months enormous demands came to be made on us. Whether one liked it or not, one had to extend oneself and one's strength. There was the parting from our dear old Austrian party, which at one stroke deprived us of the most tried and experienced leaders. We had to build a new apparatus and find a new programme and a new orientation vis-à-vis the changed circumstances. The women's organisation needed a new constitution. Women's voting rights presented us with important educational tasks, and for those of us who found ourselves among the elected members of Parliament, with the new and unaccustomed parliamentary activity. The breadth and newness of the sphere over which leadership was now required evoked enormous and relentless feelings of inadequacy. It was a hard battle to overcome these sufficiently to be able to get on with the necessary work; only the sheer imperative of the work made it halfway possible to deal with this battle. Each one of us experienced this battle, each one stepped up her willingness as her responsibilities grew. Proof of this lies in the fresh intellectual life pulsing among the socialist women of Czechoslovakia, which enables our movement to reach out more and more confidently both in breadth and in depth.

For me, socialism has become more than I could have foreseen, the only thing to hold on to in life, and its only pleasure. For the circle of human love around me is growing smaller: a brother and a sister [Ludwig and Jenny] died not long ago and during the last, dark, year I have had to bury my beloved only son. There is only one thing I can still give him: to give that part of my love which belonged to him to the party as well, and to feel, instead of being the mother of one, that I can give some humble aid to the stepchild of society, its working people. If the lot of the many can be improved, the sadness of the individual may fade.

It was Fanni's colleagues who persuaded her to go back into Parliament after the shattering blow of losing her son. In her parliamentary work Fanni was particularly interested in social questions and in the condition of women and women's work. She took part in various enquiries of the International Labour Office and represented Czechoslovakia there. She was involved in prison reform and got a bill through Parliament that abolished illegitimacy as a legal status. She was President of the Women's Committee of the German Social Democratic Party of Czechoslovakia and a member of the Women's Committee of the Labour and Socialist International.

Fanni's particular quality seems to have been to engage at an international level with the various women's movements (this term has a quite different meaning today: in the first half of the twentieth century it referred to the women's sections of social-democratic parties throughout Europe) and here she made many personal friends. After her death, all wrote and spoke of her love and modesty, her warm-hearted simplicity and her personal generosity to any who were in need, sharing what little she had.

Before 1933 she had often addressed meetings in Germany, and she knew the strength of the social democratic movement there. Even during the war she did not take the easy position of condemning all things German. It was due to her initiative and her personality that an International Socialist Women's Committee was founded in London, which as a matter of course included German and Austrian women working together with those from Belgium, Holland, Poland, Czechoslovakia, and other occupied countries. The Committee included Lucy Dujardin and Isabelle Blume from Belgium, Marthe Louis Levy and Mabel Hauck from France, Barbara Gould, Mary Sutherland and Lucy Middleton, whose husband was General Secretary of the Labour Party, from England, Marianne Pollack, Shella Hanzlik and Trude Magaziner from Austria, Lidia Ciolkosc, Anna Fiedler and Chrystina Marek from Poland, Ragna Hagen, Dagny Sanness and Rakel Seweriin from Norway, Herta Gotthelf, Dora Segall and Helene Schöttle from Germany, the widow of the Italian socialist Claudio from Italy, and from Czechoslovakia Marie Jurnecková, Marie Neumann, Irene Kirpal, with Fanni herself as Chairwoman. She felt strongly connected to the German and particularly the Austrian socialist movements and often defended the record of German socialism, which had been one of the strongest movements before 1933. Unlike the men, who throughout the war drew a distinction between allied socialists and enemy (German and Austrian) ones, the women made no such distinction.

In 1937 Fanni and a colleague, Alfred Kleinberg, published a book entitled *Das Denkmal der unbekannten Proletarierin (Memorial to the Unknown Working Class Woman)*[7]. It describes the lives and fates of Sudeten-German women over some one hundred years up to the beginning of the First World War, the historical and economic context that shaped those lives, and their emergence as a political force. Fanni's part seems to have been to get all kinds of individuals and organisations interested in the project and contributing material, and Kleinberg's to organise the mass of material which resulted.

The book documents numerous individual and family lives, through the budgets of weaver employers and the accounts of lace makers, embroiderers and other home workers; personal letters – and indeed a suicide note – from ill-treated domestic servants; reports of factory inspectors; and detailed researches of some historians. The stories tell of poverty, overcrowding, disease, child labour. A four-year-old is told that if she works hard at the lace making she will be able to eat maize gruel, which has more maize corns

[7] Karlsbad, Graphia, 1937.

in it than maize soup. Amid Dickensian vividness they show detailed documentation. The context for these conditions is provided by the political and economic history of Hapsburg Austria and the industrial revolution which, as in Britain, replaced men with machines that could be worked by cheaper women and children. Textile, tobacco and china industries went through radical upheavals, traditional hand embroidery was replaced by machine embroidery. In addition there were the ever-present cultural and language problems between Czech- and German-speaking peoples.

The authors describe with passion the strength and courage of these women as, despite the wretched conditions in which they and their families live, they muster the energy to evolve gradually into political organisation. Here the base material is personal accounts, minutes of political meetings, newspaper accounts, and trade union resolutions down to the strength of the votes cast.

It all seems far away to me now, in my comfortable flat and with today's constrained and tepid politics, where artificial passion is whipped up to sell newspapers. I am writing this as Nelson Mandela is visiting Britain, described as possibly the last real political hero. A leading article in the *Independent* says: 'The idea of political heroes, people . . . ready to die or spend decades in prison, has become anachronistic. The tyrannies that forced ordinary people to become heroic are dead or in retreat', later adding, 'Thank God'. Nevertheless, distant as it all seems, if the house burns down this book is the only thing I would want to rescue.

The Sudeten-German dilemma was pervasive. During the war the social democratic exiles in London split into two: one part, which Fanni helped to organise, was led by Josef Zinner and was strongly committed to the Czech state; the other, led by Wenzel Jaksch, was strongly German in orientation although of course not Nazi in their politics.

But there are other perspectives. In 1947 there was a Youth Festival in Prague. It was the first of a series, a few months before the Communist take-over in Czechoslovakia. Later these Youth Festivals came to be more or less limited to the young people from Communist countries, but this first one was a broadly based, idealistic first getting together of young Europeans after the war. Many of them went on afterwards to help build railways in Yugoslavia.

I was at university at the time, and for me it meant primarily a chance to go to Czechoslovakia because there were cheap rail fares. I met the family friend who had been with our relatives in the camps, and learned some of the details of what had happened to them. Fanni gave me some packages to take to her former comrades, and in this way I came to meet the former mayor of a suburb of Karlsbad. Weeping, he told how he had hidden his daughter in the cellar when the Russian soldiers came. Then he suddenly turned on me in fury, raging against the way in which the party, in comfortable exile, had indulged in the luxury of schism.

The Thirties

When I was five we spent nine months in the south of France. It is a momentously long period when you are small, and as a child I always thought of my life in terms of before we went to France and after we went to France. Just why we spent the best part of 1934 in the south of France I have never been able to discover. Once my mother said my father had pointed out that the depression which was hitting the whole of Europe was actually cheaper to ride out on the Riviera than at home. Her sister Trude hinted at darker reasons, but would never explain. Another time my mother explained that he had said, 'She'll be going to school next year, then we won't be able to travel.' There may be some truth in this: he was an adventurous man who had not married until he was forty-seven, having travelled a lot before then. Settling down must have meant giving some things up. He had been in the navy before and during the First World War (sounds strange for a Czech, but it was Austria then and the Austria of that time had a navy) and it is his excitement at seeing the sea again that strikes me now more than my own.

Juan-les-Pins

We were walking down a wide street in Nice, my father holding my hand. The pavements and houses glittered in the sunlight, and at the end of the street there was something wide and blue. 'Look down there, what do you think it is?' my father asked. It was February, and the only thing I could think of was that it might be an enormous skating rink. At home the pond on which we skated was of a shape and size that, no sooner had one worked up a satisfactory speed, one had to swerve round and come back. A skating rink on which you could just go on and on to the horizon, which this looked as if it might be, was my idea of paradise.

We settled in Juan-les-Pins, which was then a small village although it was said to be 'rising'. Much has been written about the Riviera and its colourful, extravagant inhabitants. The strange thing is that the life we lived there was nothing like the life that has been written about. We lived in a simple apartment block, in an apartment shared with a Dutchman and a Belgian woman called Daisy. If you leaned sideways as far as possible out of the lavatory window on the landing, you could just see the screen of an open-air cinema at the back. Children in the building took turns at this, and it was wonderful. Daisy was said to be there to get over an unhappy love affair. That was how you did it in those days. (My mother's prescription for unrequited love was seasickness. She said that if you are seasick you really can't worry about anything else. My father had useful advice for living, too. He said that if you are ever chased by a crocodile you should run zig-zag, because they have difficulty in turning corners.)

I also don't know how we met and got together with Daisy and the Dutchman; that was all part of an extraordinary carefreeness and holiday mood which I had never experienced in my solid, sober parents before, and never did again. It began when we had to register with the authorities in Nice. French bureaucracy required a lot of detailed information, including the visitor's mother's maiden name. In my parents' case both their mothers had been called Kohn before marriage, although in no way related to each other. It is difficult enough to find a clear way of putting this in English now. In French then it must have been pretty well impossible. It took a very long time, the official's suspicions becoming more and more sinister, and the scene became one of hysteria:

'Kohn?'
'Oui.'
'Et votre mère?'
'Kohn.'
'Toutes les deux Kohn?'
'Oui.'
'C'est votre enfant?'
'Oui ...'

All kinds of things were upside-down that year. Whereas at home I was used to going to the market with my mother, in Juan-les-Pins it was my father who shopped for food. We went to the market together, revelling in the smells and sights, and he wrote home to his brothers and sisters about grapes the size of plums and plums the size of eggs. With Daisy and the Dutchman we sat in the cool sitting room eating the huge grapes and spitting their skins over the balcony railing. The police came to complain, and we couldn't understand what was wrong until we looked over the railing and saw the pavement below black with grape skins.

The concierge had a little girl about my age. On her birthday she was given a yellow dress, all frills and flounces. All the tenants of the building stood round her on the pavement to admire, and quite casually someone said to me, 'Of course, yellow wouldn't suit you.' For the next thirty years it did not occur to me to question this pronouncement. I was in my thirties, working at Imperial College in London, when I saw a yellow dress I liked in the window of a shop by South Kensington station. I went in and asked if they had it in any other colours, but they didn't. Saying, 'That's a pity, I can't wear yellow' I turned to go. I had reached the door before it occurred to me to wonder why on earth not. I went back, bought the dress, and had a lot of pleasure from it. The incident has been very useful to me in explaining to people how psychoanalysis works. By recognising the origin of some taboo or other restriction on your life, you loosen its hold and your life becomes that much richer. Seven years of analysis and I can wear yellow. Whoopee.

But most of the time and all the time, there was the beach. All day spent in swimming trunks, hair getting lighter and skin getting darker. A large rubber ball was half-buried in the sand, and every morning a gymnastics instructor supervised classes of children bouncing on it. Again and again one lined up: kneel and up was the easiest bounce, sit and up a bit more difficult, a somersault the hardest of all, which I don't think I ever managed. After we got home in the autumn I ruined a sofa re-living the beach at Juan-les-Pins.

It was in that row of children of different shapes and sizes lining up to bounce on a rubber ball that I first realised that some people are beautiful and I wasn't one of them. I was little, and people seemed to like me. But others triggered off admiration and even awe because they had glamour, and that was something quite different.

I was five, and for some of the time in Juan-les-Pins I went to school. The first day I cried all day, and remember the other children standing round helplessly, not knowing what to do. But after that it was all right. The school was a simple wooden hut, with dusty floors, on which we sat in two groups, the youngest ones and the older ones. The teacher gave the younger ones notebooks and showed us how to make an 'a'. Then she went to deal with the other group. One went on making 'a's for line after line and page after page, until they started to look right. Then she came and showed how to make a 'b'. It meant you could progress at your own pace and without disturbance, and was pleasant in the hot, dusty calm. Sometimes there was a change of activity – singing a song or stringing coloured beads. This regime would be greatly disapproved of nowadays, when primary schools are filled with activity, colour, projects. I'm sure this is good, but I do wonder what happens if a child just wants to be quiet and think or dream.

We got to know another family, with a daughter called Sonia. The parents became friends and the children were supposed to, because we were the same age. It was uneasy, though; in some mysterious way we were each jealous of the other.

But the best thing that whole year was Easter Sunday. The two families went to Cap d'Antibes, where there was a large park, to look for Easter eggs. These are hard-boiled eggs, dyed and painted in bright colours, which the Easter hare hides in fields and woods and gardens. Finding a chocolate egg on your breakfast plate, as children do in England, is unmagical, as is decorating your own Christmas tree instead of coming upon it, decorated and alight with real candles, when you come home from skating in the dusk on Christmas Eve.

The two fathers walked ahead – quite a long way ahead, since not only did they walk faster anyway, but the children were slowed down by their search. Whenever we found an egg we gave it to the mothers, who had brought baskets, to look after. If we missed an egg, one of the mothers would drop a hint, or stare in the right direction, or even on occasion find it herself. Somehow they managed to convey the found eggs back to the fathers, who hid them again. And again. It was as if they were scattered throughout the whole park. We must have found dozens, peeping out from the shining spring grass, half hidden by a palm leaf, lodged in the fork of a scented mimosa tree. It was an exotic setting for a northern custom, and it was totally magical. When, at the end of the excursion, we actually ended up with ten eggs each, I was passionately grateful for having been thus deceived. It was the cleverest and most marvellous thing my parents ever did, and I treasure it the more because I have never succeeded in being deceived by anything since.

Karlsbad

After we came back from France I started proper school. This time I didn't cry, but I was still very reluctant. I trailed along behind my father who took me there on the first day, the gap between us growing until it was very wide indeed. My fear of venturing out beyond the shelter of home was metamorphosed into simply not seeing the point of schooling. I was going to be a Kindermädel when I grew up. This is simply a girl who looks after children, not the same as the British idea of a nanny. Having met some of these among my friends' families, as well as our own Resi, it seemed clear that this was a job that did not require school learning, so what would be the point?

I was nearly the smallest in the class, which was bad, and I had a sun-tan, which was good. I also had a very peculiar haircut: in the rush of clearing up and packing before we left Juan-les-Pins, I had heard my mother say, 'We must get her hair cut before we go.' Wanting to be helpful, I had cut it myself with her nail scissors.

Before we went to France I had been to Kindergarten once a week and to a children's gymnastics class. The gymnastics class was nearly spoiled for me by the intricacies of the bathing costume I had to put on. There were straps that crossed over at the back, and these made it so complicated to work out which opening to climb into, even when somebody was helping (especially when somebody was helping!), that I was generally late and flustered when I joined the class. In the Kindergarten I noticed that when children smiled in a way that showed their teeth, this had more effect on grownups than when they smiled with closed lips. I practised at home in front of a mirror, showing my teeth while smiling, but it didn't come naturally. It still doesn't.

Now school was full-time. On Sunday afternoons in summer the family gathered at the Richmond Park Hotel and I watched the dancing, hero-worshipped Mr Dvorsky, and chatted with the waiters. When my mother's relatives were visiting they gathered there as well. But my life was now dominated by school, and the Richmond and the whole spa aspect of the town was only a small part of it, and that only in summer. My father was no longer working in the linen shop but for an insurance company, and uncle Luis seemed a rather remote figure. Aunt Ida still provided lunch once a week but now she sent it in the form of cold cuts, which I took to school and shared round at elevenses.

Once there was a composition to write for school, with the title 'A Mother's Hands'. I wrote: 'My mother has a cigarette in one hand and bridge cards in the other.' Since the assignment was meant to produce something Germanic and sentimental about loving comfort and fevered brows, the teacher was not pleased. But the family enjoyed it and the story was passed round. I had started to make my contribution to the fund of family stories.

Our cook, Julie, had already been with us before we went to France, and her admirer often appeared in our home and generally joined us when we went for a walk. I knew him only as the man with a feather in his hat. While we were in France they married, but the man with the feather in his hat died not long after we came back and Julie, widowed after only a very short marriage, came back to us.

I don't know why Julie was called a cook; the reality was that she and my mother shared both the cooking and the other housework. On Mondays she and my mother worked in the steam-filled basement of the apartment house doing the laundry, with the help of a corrugated rubbing board and a hand-turned mangle. When the sheets were drying, Julie and I would sometimes take them and spread them out on the meadow by the river to be bleached by the sun. And sometimes the two women, or all three of us, would go to a place set up for housewives to hang rugs and carpets over ropes and beat them with cane carpet-beaters.

These now seem like very antiquated methods. On the other hand, Karlsbad had district central heating, the tiled stoves in the corners of our rooms only supplying top-up heating. Cooking was done on a large stove in which a fire was kindled with wood every morning and then kept going with coal. Once the door was closed on this fire it kept going long enough for cooking the main meal at mid-day, and was then allowed to go out. Along its side ran a rail on which tea-towels hung comfortingly to dry. Part of the skill in cooking lay in knowing the different levels of heat – cooler at the edges, hottest in the centre – reached on different parts of the stove's large surface, on which one moved the pans around as needed, and how this heat varied in the course of the morning. Snacks and small supper dishes were cooked on twin gas rings.

After lunch Julie would go home. My mother would have a rest and then emerge into what in England would be seen as the more middle-class aspects of her persona. This was a common pattern and is different from English lifestyles, where differences in activity and manner and style tend to be between different people and not within them, part of the same person. For my mother, basic housework and cooking in a no-nonsense apron, and sociable and leisured afternoons in good clothes, were parts of a seamless whole. This must be why now, as an elderly social scientist, I still do field-work in projects my Institute gets involved in, when others of my age and stage have long left this part of the work behind and drawn boundaries round what they believe is appropriate for them to do. Such boundaries have no meaning for me – getting into the field is necessary to understand any project, and a normal part of the job.

At school there was milk for elevenses, but no school lunches. Both my father and I came home for the mid-day meal. At one time the school instituted a very ill-conceived way of trying to ensure that the poorer children were well fed. The children in the class were crudely divided into 'rich' and 'poor', and once a week a 'rich' child took a 'poor' child home for lunch. It was a horrible experience for both of them.

My father was now working for an insurance company. He had a colleague called Mr Schenker, who sometimes came to the house. I felt very uneasy about the way he wanted me to call him 'uncle' and sit on his knee. I never did, and he never gave up asking.

England was a far-away place, about which there were stereotypes.

Newspaper cartoons depicted Englishmen as very thin, aristocratic-looking gentlemen wearing plus-fours. The bubble coming out of their mouths usually said, 'Shocking!', which was the only English word I knew. My parents both spoke a little English and used it when they didn't want me to understand what they were saying.

I knew that England had a new king and queen. When my mother explained to me about menstruation I found the idea ludicrous and difficult to believe. Again and again I asked, 'Are you sure? You really mean everybody?' Yes, everybody. And finally, 'Even the queen of England?' Yes, even the queen of England. That seemed to clinch it.

But alongside, and behind, and weaving itself into this ordinary domestic life there was the increasingly frightening news from Germany. A family friend who had married a German and moved there came back with her husband and children. Hitler's demands became more strident and most of the Sudeten-German population responded and met him half-way with their cry of '*Heim in's Reich!*' ('Home to the Reich!') In addition, the country was shaken in 1937 by the death of President Masaryk. At school we made drawings of laurel wreaths to mark the occasion. The country's motto, 'Pravda vítězí' ('Truth will prevail') seeped into my consciousness and stayed there.

In 1937 Julie joined the Sudeten-German equivalent of the Nazi party, led by a man called Konrad Henlein, and became an increasingly committed member. At the same time she was very attached to us and loyal. For my ninth birthday she gave me a cushion cover on which she had embroidered a red carnation, the symbol of the Social Democratic party. In the circumstances it was an extraordinary gesture of loyalty and affection, though a rather strange birthday present. But she was fascinated by Hitler, and after the annexation of Austria in the spring of 1938 her longing got the better of her and she left us to move to Vienna in order to be nearer to him. In this fascination she was like thousands of German, Austrian and Sudeten-German women. In Britain, too, I have met women who are in thrall to power and evil in a man.

For the two main political parties, the National Socialists and the Social Democrats, the first of May had great symbolic significance, and for May 1st 1938 both planned to organise parades.[8] Karlsbad lies along a narrow valley

---

[8] It was a few days after Henlein had made an inflammatory speech in Karlsbad, demanding German local government and freedom to profess German racial identity (Volkstum) and outlook (Weltanschauung). I hadn't known that. For grown-up accounts of the events of that summer and autumn, see J.W. Bruegel, *Czechoslovakia before Munich*. Cambridge University Press, 1973; David Faber, *Munich: the 1938 Appeasement Crisis*. Simon and Schuster, 2008.

and has just the one main street, so in order to avoid clashes it was agreed to hold these parades at different times. The National Socialists were to hold theirs in the morning and the Social Democrats theirs in the afternoon. Fritz and Ida lived on this main street, and I spent the day hanging out of the window of their first-floor flat.

First came the Nazis: a very large parade, disciplined, with flags and banners, singing and at intervals chanting slogans in chorus: *'Wir danken unserm Führer! Wir danken unserm Führer!'* ('We thank our Führer! We thank our Führer!') and *'Ein Volk, ein Reich, ein Führer!'* ('One people, one country, one leader!', a reference to their demand that Sudeten-Germany should become part of the German Reich). The streets and side-streets were packed, there were thousands of people shouting and cheering them on and waving flags, and children ran along by the side of the marchers.

There was the mid-day pause and then, at three o'clock, came the socialists. It was a much smaller parade, tiny in comparison, also disciplined and also with banners but just walking along, not marching in step. Fanni was among the front row, wearing her blue shirt with its red carnation pinned to it. The streets were empty; the crowds had vanished as if wiped away with a cloth. No one was in sight. It was eerily quiet.

I think of this scene every time I hear about the 'injustice' done to Sudeten-Germans when the Czechs expelled them after the war. This debate goes on down the generations, and is now conducted mainly by people who did not experience what happened. I know that there were injustices done; the expulsions were indiscriminate, sometimes involved cruelty, and hit children as well as adults, some socialists as well as Nazis. And yet I cannot shake off this image of the streets that 1st of May, packed with cheering crowds one moment and empty the next. There cannot be any doubt about where the loyalty of most of the Sudeten-German population lay.

That semester my best friend Norli suddenly stopped speaking to me. One morning in school she just didn't respond when I said hello, and she never addressed another word to me. For a few moments I was puzzled and then I realised that it must be because I was Jewish. I was also quite certain that this was not her own idea, but that she was doing what she had been told to by her father. So I was not too upset. But when I told my parents they were hugely upset. Norli's father was the manager of the local swimming baths, two open-air pools constructed along the bank of the river. He and my father had known each other since boyhood, in fact had also been at school together. It was my parents who pointed out that, when Norli had been ill for some weeks with pneumonia, I had gone to see her every day after school to tell her what had been happening, so that she wouldn't fall behind. The hurt to my father was so great that later, during the war, I heard him say that he wanted to survive the war so that he could go back and kill Norli's father.

Because I was so sure that Norli herself would not have thought of this, I really was not badly hurt. Or I think I wasn't – I have no way of knowing whether I was rationalising something because I couldn't bear it. But nearly forty years later something happened which showed me what an impact it had made. In the 1970s I was working in the Tavistock Institute of Human Relations in London. The Institute had many visitors, and one day there came a letter from a South African psychologist who wanted to visit. One of the young radicals who were dominating the Institute at the time sent a memo round to all members of staff, forbidding them to talk to this man because he was South African. For me this meant that I had to talk to him, although I was not particularly interested in his letter and had not planned to. I also sent a note round, explaining that not since Nazi times had anyone tried to control whom I could speak with. I then spent an afternoon with the South African. Nobody tells me whom I may or may not talk to.

Leaving

Prague

It was September 1938 and I was ten. I had skipped a year of elementary school and just started at the Gymnasium, the grammar school. The entrance tests had been difficult. They involved an entirely new concept – 'grammar' – and, since this had not featured in my schooling before, there had been some private coaching. It felt artificial and unreal: I memorised some rules, unconnected to any context, just long enough for the test and promptly forgot them. But the actual school was more sensible and, during the two weeks I was there, the new pattern of lessons and the new people felt like the beginning of something good.

On the table by my bed was a pile of new school books, pristine in their new covers. The custom was to protect schoolbooks by covering them with dark blue paper and sticking a label with the subject and the pupil's name on the front. My father took particular pride and pleasure in doing this for me. We had spent an evening at the kitchen table: he would first prepare a sheet of paper so that it was about five centimetres bigger all round than the opened book. Then he would mark the place on the paper where the spine would come and cut a flap, top and bottom, bending the flaps inwards. This was the tricky part: if the folds of the flaps did not end up aligning with the top and bottom of the spine, the whole thing would never come right. If they did, folding the paper round the front and back covers was then fairly easy, and I was allowed to do some. Then the label had to be straight and in the right place, about a third of the way down the front, and neatly written. His handwriting was even and neat, and he was expert at wrapping parcels. He had, after all, been a draper.

A glass-fronted cupboard in the hall was filled with the summer's preserves: strawberry jam, redcurrant jam, apricot jam, bottled blueberries and gooseberries, two sorts of pickled cucumber: small whole ones which suddenly became plentiful and cheap for a short time in July, and 'mustard cucumbers', so called because mustard seed was used in the pickling brine.

These had to be peeled, sliced down the middle, de-seeded and cut into chunks. They were a special delicacy, not only because they were good but also because more work was involved. My mother would sometimes just open the cupboard door and contemplate the rows of bottles. She always liked to mark the seasons: in early spring she would almost ceremonially serve the first early rhubarb as a sign that the season was beginning to turn, though none of us actually liked rhubarb much. For my birthday in June there would be the first strawberries. Now it was September, the time for conserving.

The Sudeten-German crisis had been escalating and it seemed likely that Hitler would soon settle the issue by force and invade. He was expected to announce his decision during the Nazi party rally in Nuremberg in September. On September 12th he made the closing speech at the rally. It was a virulent attack on the Czechs, who were an irreconcilable enemy, and on their President, Dr Beneš. The world should note, he declaimed, that the Sudeten Germans were neither deserted nor defenceless. It was clear, as it had been in diplomatic circles for some time, that he was going to invade. On September 13th the Czech government declared martial law in parts of the Sudetenland. On the evening of September 14th my parents packed two suitcases and a rucksack, and we took the train for Prague. The schoolbooks and jams and pickles stayed behind.

I took with me a volume of *Nesthäkchen*. This was the story of a girl, by Else Ury, following in ten volumes her life from when she is five until she is a grandmother. I had all ten volumes and knew them all by heart. Many years later, when I sometimes worked professionally in Germany, I tried to reassemble a set. When I visited the Institute of Social Research in Munich the Director asked what I would like to do while I was there. 'Look for volumes of *Nesthäkchen*' was not the answer he expected. I do have the complete set again, but it is mostly made up of newer editions. It was difficult to find copies of the old edition, and the illustrations in the new ones are not nearly as good or as evocative.

Fanni shared my love for the old German stories for girls, so sentimental and highly moral in their content and phrasing as to be wonderfully funny. She acquired quite a collection and, since they were almost the only books that were not spirited away from her bookcase after she died, I have it now.

We lived in Prague for two-and-a-half months, taking rooms in the flat of a platinum-blonde landlady. Everyone was expecting war. Czechoslovakia was well prepared: there were strong fortifications as well as natural defences in the form of mountain ranges on three sides of Bohemia. France and the Soviet Union were bound by treaty to support her if attacked. Later analysis has shown that in Germany much of the population did not want war, and opponents of Hitler were confident of support for overthrowing him if he started one now. But the British Prime Minister, Neville Chamberlain, provided a way out for him. Three times during September he visited Germany, in strenuous efforts to find a way of getting Hitler what he wanted without a war. In a broadcast he spoke of this quarrel 'in a faraway country between people of whom we know nothing'.

The third visit was the triumphant one. Chamberlain had succeeded in involving Italy, and on September 29th an agreement was signed in Munich by Hitler, Mussolini of Italy, the French Prime Minister Daladier and Neville Chamberlain, assigning this part of Czechoslovakia to Hitler. The Czech government had been bullied into agreeing and was not represented at the conference. On October 1st Hitler's troops crossed the border into Czecho-slovakia without a fight. As for any German opposition plans to overthrow Hitler, the ground had been cut from under their feet.

Meanwhile in Prague I was sent to school, the German-language Stephans-gymnasium off Wenceslas Square, and the grownups went into an intensive, endless-seeming round of discussions and consultations with the family about what to do. Fritz and Ida, Luis, Fanni, Marie and the Siegfried Kleins had also fled from Karlsbad to Prague, as had my cousins Hans and Richard and their families. Trude and Rudl were already living in Prague. My grandmother Rosa with Grete and her children was living in Pilsen, as were my grandmother's sister, aunt Else Glaser and her husband, and there was much coming and going between Pilsen and Prague.

At school I lost a fountain pen which the Dutchman had given my mother, and got into trouble. My other memory is of an elderly professor coming into the biology class with a human embryo in a bottle. In England, years later, biology began less disturbingly with the amoeba. In the cinema Walt Disney's 'Snow White' was playing.

The consultations went on. To leave or not to leave? America or England? The word 'affidavit' began to feature in these discussions – I must have heard it a hundred times. An affidavit was a magic ingredient you needed to get into America, but how to get one? My father on the phone to my cousin Hans, who did manage to get one and ended up in California, where he and his wife first worked in domestic service, she in the house and he as a gardener. Later he worked at the Scripps Oceanographic Institute in La Jolla. He distinguished himself by devising a new method for charting the ocean bed, but was deprived of the pleasure of using it himself because he got seasick. My father and Hans, with their families, were the only ones to escape at that stage.

Once during this period my father went back home across the new border. He took a rucksack, packed the silver cutlery that had been a wedding present from my mother's parents, and came out again. It was a terribly risky thing to do; I have that cutlery now.

America or England? I think in the end it was England because the Social Democratic Party organised a transport. They decided to send men first, because they were thought to be in greater danger than women and children. Meanwhile outside, in Prague and in the country as a whole, there was mobilisation and an overpowering bitterness about Neville Chamberlain and the English. With the Sudeten-German region he had signed away the country's natural mountainous defences. What gave them the right to do this to us? What business was it of theirs? As a matter of fact, I still don't understand that. It is hard to appreciate nowadays what great prestige and influence Britain had at that time. Thinking about those newspaper cartoons, there did seem to be a great many British aristocrats involved in diplomatic activity around 'the Czech question' – the Foreign Secretary Lord Halifax, Lord Vansittart, Lord Runciman ... Later accounts tell of shuttling back and forth between London and the grouse moors of Scotland.

Family consultations merged into the round of goodbyes. I needed a new winter coat, and there was a battle. I thought the coat my mother picked out too babyish; she didn't like the one I wanted. We found one that was an acceptable compromise. The platinum-blonde landlady warned me about England: they send naughty children to boarding school, she said, so I had better be on my best behaviour. My cousin Peter was into collecting matchbox tops, and asked me to send him some from England. I never did, and the guilt of it is with me still. My grandmother wrote recipes into a cookbook for my mother. I have it now, but many of the recipes are of little use to me because she tends to give ingredients and quantities but no instructions, assuming that you know what to do. In the section for starters there is a note: 'Herring cream. Very good. Has strayed into the tortes.' Sometimes there are cheaper and more extravagant versions of the same recipe. Sometimes there is acknowledgement of whose speciality this is; which friend or cousin has, as it were, the copyright: 'Bonbons (Selma)'. Sometimes there are instructions that I want to argue with. A sour cherry torte begins with sugar and egg-yolks being beaten for half an hour. Half an hour? Would it really matter if it was only ten minutes?

But by the time I was taking notice of recipes she had died of starvation. She died in Terezín (Theresienstadt, the 'holding' camp), of malnutrition because she gave her food ration to Peter. To the end, she was providing food. Someone who was with them and who survived told me that as she lay on her bunk she scratched my mother's name and mine on the wall. After all those eggs and almonds and sugar, butter and hazelnuts, marinades and preserves. A touch of bitter irony is that my grandmother was very worried about us going to England, because one heard and read so much about the IRA planting bombs in English letterboxes.

Uncle Viktor, happily married and farming in Austria, divorced his wife because she might be safer if she was not married to a Jew. This turned out to be true: unlike the others, she did survive the war. Then, aged sixty-nine, he walked from Vienna to Prague and joined the others. Several months later, one of his letters to my father in England describes the trouble he was still having with his feet because of that walk. Somebody once asked why didn't he walk in the other direction, towards Switzerland. It seems to me obvious that the impulse to be with the brothers and sisters would be stronger than any other.

The American connection

As grandfather's carefully researched family trees show, in the nineteenth century somebody in every generation of my father's family had emigrated to America; it was part of the broad movement that created the United States. One of these was his mother's brother Rudolf or Rudolph Kohn (already Jewish names are getting mingled with German ones). He was brought to the United States in 1865, aged nineteen, by his eldest brother, Edward Nathan Kohn, who had come earlier, prospered in the lumber business, and lived in Camden, New Jersey. A middle brother, Siegmund, had also emigrated and married there; he was killed in the Civil War. Among Edward Nathan's enterprises was a sawmill in Princess Anne, Maryland, conveniently situated on a railway line. Rudolf was sent to learn about and later manage this business, and married there.

The brothers became Protestants, Rudolf an active and devoted Presbyterian. He and his wife had seven children and later moved to Norfolk, Virginia. I think this is the uncle whom my father met when he visited New York and recognised by the shape of his hand. But Rudolf died in 1909 and the contact between the families faded.

The crisis of 1938 led to renewed contact, nearly thirty years later. One granddaughter of Rudolf, Alice Rice Jaffé, carefully kept the correspondence of that time, and later renewed and maintained the contact with those of us who escaped to England. In the autumn of 1938 the Cohn family in Virginia (the spelling by now changed) suddenly found themselves besieged with desperate requests for 'affidavits' from relatives they barely knew about. Alice Rice Jaffé wrote an account:

> ... Alois, spearheading the requests for affidavits, turned to the Cohn cousins for help. In the turmoil of their lives, they had lost the pertinent addresses, but the letter sent to my two [great-]uncles (one long deceased and the other living in Princess Anne, Maryland) and addressed to them only as 'proprietors of a sawing mill, Norfolk, Virginia' was, amazingly, delivered to my aunts, all married and with different names! Such was our postal service then.

Luis wrote the letter to unknown uncles, of whom one was long dead and the other not living in the town to which the letter was posted, on December 6th. He already had an affidavit from somewhere for himself and Siegfried, but asked for affidavits for Viktor, Fanni, Marie, Ida and Fritz. Miraculously the letter reached the next generation in Norfolk. One of Rudolf's daughters was Anna Rose, who had married a Fred Outland. The letter reached the Outlands, but they had no idea what the word affidavit meant. They immediately cabled 'agreed' anyway, and then set about trying to find out. Their representative in Washington, Lindsay Warren, was a friend, but he didn't know either. His letter to them, saying, 'I am at a loss to know what he means by an affidavit ...' is dated December 21st and is on House of Representatives paper.

Alice Rice (not yet married to Louis Jaffé) also didn't know what an affidavit was and had also been making enquiries about this mysterious talisman. She got an explanation from the Department of State Visa Division, confirming the need to establish that aliens seeking an immigration visa were not likely to be a public charge. '... The affidavits of friends or relatives showing their ability and willingness to assist the alien, in case of necessity, are helpful in this respect ...'

The American relations gathered in Norfolk for Christmas and decided to parcel the Czech relations out among themselves, taking on one each. It was not to be undertaken lightly: the Czech relations had been able to take very little with them to Prague, and there was no guarantee that they would be able to take anything at all out of the country. So the American relations had first to accept that they might have to support these unknown relatives, and then had to establish their own credibility for doing this, obtaining bank references and references from employers. And yet, by December 28th, Lindsay Warren was able to write to the American Consul in Prague:

My dear Mr Bruins:

The following have all received their passports in order to emigrate to the United States within the quota:

Viktor Klein

Mrs Fanni Blatny

Dr Fritz Feldman-Fisher

Mrs Ida Feldman-Fisher

Mrs Mary Mendl ...

Affidavits of support have been sent them by close relatives in the United States who live in North Carolina, Virginia and Maryland. These affidavits will be signed by members of the Cohn, Rice, Outland and Bell families. I am well acquainted with these families, all of whom are prominent and outstanding citizens. The Outlands, my neighbors, live just a few doors from me. Any affidavit signed by any of them is sufficient for the purposes stated.

Anything that you can do to expedite these cases will be personally appreciated by me ...

He also wrote to the Secretary of State, the Hon. Cordell Hull, enclosing this letter and asking that it be placed in the Diplomatic pouch, so that there would be no question of its delivery. He further asked that, if Mr Bruins was not in Prague, the letter be delivered to the proper Consul.

It was a remarkable response, individually and collectively. Sadly, having made so much effort and incurred so much risk, the American families did not feel able to make as committed a response to another request they then received from a branch of Czech family called Prossnitz. I don't know these, though they feature in a family tree which Alice compiled. I only have here in front of me copies of their increasingly desperate letters begging for the magic affidavits.

And, of course, it was all for nothing. The affidavits arrived during the first days of January 1939 and were received with immense and touching joy, relief and gratitude. But all they meant was that one could now apply for a visa. Then one had to sit and wait for one's number to come up under the quota system. Luis and Fanni decided to wait in England, to which entry was possible only because their stay was meant to be temporary. Luis got an exit permit on condition that he left all his possessions behind, and travelled to England with one small suitcase, landing on March 30th, the last day on which it could be done without an entry visa.

He did, however, take with him an envelope with two small yellowing sheets of paper, letters written to him when he was a boy away from

Udritsch at school, Udritsch being too small to have more than a primary school. The first letter is from his mother. There is no date, but as she died when he was fourteen it was obviously before 1885. It says:

Dear Luis,
As we will not be able to come to see you at ... you must say the necessary prayers on your own. God give you His blessing and give you health, strength, and a firm will, so that you will always fulfil your duties and that we will have the happiness of experiencing joy in you.
    I am sending you some cakes, when I come to see you I will buy what I promised. Also your dear father is sending something for the rabbi. Be sure to be diligent, so that you get good marks, and write to us all about it. I kiss you many times, your loving mother
Karoline.
Don't eat too much at once.

The second letter is from both parents, his father adding the final paragraph:

Dear Luis,
As I cannot leave Ida for such a long time, and promised to come and see you, I will come to Karlsbad on Sunday morning. So you come on Sunday with the morning train as well, and I will wait for you at the station, we can be together till four o'clock in the afternoon. Do your homework on Saturday afternoon, learn what has been set for you, so that you don't miss anything. Be careful altogether, for in your letter-writing you make quite a lot of mistakes. Make the effort, and always learn with enthusiasm and love.
    I kiss you many times, your loving mother
Karoline.
Be careful when you get into the train and be sure to do your homework well on Saturday. Your dear mother will wait for you on Sunday morning in the station in Karlsbad. Don't get your school reports dirty.

Fanni, who was in greater danger than all of them once the Germans had taken Prague in March 1939, was helped to escape by colleagues in the British Labour Party. She described her escape in one of her letters to Alice Jaffé after the war, written after an illness. In old age Fanni was rather fat.

She made a joke of it; the American relatives sometimes sent clothes that she could not use:

> Now as I am allowed to go out, my first way was to the dressmaker with your black dress. She only laughed heartily and couldn't recover laughing when I asked her whether this dress could be changed for me. So it has to go to my sister in law Valli Klein in Styria, the widow of my poor brother Viktor ... But don't worry about me, as I quite forgot to mention to you that my brother has sent me a black woollen dress some years ago.
>
> Now I will tell you how it came about that I could not bring more of my clothing to England.
>
> On the 12th of Sept. 38, our friend Adolf Hitler held his well-known speech at Munich.[9] That was the signal for thousands of people, including my brothers and sisters, to leave as quickly as possible (meaning the next day) the German border country and to take refuge in the inner part.
>
> It was different with me. Just at that time, beginning on the 15th September, I should have presided over a fortnight's school for women in another part of the country. So I just packed a small case with sufficient clothing to last me for a fortnight. I went to Prag to our political headquarters to ask them whether it was not too dangerous to separate women from their families at such a critical time. The school was cancelled, as well as any other political activity, and I therefore had to go back to Karlsbad, only to preside over a women's [meeting] to tell my comrades to prepare for flight and only to take as much with them as they could carry. Advising them like this, it was only natural for me to do the same.
>
> I stayed with my sisters and brothers in Prag until the end of March, when Hitler had invaded also the Czech part of the country. Brother Emil and his family had left already for England and Luis had gone some days before. I, as the most endangered, had to leave too, and left with false papers and my old M.P. passport. The farewell from my remaining family was terribly sad, although we did not know then that we would not meet again.
>
> Nothing happened on the way through Germany. Two English people who shared the compartment asked me whether I had any written or printed papers among my belongings. I said no, except my

---

[9] She has misremembered. It was Nuremberg.

address book, a book I wrote myself, and the family history. They thought me careless and so the gentleman took all my treasured books so as to throw them at the first opportunity into a river. (Just imagine, that months after that I was informed by the Society of Friends that a parcel of books belonging to me had been sent to them, to be forwarded.)

My trouble started at the German-Dutch border, the reason being my old M.P. passport. After being searched thoroughly they took my travel ticket, so leaving me completely helpless, as the Dutch only accepted transit emigrants. My English lady friend gave me her ticket, and in the last moment I slipped into the Dutch train and so the Germans saw the last of me (thank heavens).

I believe that the 'two English people' who shared her compartment were members of the British Labour Party who had come to get her out, and that the 'English lady friend' was Mary Sutherland, its Chief Woman Officer.

The other brothers and sisters, brothers-in-law and sisters-in-law stayed waiting in Prague.

England

We docked in London on November 28th 1938. There may have been reporters on board by then, because the children in the group were lined up on deck and told to point at something while photographs were taken. The ship was the SS *Baltrover*, with about a hundred Sudeten-German Social Democrat women and children on board. It was a small ship, but to me it had seemed huge when we boarded, the dark grey hull looming up against the lighter grey surroundings in the dusk. It had left the port of Gdynia five days earlier, and we had left Prague by train two days before that. I can still see the cluster of relatives standing in the dim light of the platform as the train pulled out at nine in the evening. The Pilsen relatives had come to Prague, and even ten-year-old Peter had been allowed to stay up.

(Recently I travelled to Prague by train, which meant arriving at the same Wilson railway station. They were still there, ghosts in old-fashioned clothes, puzzled by what I have been up to in the meantime, and sad that I don't have children. But loving me unconditionally anyway.)

We were obliged to go the long way round, via Poland, because it was not possible to go through Germany. Even at ten I had a vague feeling that there was something wrong about this. Czechs were generally snobbish about Poland, its peasant culture and bad roads, and now, it seemed, we had no scruples about using their country for transit and their facilities for escape.

The sea voyage took five days, because we could not go through the Kiel Canal but had to go round between the islands of Skaggerak and Kattegat, and it was rough. My mother stayed in her bunk the whole time, and to leave the cabin shared by about twenty people one had to skip over puddles of vomit. The worst part was the smell. So, left to my own devices, I became friendly with one of the sailors, a Pole; it was my first experience of flirting. On the Sunday the sailors, who felt sorry for the refugees, had clubbed together to provide a special lunch for us. But the whole group was by then sea-sick, and I remember sitting alone in the dining room, waited on by the sailors, eating roast duck.

Then we were moving up the Thames, through the gap of Tower Bridge which we had watched open up, and docking at Tower Hill pier. It was six o'clock in the evening. By ten o'clock the ship was cleared, except for my mother and me. She was refusing to land. It was the fault of the English that we were in this situation, she said, and she wasn't going to set foot in their country. This feeling about England stayed with her for a long time, and as I was to become more absorbed and assimilated and British, it became a big problem between us. So there we sat, in the now empty ship, while various people came to try and talk her round. The men had been sent about four weeks ahead, so my father was already in England somewhere in a refugee hostel. Finally one of the party officials talked my mother round. By this time it was late evening and dark, and we came down the gangway into the sudden glare of a circle of lights and whirring of newsreel cameras. Next thing my mother was standing in front of a microphone, making a speech about gratitude and hospitality. They stood me beside her, I suppose for added pathos. But I knew what she was really thinking, and the sight of my mother lying in her teeth brought on a fit of schoolgirl giggles. So they were filming this idiot child, gazing up at its mother, simply not able to stop laughing. That newsreel must have been unusable.

Our first stopping place in England was a refugee hostel in Sussex. An elderly couple, who owned a large old house surrounded by beautiful parkland near West Hoathly, had had a modern house built in the grounds for their daughter when she married. They were very philanthropic, and had already housed and given help to refugees from the Spanish Civil War. Now they took on the Sudeten-German socialists and Jews and offered this house to the British Committee for Czech Refugees, which had been formed after Munich. So it was there that we were reunited with the men of the party, including my father.

Before the actual transfer could be arranged my mother and I were housed for a few days in Wimbledon with a mother and her grown-up daughter. My mother spent the whole time in bed, trying to recover from the journey and its traumas, while the daughter of the house gave me my first English lessons. I would draw, say, an apple, and she would write underneath the word APPLE. This went well, until I drew a cooking pot. It did not resemble anything she could identify. After various attempts she tried drawing, and showing me, a saucepan but that in turn was unfamiliar to me. The puzzle remained unresolved.

In West Hoathly it was a tremendous irony to be settling to live in idyllic surroundings in the dreadful situation in which we found ourselves. The three children in the group squabbled about who was going to wash in the blue bathroom and who in the yellow bathroom, while the refugee organisation issued pocket money to the adults, to buy toothpaste and get shoes mended. A very interesting lady, who had travelled alone in the Far East and had turned her letters home into a book,[10] came and gave English lessons. It was difficult to understand that you say 'he is, isn't he', 'he does, doesn't he', but not 'he goes, goesn't he'. Some years later a friend of my mother's made a dress for me. As I tried it on she stood back with satisfaction and said, 'It fits, fitsn't it!' It seems much more logical than the correct version.

Refugees were still rare at that time, and we were the objects of much curiosity. Strangers would drive up in their cars, knock on the door and ask if they could come in and watch us eat. There were country houses and estates in the surrounding districts, and we received many invitations. The people in the neighbourhood included Harold Macmillan and his wife Lady Dorothy. They eventually offered to have me educated with their daughters. From some level of wisdom with which I would not have credited them, my parents declined with thanks. Our relationship, especially that with my mother, became difficult enough as I was to become more and more English. I cannot imagine how things would have turned out if I had gone to an upper-class boarding school.

Having had no address to give them, we had no news for a long time from the relatives who had been left behind, and we worried about them and missed them badly. And at the same time there was safety, comfort, beautiful countryside, and generosity. And, at the same time again, there was an over-riding resentment at being in this situation at all, at having to be grateful to the people who had brought it about. And there was bewilderment at their peculiar habits: they had open fires that burned your front while your back froze, and their food was horrible (there is a recipe on the women's page of the *Daily Telegraph* in November 1938, for 'making winter greens more palatable': add a little vinegar or horseradish to the water in which you boil them). They seemed to value manners above everything (my father came back from a visit to London saying they could stamp on your feet and knock you over, but it didn't matter as long as they said 'sorry'). They knew very little of politics or geography, and regarded foreigners like something from the zoo. And yet again, in my father's mind they could be summed up as 'This is a country where you can leave your bicycle outside the door.'

When Christmas came we were overwhelmed with presents, especially the children, and with hospitality. This had its problems. The people in the big house wanted to make a nice Christmas for us and consulted my mother, the

---

[10] Audrey Harris, *Foreign Visas* (1939). London, Collins.

only one of the women with a few words of English, about what our customs were. Now the custom in our Catholic part of Czechoslovakia had been to have the main Christmas meal on Christmas eve. And, since there was some vestigial connection with fasting, the meal was fish. But in no sense was this a privation – the custom was to do very elaborate things with carp. The only thing my mother was able to convey out of all this was fish, so we sat down in the handsome Elizabethan manor hall to pieces of fried cod. This was followed by Christmas pudding, which is a terrifying object when you first encounter it. A huge lump of black stickiness was brought in, frighteningly engulfed in flames; and my father broke a tooth on a three-penny bit.

And then there was the problem of Christmas cake. Wherever we were invited during this period, we were confronted by small pieces of what was recognisably cake, encased in seven or eight centimetres of concrete. Having gathered how important table manners were in England, we simply didn't know how to tackle it. At one such tea party the hostess asked my father if he would like a second helping. He politely said no thank you, but then pointed to the plate of one of the other men and said, 'My friend here likes it very much.' His hapless friend, who didn't have enough English to defend himself, stared miserably at yet another cannonball. Inwardly he was so enraged at the trick that had been played on him that, when we got outside, there was a fist fight.

After Christmas the three children in the group, two girls and a boy, were sent to the local village school. The schoolmistress didn't know what to do with us, and gave us cards with nursery rhymes to look at. Nursery rhymes may be for children, but at the same time they are very puzzling. A tuffet? Curds and whey? Humpty Dumpty? Whenever the class did something we could follow, such as arithmetic done on the blackboard, it was stuff that we had already done at school at home long before.

I made a friend, the daughter of a farm worker. The children had been told that we came from Czechoslovakia. But when she asked whether Czechoslovakia was a village bigger than West Hoathly, I didn't know the word for 'country' and could not explain.

One day a lady from the refugee organisation came and asked some questions of the two girls, who were about the same age. There was a girls' grammar school in London whose Christian Board of Governors felt guilty about what had happened at Munich, and had decided to give two free places for children who were in England as a consequence. (I have met this phenomenon again, in odd places. Many years later a Harley Street oculist refused to give me a bill when she heard where I came from.) And so, by a stroke of the most enormous luck, Marianne Lischke and I got the opportunity to go to the Grey Coat Hospital in Westminster. Marianne's parents moved on to Canada a few months later, taking her with them, but I stayed at the school. I learned the story of how we got this opportunity on the day I left school eight years later, when the headmistress, the redoubtable Miss Chetham-Strode, asked me to her room and explained it. I stayed at the school before, during and after the war, through war-time evacuation and beyond, winning a scholarship at fourteen but always supported in any case, down to socks and toothpaste and a holiday for my mother when we were away from London. And when I later went to university, they collected some money to supplement my scholarship.

At first, however, it meant leaving our parents in Sussex and moving to London. We were taken to London and from Victoria to the school in Westminster. In a taxi! Whoever took us was inspired enough to get the driver to make a detour via the Mall – I can still see it vividly.

It had been arranged for the widowed mother of one of the older girls in the school to put us up. On our first night in this billet we came up against a problem. Our bedroom was the downstairs back room. I woke up during the night needing to go to the lavatory, and found my way upstairs to the bathroom. But I couldn't open the door. There was a smooth, round doorknob to be turned, where I had only ever dealt with door handles which you press down. I knew that Marianne could manage the handle and went back downstairs, woke her up and asked her to do it. But she was afraid of the dog and could not be persuaded to leave the bedroom. By the time we had argued about this for some time, she too needed a lavatory and the problem was still unsolved. The room had one of those old-fashioned washstands with a china washbasin, and in the end we used that. In the morning I carried it up to empty it in the bathroom, and on the way encountered Mrs J. She did not make a fuss, but when I wrote and told my parents about this episode, my father wrote to her and apologised. I wish he hadn't done that.

School became a good experience, the billet less so. Mrs J thought it her duty to teach us English customs and manners, and any infringement pro-voked a stern lecture. She bathed us, not trusting us to wash ourselves (we were ten years old). At night she came and planted a formal little kiss on our foreheads. Tea after school consisted of slices of bread and butter, which one turned into sandwiches by spreading on some fish-paste from a little jar, laying a lettuce leaf on top, and then another slice of bread. When my father came to visit once he found this ritual strange, which must have provided further proof of the uncivilised nature of foreigners. Mrs J's great source of pride was that, in a street of identical terraced houses, hers was a little different from the others because it formed the corner with a side-street.

On Sunday mornings we were sent to Sunday school and in the afternoons we visited Mrs J's husband's grave, to cut the grass on it with a pair of scissors. In six months the only time we saw anything of London apart from the bus-ride to school, the Sunday school and the cemetery was on my birthday in June. We were taken to Wimbledon Common for a picnic. It was a pleasant outing, but disaster struck on the way home. There was an ice-cream man. Mrs J exceptionally handed Marianne a sixpence and told her to get three twopenny ices. Marianne, whose English was still uncertain, misunderstood her and got two threepenny ones. We thought the punishments were never going to end: lectures about how selfish and ill-mannered foreigners are, pocket-money stopped, early to bed – there was no end to it.

At school we were put into the last year of the lower school, so I lost the year I had skipped at home. There seemed to be a lot of knitting and handicraft and games, not much of what you could call real school work. But one of the language teachers took on the task of teaching us English. She gave us extra lessons, and we were told that she was teaching phonetically. I am not sure now exactly what that means, but in any case the only reminder I have that English is not my mother tongue is that I tend to pick up the accent of anyone I am speaking to. It happens quite automatically and can be embarrassing – people sometimes think I am mimicking them deliberately.

The children in the class supplemented this teaching, or rather they didn't. They would sometimes stand in front of us and say a word and, when we asked what it meant, giggle and run away. It is actually very difficult to learn the meaning of 'rude' words, since nobody will tell you. There are some I am not sure of even now.

It has been strange sometimes, being as it were on the other side of the table. In 1985 I was a member of the Norman Thomas Committee, which was looking at primary schools in London for the Inner London Education Authority. Some of the people giving evidence to the Committee made a passionate case against the teaching of English. Children coming from ethnic homes should not in any way be made to feel that what they heard at home was not correct. There was no such thing as 'correct' English; any formulation was as good as any other. Never mind that many ethnic minority people had come to Britain precisely because they wanted their children to have a good education and chance in life, it was politically incorrect to teach language.

Finally I lost my cool with one of these activists. 'Listen,' I said, 'I came to this country without a word of English. I'm very thankful that you were not around, and that someone took the trouble to teach me. They gave me a tool, so that now I can argue with you! I have sat in negotiating meetings in companies where the shop stewards stormed out in frustration, not because they didn't have a case, but because they were not able to put it; and where management won a much weaker case simply because they could argue it. You have no right to condemn your children to that!' I don't suppose it had any effect.

In March the Oxford and Cambridge boat-race was a cause for great excitement and partisanship. With no idea of what this was about, we were challenged to say whether we were for Oxford or for Cambridge. Since I liked dark blue, I said 'Oxford', and instantly became a passionate supporter. Of what? I didn't know.

Then, one morning on the bus to school, I saw a headline on the front page of the newspaper of the man sitting opposite: the Germans had entered Prague. At school that day the teachers looked at us with solemn faces, but no one actually talked about it. They probably assumed that we knew. When we got back after school I asked Mrs J if it was true: she listened to the radio, she must have already known in the morning. Instead of answering she lifted me onto her knee, pushed my face into her bony shoulder, and said, 'There, there, have a good cry. It will make you feel better.'

I've just had a flash: this must be the origin of my loathing for some forms of 'counselling' – the kind that consists of a shoulder offered but absolute unwillingness, or more likely inability, to acknowledge the substance of a problem. Ugh.

Billets of various kinds were to be my homes for the next four years; it turned out to be a unique way of learning about the life of a very wide span of English society. None of the billets was to be as bleak again as Tooting, but on the other hand even the nicest was not home. I remember a very clear sense, in the house of a family who really treated me as one of themselves and were kindness itself, that you can't kick the furniture because it's not your furniture; and they don't have you here because they want you, they are forced to have you. In your own family you count as an individual. Without it, you may get good and fair treatment but it is because you are one of a category. In England I have never been able to shake off this feeling of only being one of a category. Perhaps it is also the difference between living in a country of thirteen million people and one of sixty million. In any case, refugee-dom and war-time evacuee-dom fed into each other, and the combination has left a permanent mark. One minor consequence is that I am still not good at accepting hospitality. In other people's houses I lie awake, wondering what they do about breakfast and how to get to the bathroom without waking anybody, as I did in all those other strange bedrooms. And I behave badly when English people invite me for Christmas dinner, especially if I find the regulation bags of toffees and bath salts by my plate. There have been so many of them.

But I am jumping ahead, the war had not yet started. When it did, I was spending the school holidays in Sussex. The refugee hostel had been broken up and the people dispersed. My parents had been lent one of a pair of farm workers' cottages on one of the estates and already at Easter I had been there for an idyllic holiday. The farm worker in the other cottage had a daughter about my age, and with her I had discovered the Sussex countryside with its primroses, wild daffodils, and bluebells. Sometimes the landowner would call in with a couple of rabbits he had shot, and my mother would grit her teeth and set about skinning them. My father threw himself into helping on the farm, and there is a photograph of him helping with sheep dipping. He also tried growing vegetables on a small plot that was attached to the cottage. But he was inexperienced: having sown a packet of lettuce seeds we watched helplessly as they all came up in the same week in the summer, and bolted. Potatoes were more successful and it was a new experience to dig up fresh potatoes to cook. He tried to convince our neighbour about the pleasures of continental food, proudly taking a plateful of my mother's potato dumplings next door, but I suspect that this was not a success.

In the spring Fanni and Luis had arrived in England. Luis found a room in Inverness Terrace in London, and Fanni joined my parents in Sussex. He wrote to her two or three times a week, the way people telephone now. The letters are about the problem of finding a cheap enough room, and the landlady, and making contact with the refugee organisation, and discovering Kensington Gardens.

Paradoxically, 1939 was a long, beautiful summer. I was with my parents and Fanni, there were friendly neighbours, some of the other people from the refugee hostel were nearby, the weather was lovely and so was the countryside. For the grownups, it remained alien. One day my mother and Fanni were invited to an afternoon with the village Mothers' Union. They came back speechlessly shaking their heads. The afternoon had been spent in a race: fish shapes were cut out of newspaper, and the ladies had raced their fishes across the floor of the village hall by flapping at them with newspapers.

We had no radio, but on the day war was declared we all, together with some of the people from the farm and a few other refugees nearby, went up to the big house to listen to Neville Chamberlain make his broadcast. Then we went back to the cottage in the summer sunshine. A week earlier, Luis had become afraid that we would be moved to unknown destinations and interned, and would lose contact with the relatives. He wrote to several of them separately ('one of the letters is sure to arrive') giving a list of people whom he would always keep informed about where we were.

The main contact in a neutral country was a woman employee from Luis's shop who had married a Swiss and was living in Lausanne. M and Mme Devaud agreed to forward letters if it should become impossible to write direct, and for the next four years they devotedly acted as a kind of post office, transmitting letters from us to the relatives who had stayed behind – both my mother's and my father's – and from them to us, as well as to and from Pepp in New York.

I have a box of letters and postcards, the ones that still came direct in 1939 and the ones that came via the Devauds once war had started. There are about 150 of them, and I wanted to translate some of them and put them into an appendix. However, that didn't work; they assume that the reader knows what is being talked about, and it would require a running commentary of explanations, some of which I don't have myself. So I made a short and wholly inadequate summary of this correspondence, which is in Appendix 1.

Evacuation

Plans to evacuate schools out of London had already been made a year earlier, during the Munich crisis. Now they were very quickly put into operation. Grey Coat was first evacuated to Brighton, where it shared the premises of the local grammar school; the girls were billeted out. I had two billets, both in small terraced houses in the same street, with families who were kind and ordinary, in the good sense of the word, meaning normal. The evacuee, or 'vaccy', was simply accepted as part of the new situation everyone was in.

The Ringshaws lived by routine, always the same food and the same activities on the same day each week: a roast and the *News of the World* on Sundays, cold meat and the washing on Mondays, shepherd's pie and the ironing on Tuesdays, and so on until it was sausages on Saturdays. On Saturday afternoons they went to the pictures, and on the way home they would stop at a pub for a drink. They took me with them as a matter of course, and when it came to calling at the pub I would wait outside. I didn't mind; it was interesting watching the traffic, there were usually one or two other children, and Mr Ringshaw would bring me out a glass of lemonade. But my mother was horrified when I wrote to her about this treat, especially at the idea of going to the cinema to see whatever happened to be playing. I loved it.

The Ringshaws had a daughter of about twenty, who shared her bedroom with me. It was so cold that we both performed acrobatics in the mornings to put our clothes on under the bedclothes before getting out of bed. That winter I developed chilblains, something I had never come across before.

Winnie went to cookery classes and one day produced a most magnificent trifle. It took three days to make, because each layer had to set before the next layer could be put on. In one of the layers of jelly there was a tin of fruit salad, and in the custard on top there were silver balls. I still regard trifle as an awesome creation.

The Akehursts, too, were kind, Mrs Akehurst being perhaps a shade more motherly than Mrs Ringshaw. She was able to put her arm round you and give you a hug, which so far no English person had done. Mr Akehurst was a builder and his treat, for Sunday afternoon tea, was to spread sweetened condensed milk out of a tin onto his bread and butter. The only time they got it wrong was when Mrs Akehurst sent me out on a Girl Guide hike over-equipped, down to a saucepan and a raw egg to boil in it. I had to take quite a lot of teasing for that.

The school had a uniform for winter, consisting of a grey tunic tied in the middle with a girdle, and a pale blue cotton blouse. I still like the colours grey and blue. The uniform had its problems; the pleats on the tunic would never stay in, the woven girdle had to be rolled up to try and keep it flat, but still ended up looking like a piece of string. But with all its difficulties (and I have skirted the problem of lisle stockings which would not stay up, hats with brims that twisted and waved, woollen knickers with cotton knicker linings) – with all these difficulties I liked school uniform. It was a relief not having to worry about some children having prettier or better clothes than others, which had been a preoccupation in the school at home.

For summer there had been no uniform. But now, being responsible for three hundred girls away from home, the authorities felt it was necessary to be able to identify them at any time. A rule was made that uniform should be worn at all times, including weekends, and a summer uniform had to be designed. For me that was fine, since I had virtually no other clothes – the problem of clothes could be put aside. When it confronted me again eight years later I was completely unequipped to deal with it. The specification given to the designer of the school summer dress was that girls wearing it should not appeal to Canadian soldiers. He did a great job, putting well-built seventeen- and eighteen-year-olds into checked gingham with puffed sleeves and Peter Pan collars. The Upper Third made its own first dresses in the weekly sewing lesson; I suppose everyone else must have done too. Mine took so long to make that by the time it was finished I had outgrown it.

That was in the summer of 1940. France fell, the British army was evacuated from Dunkirk, and moving children to the south coast turned out not to have been such a good idea. The school was moved inland, to Farnham in Surrey, and once again there were arrangements to share the building of the local grammar school, and to billet out the girls. In Farnham our evacuee status was somehow more pronounced. Perhaps it was because Farnham was more middle-class than the Preston Park area of Brighton, perhaps my own adolescence made me more self-conscious, perhaps the first spontaneous acceptance and adaptation on both sides was wearing off. It was in any case here that the sense of 'you don't have rights and you can't kick the furniture' entered my blood and bones and became a permanent part of me.

I had three billets in Farnham, the first two rather short-lived and shared with another girl. Heather and I lost contact after we left school, and it was forty years before a mutual friend gave me her address. I telephoned and her husband, a by-then retired clergyman, answered. I explained who I was and he called Heather, who came to the phone with the words, 'When you've woken up in the morning with someone's big toe in your mouth, there is an intimacy you never quite lose!'

It was at Miss Brading's that we slept head to toe in a single bed. Later we graduated to a double bed, but with single sheets. We quarrelled over these sheets, each thinking the other had more than her share. Then we tugged at them, and then they tore. Sheet after sheet got torn in this way, and each time the dreaded confrontation had to be faced in the morning.

Poor Miss Brading. She was a respectable elderly spinster lady who knew nothing about children, and who just wanted to be left in peace. Even in that modest terraced house there was a maid, Rose, and there was also a lodger. This was another spinster lady called Miss Tombs, who worked as a cashier in Farnham's drapery department store, where they had those pneumatic cash tubes that whizz round the shop and go ping. Miss Tombs paid rent and was therefore entitled to special treatment. A seedcake was baked for her Sunday tea, and in the interests of her Sunday afternoon nap we had to be out of the house. That was how I became religious. The only place to go was Crusaders, a rather fundamentalist prayer meeting. I had already found Christian teaching very appealing in my first year at the school. The teaching was good and persuasive, and I had started going to church. All the people one admired seemed to be Christians – the headmistress, the Guide captain, one's favourite teachers.

Not only were religious occasions practically the only way to spend Sundays during these evacuation years, they were also almost the only way to spend the school holidays. We were not allowed to go to London, and ways had to be found to occupy us. So holidays were divided between Guide camps, summer camps organised by a very intense religious group called the Federation of University Women's Camps for Schoolgirls and, later, harvest camps. The hothouse atmosphere of some of these events might seem unhealthy today, but there was no choice. Something had to be organised to keep us occupied. I became a Christian, was baptised and confirmed, and still like the Church of England and enjoy going to church sometimes, even though belief abandoned me long ago. It seems to me very unfair to have internalised the Protestant ethic without having the comforts of religion.

In confirmation classes the vicar of St. Thomas-on-the-Bourne seems to have found the doubts and questions of a bunch of London adolescents difficult to cope with, for one day the Head called us together and gently asked us to bring our questions to her and not to worry the vicar with them. But he was a kindly and fatherly man. We discovered that he and I shared the same birthday. One day, years later, when I visited Farnham, he spotted me on the other side of the main street. Suddenly there was this stentorian voice booming across the traffic, 'Ha! Lisl! I remember you! Always pray for you on your birthday!'

But back to Miss Brading's. There was not enough to eat, and we were quite often hungry. I think Miss Brading simply didn't realise what adolescents eat. Heather, who was braver than I, once or twice got up in the night to steal a few biscuits. Although in these cramped and pinched circumstances we squabbled quite a lot, we also observed a strict code of honour. When Rose brought a plate of bread and margarine to the table – it still seems strange to think of a maid in such a poor little house – we instinctively counted the slices. If it was an even number one could relax in the knowledge that one would get one's share. But if it was an odd number it was a race to get through one's share to the extra slice.

Having been told that I came from Czechoslovakia, Rose once asked me whether people there lived in houses. I said no, we had been nomads and carried our tents around with us, and my father had been head of the tribe.

I don't remember how it came about – I imagine she must have complained about us – but from Miss Brading's we were moved to the house of a retired general and his wife, General and Mrs L. It was a tremendous contrast – a very large house with a servants' wing. We lived with the servants; it was unthinkable that we should live with the family. It was also much more comfortable for us: the servants were relaxed and friendly and the food was good and plentiful, an enormous improvement on Miss Brading's. The only time we penetrated into the main house was on Sunday mornings, when we had to present ourselves to Mrs L for inspection before church, to see if our gloves were clean and our stocking seams straight. We never met the general.

Between the family and the servants there was what would now be called an interface, in the shape of a housekeeper. This was a thin, prim lady with an encyclopaedic knowledge of etiquette, neither family nor servant, who managed the communications in both directions. My mother came to visit once, and rang the doorbell. The housekeeper came to the door and sternly rebuked her for going to the front door. She ought to have realised that her place was the servants' entrance.

But in some ways we were also treated as family. We recognised it for the privilege it was that we were subjected to the same kinds of discipline as the Ls' own children had been. This meant a cold bath every morning, a hot bath every evening, and lying on the floor for half an hour after meals so that our backs should grow straight. And Mrs L came every night, before their dinner in the main house, to wish us good night. On the housekeeper's instruction we had to receive her propped up in bed on one elbow. It was the bedtime equivalent of standing up when she came into the room. Once the dinner dress she wore was an Austrian dirndl, bought during some tour of duty in Vienna. She had put it on thinking it would remind me of home, not realising that it represented the way Nazi women had dressed.

The Ls made no bones about the fact that they only had us there because they were forced to. People with spare rooms had to make them available as billets, and the alternative would have been Commonwealth soldiers; London children were the lesser evil. So when news came that their son was going to be sent home wounded from the Far East it was an opportunity to get rid of us. At that stage Heather and I became separated, each going to a different billet. Mine was to be the house of a retired colonel and his family, only a few minutes' walk away from the Ls. My mother came to help me pack and move, and when we got there with my suitcase we anxiously looked for the back door, mindful of her earlier experience. It was nowhere to be seen, being hidden behind a wooden palisade. Eventually we decided that we would have to brave the front door. It was thrown open by the colonel, who cried, 'Ah, there you are! Let me take your case and show you to your room!' It was staggering.

I lived with the Days for three years, and we have kept in touch ever since. Colonel Day had served with the Royal Engineers in India as Director of Army Signals, but had retired from the army early because of what he called his 'dickey heart'. Mrs Day was his second wife, and there were two little girls, aged five and nine. There was also an older son, from the colonel's first marriage, who was abroad serving in the Royal Marines. These three sprang an enormous, and enormously moving, surprise on me by coming together to celebrate my seventieth birthday. I didn't even realise that they knew the date. They did it in style – a champagne lunch, birthday cake, balloon, candles, the works. More than fifty-five years later.

The Days too had been used to having servants, but these had been called up, either into the forces or to war work. So Mrs Day took on the cooking and housework, scrubbing the kitchen floor with the same poise with which she presided over meals. The colonel organised us children into doing some of the 'chores': every week he worked out a rota and this was pinned to the larder door. It was quite complicated, since the five-year-old was excused some of the chores. She could lay the table, for example, but not wash dishes. The colonel, on the other hand, did wash dishes (his cry of 'any more for any more?' still echoes in my head) but found drying them somehow unmanly. One was allowed to swap chores by mutual agreement.

The colonel also weighed and measured out the weekly rations. Each person had an identifiable saucer or plate for the butter ration, which was two ounces. He shaped these into pats and we marked them out into eight portions, which was easier than dividing them into seven. That gave one portion per day, and an extra one for Sundays.

The Ministry of Food had set up an institution called the British Restaurant, and Farnham had one of these. It was a Nissen hut on a piece of waste ground where cheap, filling, non-ration meals were served. They produced things like dumplings with carrots and gravy. To eke out the rations we all went to the British Restaurant once a week, sweeping in as if we – or rather the Days – owned it, and after the meal Mrs Day would go backstage to meet the cooks and congratulate them on the meal, as if it were the Savoy.

One day, during the so-called darkest days of the war, the Days decided to show the flag and give an old-style dinner party. They invited the vicar and his wife and another couple, looked out their evening clothes, and from somewhere the colonel produced a bottle of sherry. I entered into the spirit of the thing and offered to act as maid, and Mrs Day found me a maid's apron and cap. Then she taught me how to serve at table – from the left and a little behind.

The only food that could be got without ration coupons was fish and chips, when there was some. On the morning of the dinner party Mrs Day cycled into town and came back with a large bag of fish and chips. During the day it must have congealed, but in the evening we heated it up in the oven. Then, when the guests in their dinner jackets and long frocks were seated in the dining room, aged fourteen and wearing the cap and apron, I served the warmed-up fish and chips, on silver dishes, in the way I had been taught: from the left and a little behind. And I thought that nowhere else in the world could such a thing happen. I think this is why we won the war.

(We? Two men are sitting on a park bench and hear the drone of an aeroplane. 'Is it one of ours?' asks one, in a Polish accent. 'No, one of ours' replies the other through clenched teeth.)

There is a strength that comes from tradition and custom and does not have to rely on what is inside. Living across the road was the family of a brigadier who was on active service. Many years later, when I was visiting Farnham, I called to see them. The brigadier opened the door, smiling and welcoming, and ushered me in. Then he excused himself: he had been working in the garden wearing old clothes, and would go and change. Foolishly I said, 'Oh, you don't need to change for an old friend,' but he frowned. 'I change for the drawing room,' he said stiffly, and I knew myself to have been rebuked.

Paradoxically the very quality of the life with the Days presented me with a greater dilemma than any of the other billets had done. I was not aware of this at the time but see it now from a distance. It was here that the difference between cultures presented me with a conflict, because I was seeing the best side of the other culture – or at any rate one of them, for there are many British cultures. The renowned English stiff upper lip was there, but came not from insensitivity but from a strength based on I don't know what, certainly in part on Christian belief. The renowned class distinctions were also there, but tempered by grace. Protected as she was by her assured place in a benevolent society and by having no money worries, Mrs Day presented the model of a mother who was not herself in turmoil, who had the attention and interest available to encourage children, to let them experiment with cooking, to sing to them songs out of A.A. Milne, to turn coping with shortages into a game, to make sure that they practised the piano, to make Christmas or a birthday into an occasion (and who was always dressed by breakfast time!). Her aim was to provide a stable setting for her family no matter what the war might bring, and she succeeded in this, and I was included. How could my mother compare with this, in the situation she was in? And what part of it was due to different situations, and what to something else? And which way was 'right'? A lot of my later difficulty came from these unacknowledged comparisons.

There was an episode that shows the dilemma clearly. Mrs Day had a brother who was a senior officer in the navy and had lived in New Zealand. He was due to come home and there was to be a family reunion, after several years of separation, at their mother's home in Godalming. The Days planned their visit to Godalming and took it for granted that I would come too. Now my mother also had a brother living far away, in Australia. If this had been Paul coming back to be reunited with her after war-time years, the occasion would have been so intimate and emotional that an outsider would have been out of place. So I assumed that they were only asking me because they felt they had to and that I would really be in the way. I said that I would rather not go. This became a big issue; Mrs Day thought I was being difficult, and couldn't understand why. It happened that my father came down for a visit, and she asked him to try and talk me round. Then I gave way, mainly just to put an end to the trouble. So we all went to Godalming and the day was calm and pleasant, the family catching up with each other's news. None of it was so intense or intimate that an outsider could not be present. I was bewildered.

At the same time I was never really part of this life, with my permanent school uniform, my pocket money that was a charitable gift from the school, my parents with their foreign accents, and my too-good school results (when the younger daughter later married, the older one introduced me to guests at the wedding with the words, 'This is Lisl. She's a female academic'). I used to lie in bed going through a mental inventory of our flat at home. Perhaps I wanted to make sure that I didn't forget it. Perhaps I also wanted to reassure myself that there was a place where I *could* kick the furniture.

Protest at these incongruities took the form of untidiness, and I became monumentally and spectacularly untidy. The Day children still speak of 'the Lisl trail'.

The Days' self-confidence remains for me utterly admirable and enviable. Even their own daughter-in-law later told me how awed she was at the confident way they would walk to church, strung out across the quiet Sunday morning street as if no car would have the audacity to get in the way. Nothing seemed to faze them; there was nothing that could not be incorporated into their scheme of things. One day my aunt Fanni was invited down to give a talk about Czechoslovakia at the school. I was to chair the meeting, partly to help her out with English, and Mrs Day invited her to the house for tea before the lecture. The two women came from utterly different worlds, but I think each sensed the quality of the other. It all went well, and I was proud and happy. And then, afterwards, Mrs Day started referring to me smilingly as 'our little Red'. It shows such an exquisite blend of affection and patronage, managing to incorporate another world in a way that makes sure it will not disturb things, that once more I am awestruck.

But eventually, of course, the other world did come in to disturb. In the summer of 1945 there was a general election. Labour won a landslide election victory, and Clement Attlee became Prime Minister. The colonel was devastated. He could not grasp how an ungrateful country could have rejected a leader such as Churchill. As he sat in his study, his head in his hands, utterly downcast, his loving wife, wanting to comfort him, said, 'Dear – they *are* British!'

(A letter from Mrs Day, some time after the war: 'There is a new shop in West Street, called a Delicatessen. I thought of you, and went in and bought something called salami. But I must admit that when I got it home I didn't know what to do with it. I tried grilling it for breakfast, but I'm afraid the colonel didn't like it very much.')

The organisation of refugees had changed soon after the war started. German and Austrian refugees were interned; Czechs were not interned, being classed as 'friendly aliens' as distinct from 'enemy aliens'. (When the Pioneer Corps was formed in which foreigners could do some of the army's work but without being armed, the regiments were known as 'His Majesty's Own Enemy Aliens' and the 'Hampstead Highlanders'). But they were not at first allowed to take jobs. My father desperately wanted to make a contribution to the war effort and wrote many letters, but without success.

My parents and Fanni had been moved to London. Fanni and Luis were lent a small flat in Norland Square by an English friend who had joined the army, and my parents were moved into Canterbury Hall. This was a student hostel of London University, which was used by the refugee organisation, the university having been evacuated out of London. Here several hundred refugees spent some of the war years, made friends, argued, worried about their relatives left behind, and fretted at their enforced inactivity. As always, there were stories. My father talked of fire-watching during the blitz, standing on the roof of the building watching, as he put it, the bombs come down and the houses go up, while a terrified fellow firewatcher moaned, 'Mr Klein, Mr Klein! A Jew should emigrate to an island?'

Eventually, local labour exchanges were able to offer jobs to aliens if they could not find a British person locally to do the job. My father found a job as storekeeper in a Hammersmith hotel, and my mother in a small jobbing factory in Blackfriars. Later she moved to a slightly better-paid job in the kitchen of Lyons Corner House in Coventry Street. There were several other refugees working there, and some lasting friendships were formed.

This meant that my parents were at last able to look for a home and they found and furnished very sparsely a small flat in a 1930s block in Hammersmith. The flat had one room, there was a tiny kitchen and a bathroom, and they were immensely proud and excited about this achievement. I went on an illicit visit to London to be shown it. My disappointment when I saw the little flat must have been obvious and very hurtful. It shames me still. I don't know what I had been expecting; I had been living in large houses for several years and was simply unprepared.

London

In any case, there was now a home to return to. By the spring of 1943 air raids on London had died down. The school moved back to London, into a partly destroyed building, and the children had to reconnect with their families. I moved into my parents' one room. To make up a third bed my mother bought a mattress at a bombsite. It was very dusty and stained, and we spent ages scrubbing it. A wooden crate from the greengrocer made a bedside table. A Czech couple in the same block of flats lent us a carpet which they had in store, and I brushed it with a stiff brush and dustpan, square foot by square foot, to get rid of the dust of several years. There was, of course, no vacuum cleaner or even carpet sweeper.

Then we settled into a pattern. The week was taken up with work and school. On Saturdays we did the housework and shopping and went for walks in Ravenscourt Park, or sometimes to the pictures. My father was intrigued by the strange kinds of homework I was struggling with – things like algebra and Latin – and enjoyed helping me to puzzle things out. I can pinpoint exactly the park bench on which we were sitting the first time I saw the answer to an algebra problem before he did. It was very upsetting, and I pretended I hadn't seen it. But something changed that day.

On Sundays we generally visited Fanni and Luis. Fanni had become the centre of a circle of émigré socialist friends and colleagues who usually gathered in her room on Sunday afternoon for coffee. She was also involved with the Labour Party and the Fabian Society. English politicians, for instance Lucy Middleton, sometimes joined in. Ellen Wilkinson who has been described as 'the Member for refugees', was a good friend. Luis might make a brief appearance, but mostly kept out of the political discussions as well as the gossip. The friend who had been his manager in the Richmond had also escaped to London, where he worked as a cook and lived in a furnished room. He was a skilled and lavish cook, who did not seem to be able to adapt to rationing and shortages. When he occasionally cooked Sunday lunch for us all, he would use up not only a month's rations, leaving

Fanni and Luis short for the rest of the month, but also every single piece of crockery. He also did not seem to grasp that Luis was now very poor.

I enjoyed being on the edge of these conversations, listened avidly to the politics, and especially could not get enough of the old family stories being told over and over again. In this way, I think, my roots were being nourished. My function was to do the washing up, whether it was for the coffee afternoons or for one of Mr Petter's unsuitable meals with their mountains of crockery.

We had found a kind of equilibrium. But in the autumn of 1943, only six months after the return to London, it was destroyed. My father was taken to hospital with a heart attack and it was in hospital, three weeks later, that he had a second attack and died. I am sure that a heavy physical job, after several years of enforced virtual inactivity, brought this about too soon.

Thinking back, there were some signs beforehand that he had not been feeling well and was keeping this from me. In the three weeks he spent in hospital before the second attack, my mother also had a misplaced notion of 'protecting' me by not allowing me to visit him. She said I should think of him as I had known him, looking well and full of life. I don't know if that was a joint decision of theirs or only hers, but by 'protecting' me in this way my parents also somehow excluded me; I was both protected and shut out. It has left a curious blank in my life, an unfilled gap, as well as a big sense of guilt – should I have insisted on going to see him? Could I have insisted?

On the surface the pattern went on: my mother went to work, I went to school, and on Sundays we visited Fanni and Luis. But now there was nothing to balance my mother's unhappiness and to contain it. Equilibrium had gone for good.

In the summer of 1944 there came a renewal of air attacks, this time the V1 and V2 rockets. The V1s were the more frightening, because you heard them coming and you heard the motor stop, which meant the rocket was on its way down. The V2 may have been more powerful and destructive but, as you did not hear its approach, by the time you heard the bang you knew it was somewhere else.

In the middle of this we had important exams, the precursor of today's GCSEs, called the General Schools Certificate. The results that year were brilliant: no one, at least in our school, failed, and most had very good grades. I imagine the examiners felt sorry for children having to sit exams in those conditions, sometimes literally under the desk. Moreover, we probably did much more work and revision sitting up at night in air-raid shelters – or, in my case, in the window-less corridor between two rows of flats – than we would have done normally. It was strange coming out in the morning to pavements deep in broken glass.

A few weeks before these renewed air raids, the second front had opened up in Europe with the Allied invasion of Normandy. The timing of this had been hotly debated for months. Many people believed that the Allies were delaying the invasion so as to weaken the Russians who were taking the whole brunt of the German forces in the East; the invasion of the Continent was awaited with explosive impatience. On the day it happened I had time off from school to go to the dentist. So I saw the evening paper placards as soon as they were on the streets at midday, and rushed to school to spread the news.

And then, at the beginning of 1945, the Allied armies were pushing eastwards, into Germany, towards Berlin, and towards the end of the terrible war. As Belsen and the other concentration camps were discovered and opened up, the International Red Cross began to compile lists of the survivors who had been found there. The headquarters of the Red Cross were not far from my school, and I went there about twice a week on my way home from school to read through the lists. I never found a single one of the names I was looking for, and to this day I am haunted by the possibility that I didn't look properly. A rather slapdash schoolgirl, untidy and careless about homework, why would I not have missed some name among the hundreds? For years I used to look at faces in the London Underground, speculating about what Peter or Stefan might look like grown up and wondering if this or that man might be one of them – as unable to find us as we were to find them. Once a man clearly thought I was trying to pick him up and moved away with an expression of disgust.

The incongruity of the double life we were leading strikes me more now than it did then, and is difficult to put into words. At one level there were these desperate things, and at another level the normal problems of school, my mother's job, her worries about money, my worries about exams and getting into university. Then, it seemed normal, and the normal part of this 'normal' was bad enough.

For the older generation in particular, 1945/46 was the time of trying to piece together what had happened to our relatives and trying to work out whether, and how, to go back. At first, Luis tried to get agreement for the return of the smaller of his hotels, the Atlantic, so that the relatives would have somewhere to stay. Other people also asked him to put them up as a temporary measure, and he said yes to all of them. But he didn't get the hotel, and there turned out to be no relatives. For Fanni, in the midst of enormous grief, there was also the renewing of contacts with old political colleagues, learning how they had fared and discussing the future. There is a letter from a social-democratic colleague, asking Fanni to intercede with the Czech authorities who were refusing to grant her renewed citizenship because she had made the mistake of staying behind. So I know that there were injustices done; it's just that I cannot get those images of 1938 out of my mind. There is also a very friendly letter to her from President Beneš as he was preparing to go back home.

Gradually, with much correspondence with friends and survivors, and many false starts, most of the story of what had happened to the family came together. As late as 1943 the Siegfried Kleins, as well as Fritz and Ida, Marie and Viktor had been sent to Theresienstadt (Terezín). This was not explicitly an extermination camp, although many people died there from hunger or illness or ill treatment. It was from there that people were then sent to Auschwitz and the gas chambers. Marie was the first to be despatched there. She was very afraid, and Viktor went with her voluntarily, so that she should not go to her death alone. Fritz was for a time allowed to work as a doctor among the other prisoners. I have two versions of what then happened to him and Ida. In one, Fritz caught TB from his patients and died in Theresienstadt; in the other he died there of prostate and heart problems. According to one version he was able to get hold of some poison, having access to the pharmacy, and before he died gave it to his wife, telling her to take it when they came to take her away; so that is what she did. According to the other version they all had poison but the Germans took it away from them, and Ida was sent to the gas chambers in Auschwitz a few days after Fritz's death. Fanni said Ida had already been terrified in Prague, before they were in Theresienstadt. It was not known how Friedl and his wife died, only that it was in Auschwitz. Friedl was beginning to be a little senile, and the hope was that he might not have realised what was happening.

Richard, Frieda and little Stefan had hoped in 1938 to go to England, and had sent a trunk of possessions ahead with some Neubauer relatives. But they did not manage to get out. Frieda and Stefan were gassed in Auschwitz in October 1944; Stefan would have been nine years old. Richard had been pressed into a work gang. He was shot by an SS death-commando on January 27th 1945, a few hours before the arrival of the Red Army. The friend who found all this out and let us know about it was devastated by the fact that he had himself been quite near by but had not known what was happening to Richard.

Neubauers eventually gave me some of the things that Frieda had sent ahead. They are the fresh, pretty possessions of a smart, newly married young woman: towels edged with a band of coloured polkadots and a blue printed cotton drawstring bag to store sewing materials. The towels have long since worn out, but I still have the sewing bag. I tried to wash it once, but it started to fall apart. So now it is very dirty.

Fanni wrote in a letter: 'I have to fight against these haunting thoughts in the sleepless night hours, when I suffer not so much their loss but their suffering. But I am able to think of the greater family of mankind in the daytime.'

As for my mother's family, I don't know what efforts Grete made to get herself and Peter away in 1938. I once heard it said, but don't know if it is true, that she was having too good a social life to recognise the dangers or give up a pleasant life for unknown privations. In 1942 she and Peter and my grandmother Rosa were also sent to Theresienstadt. My grandmother's last letter before they left is dated 17.1.1942 and addressed to the Devauds in Switzerland:

My dear friends!
Shortly before my departure I am writing to say farewell to you and to thank you for all your love and goodness. I am going away with my daughter and my grandson, we are very sad and unhappy. As soon as I am allowed to tell you my new address, I will write to you. I hope with all my heart to see you all again in good health, God will help us. Now just hearty greetings to you and all our loved ones.
Your
Rosa

She died in Theresienstadt, as I have said, of malnutrition. Grete and Peter were sent to Auschwitz. At the point where some prisoners were selected out to be sent to labour camps instead of to the gas chambers, Grete didn't stand a chance, and even Peter didn't make it because he was by that time too thin and weak to be suitable for a labour camp. He was sixteen. About my grandmother's sister, aunt Else Glaser and her husband Emil, I also have two versions. In one they died in Auschwitz. In the other they were sent to the Warsaw ghetto and died there. They had no children and I remember aunt Else as a fussy, dainty housewife, in whose home one did not dare touch things.

So that makes fourteen people. I have counted them and recited their names, over and over. But a couple of weeks ago I sat bolt upright in the middle of the night, in total panic because I couldn't remember aunt Else's and uncle Emil's names. It was a moment of complete terror, to feel that they were not even being honoured enough for their names to be remembered.

There was the question of whether, and how, to go back. Luis and Fanni were getting old. When arrangements were finally made for Fanni to go to

Prague on a visit in October 1946 to explore the possibilities, she got pneumonia and the visit was cancelled. And all of us were handicapped by not speaking Czech. The Czechs at that time were so bitter about all things German that it was unthinkable to go back speaking only German. This was something that I, at least, could do something about, and I started taking Czech lessons. Having, chameleon-like, become very English during the years of living in English homes, I was now shifting back in the other direction. There had been an international Ranger Company attached to Girl Guide Headquarters in London and during my last two years at school I belonged to it, proudly sewing a flash that said 'Czechoslovakia' onto the shoulder of the uniform.

My mother was depressed and bewildered. She had never come to terms with being in England, had always assumed that it was temporary, but going back in this situation, with no family and no language, did not seem workable either. Where to? Living how? The immediate decision was made easier by the fact that I obtained a place at London University and a scholarship, 1946 being the first year the London County Council scholarship system was open to foreigners. It seemed obvious to take this opportunity, and things might be clearer by the time I finished. I opted for modern languages. I didn't know what I wanted to do, but it seemed likely that when we went back I would teach English.

Many political émigrés of course went back as soon as possible to Germany, France, Austria and Czechoslovakia. There is a pile of letters to Fanni, both from those who went back and from those who had stayed behind, describing the situations they were dealing with: Angelica Balabanoff writes from New York, full of love and admiration for the way Fanni has remained herself in the face of such tragedy. Alice Pels writes from Belgium, Herta Gotthelf writes from Germany. She complains that British voluntary organisations like the Women's Institute and the Town Women's Guild were in Germany trying to help, but where were the political organisations, where were the trade unions? She is also angry about well-nourished do-gooders coming like tourists to look at the devastation – maybe one could charge an entry fee? For herself she is quite pleased that she is losing a lot of weight, because she had been rather fat. An Austrian couple who had stayed behind in Vienna write despairingly about the intense hunger and cold, and water coming into their damaged flat. Czechs are in turmoil about having to re-apply for citizenship and not knowing whether or when it will be granted. The government had decided to deal with the Sudeten German problem by making the people from those areas re-apply for Czech citizenship. This meant they were investigated, and if their record was considered unsatisfactory, citizenship was denied and they were expelled from the country. Marie Günzl, who had stayed behind and been imprisoned and beaten, writes from Munich that Czechs were now behaving like the enemy from whom they had been freed. Irene Kirpal, who went back, also has to apply for citizenship and tries to help Fanni get hers. Fanni and the Party in exile had passed resolutions against extradition, but this was being ignored. The political discussions in Norland Square itself became attenuated.

To these levels of underlying shock and pain and difficulty, and the need for adjustment and decisions about the future, must be added another level of ordinary, everyday life. From a distance of fifty years the combination seems crazy and impossible but at the time, as I have said, it was normal. Here is an extract from a letter from Luis to a distant cousin who had moved back to Prague, showing how one man brought these elements together:

... Personally I would decide immediately for moving to Prague, if my affairs can somehow be sorted out so that we have something to live on. Fanni is for going to Austria, largely because of the not being able to speak [Czech]. I don't see it: we don't get to talk with anyone here either, except people who come to see us, and that could surely be arranged in Prague as well. The only problem would be that when the third world war starts we would right away be in the line of fire again.

We had a visit from the son of a niece of Marie Mendl, from Prague, who survived three years of Auschwitz and then found his mother in Belsen, where she had also spent three years. The father 'went into the gas'. Mrs G. was here for only five minutes, she will come to London when she has dealt with the children. Dr R.'s wife and younger son got residence permit, the son who is over twenty-one didn't.

I don't have anything special to report. Every day from 4.00 to 7.00 I am in Kensington Gardens, the park is more beautiful than ever, I would miss it wherever I will end up. Mr Petter has fourteen days' holiday, he cooks and shops for us, so I have less to do.

Visitors are fewer, because many have already gone. Sunday afternoon was very 'weak', only Rosa G., Irma [my mother], Mrs W., and a newly widowed K. from Podersam. As there were no politicians present, the talk was of fashion. There appeared Mrs F., that ugly ink-blot, immediately took charge of the subject, and silenced all the others. Her main exposition – which might be of interest to you as well – was that the suits left behind by the dear departed (all those present were widows) should no longer be turned into costumes, but into slacks and short jackets, first because it is cheaper and then because it takes account of the broad trend in fashion! She – the blot – spoke with conviction, because she has already carried it out in practice, in that she has had a grey-striped suit of her first – not even deceased but only divorced – husband remodelled, which she had obtained when property was being divided, in exchange for a leather suitcase which belonged to her but which she let him have. 'The trousers only had to be shortened a bit in the legs, and the pieces gained in this way inserted right and left at the hips. But on no account at the back, because then the good cut of this most important part of every trouser would be lost. The jacket also only needs to have triangular sections taken out from under the arms and be shortened a bit.'

There was general attention, even aunt Rosa kept quiet. I suspected her of reviewing the departed suits of dear Emil in her mind's eye. The only one not interested was Edith E., who only called in for a moment and made excuses that she had an appointment. I can understand her, first that she ran away, and second because hers isn't deceased yet. Well, and if? What kind of slacks could you get from Hugo's trousers, with that bottom? It's really better that he should be alive and well ...

BOOK TWO

I have read a number of memoirs of refugees. Many of them end at the point where the author arrives in the new country, or at the point where the war ends. It is not surprising. First there is, pervading absolutely everything for ever after, the question of how do you live what other people regard as a normal life in the light of what has happened? It is not only hard to do, it is also hard to put into words. Also, the threads begin to go in many different directions and it becomes difficult to hold them together. But I'm going to try. Perhaps this need to synthesise has been the sub-text of my adult life.

Much of it has been played out through my working life over the next decades and quite a lot of what happened from here on has, over time, been integrated into my professional writing. I have always had trouble with the boundary between the 'personal' and the 'professional': I cannot, in all conscience, make *ex cathedra* pronouncements that 'this is how it is' – I can only explain how I arrived at seeing it that way, and this means that my professional writing has elements of autobiography in it. While I absolutely don't accept that this is unscientific – on the contrary, it gives readers the opportunity to judge the evidence for themselves – it does make it difficult to separate out what, conversely, is material for a memoir. I'll do my best not to become too boringly repetitive.

My friend and mentor, Marie Jahoda, saw the first draft of this memoir and said, 'This is really two books.' I can see her point but it has, after all, only been one life.

Transitions

I was completely unprepared for what came next. When the constraints and certainties of the war ended, and the constraints and certainties of school fell away a year later, I was not equipped for a life and a world without them and had virtually none of the necessary skills.

The war had in many ways simplified life. There had been very few choices to make, and there was great clarity about what was right and wrong, good and bad. In the 1996 newsletter of my school's Old Girls' Association, the headmistress writes of the challenges and problems that young people in the 1990s were facing: 'I get weary of hearing about the wearing of gloves in the 'fifties, evacuation is so much more interesting ... In years to come the children of the latter ten years of the second millennium, living in inner cities, will be regarded as heroes who really were presented with immense challenges ...' She is right. The end of the war brought freedom from the fear of being blown to pieces, but many of the other freedoms it brought, and the consequences of everyone else's freedom, created a baffling world in which it was very difficult to find a foothold.

Looking back from a distance gives one some new perspectives. I see now how the situation that confronted us after the war was quite different for the different generations: Luis, now seventy-four, could think in terms of himself and Fanni insulating themselves from the post-war realities with his 'we don't get to talk with anyone here either'. My mother, aged forty-five, was caught agonisingly between what had been and what was emerging now. I, at eighteen, was fully involved in the now. Perhaps too fully – hindsight tells me that going to university at this stage was too total an immersion into one of those realities, at the same time engulfing in its own right and split off and different from the others. These things happened at the same time, but they don't fit together. Try as I may, I cannot integrate the story at this point into a neat merging together, grafting onto, growing out of.

My professional life and work, it turns out, has been about synthesis. Research *and* practice, technical change *and* the human aspects that shape it and arise from it, putting together organisational understanding *and* technical understanding *and* psychoanalytic understanding. As my friend Harold Bridger used to say, 'not either/or, but both/and'. Is it too fanciful to think that this striving for synthesis has its roots in the desperate inability to synthesise what was happening to me at this turning point? Or perhaps in the scattering and loss of a family which I hadn't been able to hold together?

In any case, watching my mother's unhappiness and inability to cope; feeling guilty about being cheerful; the impossibility of religious belief in these circumstances and long discussions with the college chaplain; writing essays on the flat roof of our block of flats to get some peace and privacy; falling in love what seemed like once a fortnight, but hemmed in by inexperience and the strong sense of what was right and proper which had been inculcated by spinster teachers and which was, in any case, common at that time. That student trip to Prague in 1947 which was, after all, to a Youth Festival, with its sheer exhilaration and idealism, as well as being a first return home; the shock of seeing a bowl of hard-boiled eggs in the station buffet at the Gare du Nord on the way there, the first time in many years one had seen more than one egg at a time. A Czech student saying, 'Good God, you must be the only virgin in Prague!' The family friend in Prague who had been with our relatives in the camps and finally described exactly, one by one, what had happened to them. The mayor of Fischern weeping as he told how he had hidden his daughter in the cellar when the Russians came, and then ranting furiously about the split among the social democrats in exile. And the thought of Peter at fourteen, in tears after one of my letters because of my luck in being likely to go to university while he was not (see Appendix 1); and then at sixteen, going into the gas chamber. How is one to live with that? I see no way of 'synthesising' all this; I'll just go on with the story.

The school's preparation for adult life had been a bit idiosyncratic: in the sixth form there was a weekly lesson euphemistically called 'hygiene'. It was part sex education, part how to bring up children, part etiquette. The sex education involved passing round photographs of classical Greek statues. We should be so lucky. On bringing up children, I remember that they need indoor shoes, outdoor shoes, Wellingtons, slippers, party shoes, I don't remember the rest but it added up to seven pairs of shoes. I do remember some points of etiquette: it is bad manners to wear a backless evening dress if you have curvature of the spine, because it embarrasses people. And if you are invited to a hunt ball you should wear either black or white, so that you don't clash with the pink of the huntsmen's coats.

Thus equipped, I took up the scholarship in modern languages at King's College, London. Eventually, of course, I learned some skills of living and gained confidence. But it was a hard apprenticeship, there was no tuition or guidance, and it took a long time.

Meanwhile, I made mistakes. There were young men at college who had not come straight from school but from the armed services. They were a few years older than the school-leavers and appeared immensely sophisticated. One of them asked me out for the evening. We went to a cinema and then, walking along Oxford Street, he asked where I would like to eat. I knew nothing of restaurants, and the only guideline I could think of was that I should not cost him a lot of money. As we passed a fish and chip shop I said, 'What about here?' He seemed startled and took charge of the situation, leading me to an elegant Spanish restaurant. I never saw him again.

(Many years later I did some work for the Flax Spinners' Association of Northern Ireland. When the managing director of one of the companies came to London he took me out to dinner. The restaurant had two kinds of menu, one for the host, with prices, and one for guests, without prices. He asked them to let him have one of each to take home, because he wanted to teach his teenage son and daughter about ordering meals. A wave of envy for those children swept over me, not because of the privileged kind of restaurant they would be encountering but because of his understanding that coping with that world requires training.)

I had some talent for acting, had played a range of parts in school plays, and joined the college drama society. But I didn't know how to get noticed and was grateful, during the first year, to be allowed to be prompter in their productions. In the second year I started to get parts, and in the third year won the prize for best actress in the university competition. If ever I needed to cry on stage, I only had to think of the Czech national anthem or the slow movement from Dvořák's New World Symphony. Then I was offered the lead in O'Casey's 'Juno and the Paycock'. I don't remember why my mother took me to a doctor around that time, but the doctor found that my blood pressure was raised. She prompted him: 'So she shouldn't take on a big drama part, should she, with so many rehearsals and late nights?' The doctor turned to me. 'How important is it? Are you going to make a career on the stage?' Of course I wasn't. 'Well, then . . .' I had no choice but to turn down the part. Even as I write this now I tense up with the frustration and fury of it.

Some of my friends wanted to make acting a career. I didn't look right for the stage, but thought I could try radio. I obtained an audition with the BBC Drama Department and was thrilled to get a letter saying that I had passed it. I thought this meant that they would start offering parts, or at any rate auditions. I didn't know that you then had to get an agent and knock on

Top: Wilhelm Klein's parents, my Klein great-grandparents.
Below: Karoline Kohn's parents, my Kohn great-grandparents.

Left:
My grandparents, Wilhelm and Karoline Klein.
Below:
Grandfather Wilhelm Klein and his ten children.

EMIL JOSEPH   VICTOR   ALOIS MARIE SIEGFRIED   LUDWIG JENNIE
                                                        +   +
            FANNI   WILHELM   IDA
                            KLEIN

Top: My Robitschek grandparents, with my mother's sister Grete and her husband 'Griff' Gutfreund.

Below: My parents' wedding. They are seated in front, flanked by her sisters Grete and Trude.

Top: Me, aged 2.
Below left: With my parents.
Below right: Peter and me, aged 6.

Top & below right: The Richmond Park-Hotel in its hey-day.
Below left: Luis (on the right) and friends in front of the Richmond.

Top: Karlsbad.
Left: Uncle Fritz Fischer-Feldmann.
Right: Richard and Frieda Neubauer, with Stefan.

Top left: Letter from Peter, ca. 1940.
Top right: At harvest camp, ca. 1942.
Below: With my mother and Suse, 1948.

Top: Fanni on her 75th birthday.
Below: The Social Democratic Party in exile. They are being addressed by
              Josef Zinner; Fanni is in the bottom right-hand corner.

doors. So I did nothing, and waited. They also did nothing. And nothing ever happened.

(As I write this I realise more than I did then what a terrible story it is. And a young friend who has read it was simply not able to understand how one can be so stupid. But I also think, from the perspective of over fifty years later, that I simply could not have moved into a pleasurable and pleasure-giving career just like that, as if nothing had happened and as if life was normal by today's standards. If I work out the dates, Peter's death must have been around the time that I was playing Sir Anthony Absolute in the school's production of Sheridan's *The Rivals*. It is inconceivable that I could have turned away so abruptly from all the history without some serious consequences – perhaps inexperience was in some sense protecting me. Frivolity was to come later.)

Strangely, I had not really needed to think about money until I went to college. Basic needs had been taken care of: the school kept me in uniform clothes and books, nobody went away for holidays. Paul, in Sydney, was prospering and after my father's death sent a small monthly cheque to supplement my mother's wages. I don't think I realised how little it was. A bit in the way that Fanni had written about her life in Udritsch, I didn't realise that we were very poor. (There was a regulation that one could not spend more than five shillings on a restaurant meal, without giving up coupons. I couldn't imagine how that could be a problem.)

Not having any money beyond the basics had not mattered until that outside world impinged: the wonderful actress Edith Evans gave a talk at the school once and suddenly pointed at me with a challenge to say what would make one decide whether to go to the theatre or to the cinema. I realised that it was a question of money, and the realisation took both me and her by surprise.

I had never been to a party or owned a party dress, and went to my first college dance in flat lace-up shoes. I knew neither how to work out how to earn a living nor what to say when asked if I would like a drink. When a group from the drama society went to a pub after rehearsal and someone asked what I would like to drink, I realised that I didn't even know the names of drinks. I disliked the taste of beer, and everything else was unknown and expensive. The only name I knew was 'port', so I asked for that, drawing some strange looks. When there was something I didn't know or had not experienced, I didn't have the know-how or confidence to say so and ask for help. That came later, in large measure, and has stood me in good stead. But at that time whatever the opposite of 'street-wise' is, that was me. I must have been the most street-ignorant person in Britain.

Since coming to England I had not encountered any boys, except for one disastrous episode while I was still at school. Family friends from Karlsbad who had come to England in time to bring their possessions and get established had a son who, in the summer before I moved up to the sixth form, got in touch and invited me to play tennis. I didn't play well but, like a fool, I agreed. I didn't have tennis clothes but used to play in an old school summer dress, so it would not matter if it tore. Came the day and Paul turned up, in immaculate whites. He was member of a tennis club, and an excellent player. We went to Ravenscourt Park. Being a gentleman he allowed me to win the first game, and then went on to win the next seventeen, chasing me all over the court, sweating in the hot July sun. Afterwards we talked about school: he already knew that he was going to be a doctor like his father, and had one year of science sixth form behind him. I was finding it difficult to make the choice between science and arts but was about to opt for science, taking pure and applied maths, physics and biology. Biology was new for me.

Undaunted by the tennis experience, Paul got in touch a few weeks later to invite me to a Prom concert. As Egon Adler points out in the first chapter of this memoir, not much can go wrong at a concert. But some time later I was invited again, this time for Sunday lunch at home. That in itself held no terrors, I had known the family since childhood. But afterwards I was conducted up to Paul's bedroom where, carefully laid out on a table, were his father's rather elaborate microscope, two slabs of marble, two sets of dissecting instruments, and two dead earthworms. The idea was that we would spend the afternoon dissecting earthworms and looking for their ovaries, which, it seems, are hard to find.

I was appalled. Paul didn't know that I had changed from science to languages after only a few weeks. In biology I had never got as far as earthworms, didn't know one end of an earthworm from the other, and had no experience of dissecting. There was nothing for it but to explain, thus destroying the poor chap's carefully thought-out plans. For a moment it threw him. Then he found a solution. 'I know,' he said, 'I'll do the dissecting and you look at the slides.' But that didn't work either. I didn't know what I was looking for, and in any case I was afraid of damaging his father's microscope, which was much more complicated than the ones I had briefly encountered at school. So we gave up and went to the pictures, and I didn't see him again for over thirty years, when we began to meet at funerals. By that time he was a grandfather.

Lack of social skill was only one of the reasons why the next ten years were so awful. One of the two analysts whom I later consulted said that I should consider myself to be a war casualty. But I didn't feel entitled to that concession; after all, nothing dire had actually happened to me. My mother, deprived of the large supportive family she had been used to, was now clinically depressed (a term born of hindsight; I knew nothing of mental health or illness at the time) and had become totally dependent on me. The one-roomed flat, which I have always blamed for our problems, was in a way a symbol rather than a cause of them. Going away to university had been out of the question. It had to be London – I couldn't leave my mother.

In 1948 Paul and Alice with my cousin Sue, whom they had taken from Palestine to live with them, came on a visit from Australia. Sue was twenty-four and glamorous. She had jewellery, and dresses which Alice had bought for her in Paris on the way, while my clothes were the cheapest post-war 'utility'. The war years in Palestine had turned her into a passionate Zionist, while I had become very English. She was neurotic and egocentric, while I was too sane for my own good. The most damning thing she could think of to say to me – and she said it many times in the years that followed – was, 'Of course, you're the intelligent one in the family.' And she had lost her mother. My mother, sitting on the edge of her bath, blossomed under the secrets and sexual confidences that were shared. I, on the other hand, having been cooped up in one room with my mother since the age of fifteen, needed privacy like I needed oxygen. Sue was the daughter my mother should have had.

We were so different, but at the same time there was always a hard-to-define something that Sue and I shared, and that we couldn't share with anyone else: jokes, and reminding each other of Peter's and our fathers' jokes, slang and the Egerländer dialect, memories of Neusattl, tastes and ways of preparing food.

As we grew older, she became more sensible and I less so, and we grew closer together. But it was not until her final illness that the detritus of our differences fell away. On essentials we had a similar honesty, and it was this that now determined our relationship, conducted by phone between Sydney and London.

'Shall I come over?' I asked.

'There's nothing you can do that we can't do by phone', she answered. 'And I would only moan at you for twenty-four hours a day, instead of only some of the time. Better stay where you are, we can handle it better this way.'

She died in 1996.

I think of the letters we received at the beginning of the war, of Luis writing to Fanni from Inverness Terrace to West Hoathly, and I marvel at the change. It is difficult to convey the difference between the not knowing,

89

which may be relieved by a letter, the guilt about the letters one has not written, the recognising an airmail stamp; and the present-day ease of emails, and of talking on the phone to anyone anywhere on the other side of the world, with the enormity of the undertaking not even signalled by squeaks and crackles on the line.

But back to 1946: my mother had a different job now. An acquaintance had started a business manufacturing women's blouses, and my mother embroidered them, working at home. It was more comfortable than the Blackfriars factory or the kitchen in Lyons' Corner House, but it meant isolation, the worst possible kind of work for someone who was so depressed. It was to be another ten years before I was able to move out, at the age of twenty-eight, and during all those years my mother sat at home, stitching at the wretched blouses, waiting for me to come home and tell her about my life. She must have resented the fact that I was living a relatively normal and cheerful life; I know that she thought me cold and unfeeling. I resented her dependence on me, and her relentless depression. And at some level I must, though I don't remember it, have made wishful comparisons with Mrs Day in Farnham, and her balance. My mother had not been brought up to the stiff upper lip.

When I was twenty-four the porter of the flats, who felt sorry for us, wangled it so that we were offered a bigger flat, with two rooms. He used to hum a little tune when he saw me passing, which had the refrain 'And her mother came too'. Until then I did not have a bedroom of my own and lay in bed at night, pretending to be asleep, listening to my mother crying. If I needed to study late I draped a towel over the bedside lamp. If she had a friend to visit I took my books to the bathroom. In summer I took them up to the flat roof of the block of flats. If I wanted to invite someone home she would arrange to baby-sit for neighbours along the corridor. So I could never ask anyone home spontaneously. My dream of paradise was to be able to open a tin of baked beans for a friend on the spur of the moment. Ever since those years, baked beans have symbolised spontaneity and freedom for me.

Some aspects of our situation brought out my mother's strengths. She was a superb cook and never failed to produce good meals in our tiny, ill-equipped kitchen and from the cheapest ingredients. On Christmas Eve she would wait cannily until five or six in the afternoon, when the traders in the streetmarket on Hammersmith Broadway started to drop their prices. Then she would put on her coat with the air of a warrior going into battle, pick up a shopping bag, and announce, 'Ich geh auf die Vogeljagd' ('I'm going on the hunt for a bird'). It was quite a gamble by that stage, but she always came back with a trophy.

I have an undeserved reputation for being a good cook, based entirely on a small range of dishes I learned from my mother, nothing like the extent of her repertoire. She could demonstrate things like how to chop an onion or make a roux, but found it difficult to translate her tacit knowledge into words. If I was trying to make something, the conversation would go: 'Now put the flour in.'

'How much?'

'Oh, you know, till it feels right.'

At the time when I was applying to go to university we still assumed that we would eventually be going home. Fanni and Luis were in urgent correspondence with Czech authorities and contacts, trying to work out how to do it. But by the time I left college in 1949 the assumption had changed, and it had become clear that we were not going back. There was not a single relative to go back to. The Communist coup had taken place in 1948. Fanni and Luis were old. All my own links were in this country and my mother, too, had some links here by now and anyway none at home. So she eventually applied for British naturalisation. The final trigger was that children under twenty-one could be included in a parent's application, which made it cheaper. But the procedure took a long time and by the time it was completed I was over twenty-one. The lady from the Home Office who came to interview her talked only about what good coffee continental people make.

So I applied again in my own right. The last step in the process is the oath of allegiance. I was working in St. James's Square at the time, and looked in the Yellow Pages to find a nearby solicitor to administer the oath. This turned out to be an old-established firm in Pall Mall, impressive with mahogany and old leather. A white-haired gentleman behind a large desk asked who had recommended them to me, and was disconcerted when I said that I had found them in the phone book. He talked to me solemnly about the importance of the step I was taking, and produced a Bible. As we stood up for him to administer the oath, his phone began to ring. He stoically ignored it and I took my cue from him. To the insistent shrilling of the telephone I swore allegiance to King George VI and his heirs and successors.

In the general election of 1950 the Conservative candidate for Hammersmith canvassed our block of flats. My mother explained that she didn't have a vote as she was not yet naturalised. 'If you vote for me, I will see that it gets through quickly,' said Anthony Fell. This combination of cynicism and sheer stupidity was sign of another transition. The nature of politics was changing.

The Transition to Work

And then there was the question of how to earn a living. The only job for which a language degree prepared one at that time was teaching languages. Some of my contemporaries were planning to teach, partly because there was a scheme under which one could obtain a university grant if one undertook to become a teacher. This seemed to me the wrong kind of reason and not fair to the children; if I was ever going to teach, it would have to be because I really wanted to. Besides, the progression of school – college – school seemed too limited and stifling.

But what else to do? Fanni urged me to take some post-graduate qualification, possibly in social work, but I couldn't put off earning any longer, I had to find a job. Career guidance at school had been virtually non-existent. Once someone had come to give a careers talk to the fifth and sixth forms. During the questions period I had asked, how do you become a lawyer? Afterwards one of the staff took me aside and told me not to show off. Another time I had asked the Head about studying medicine. She picked up my hands, turned them over and looked at them, and pronounced, 'These are not a surgeon's hands.' And that was the end of that. The University Appointments Board was no better. I asked the interviewer how one might get into journalism. She said, 'How do you expect to get a job in journalism without experience?' I said, 'How am I going to get experience if I can't get a job?' And that was the end of that.

But the Appointments Board did circulate vacancies that were notified to them, and I applied for the first one they sent. I didn't even have the wit or experience – or maybe the courage – to wait to see more than one. So I became assistant to the Information Officer of ASLIB, the Association of Special Libraries and Information Bureaux. They were at that time in a tiny cramped office in Bloomsbury, the heart of which was a card index of libraries specialising in all manner of topics. Whatever anyone wanted to know, we were supposed to guide them to a relevant library. After two days my boss went on holiday, and I was left to deal with the enquiries. The phone rang, and someone on the other end of the line asked how he could find out what was the chemical composition of the human body. Desperately I scrabbled through the card index and came across the fact that there was an organisation called the Chemical Society and that it had a library. I picked up the receiver again and said, 'Could you try the library of the Chemical Society?' A frosty voice replied, 'This is the librarian of the Chemical Society speaking.'

Once the information officer was back from holiday my job was filing, since my predecessor had not done any for a very long time. She still appeared sometimes, because they were a matey little group in the office, who drank together, shared jokes and pinched each other's bottoms behind the filing cabinets. One of the jokes they shared was my pathetically goody-goody reference from school. It had said that I had been a 'useful Girl Guide', and I learned that this had nearly cost me the job. I had been quite proud of that – was I now supposed to be ashamed of it?

I was wretchedly bored and miserable; however, it didn't occur to me to look for something else, just as it had not occurred to me to wait for a few more openings. The idea of choices simply did not feature in my thinking; I just assumed that I had to make the best of it. This is really hard for me to understand now, especially as I watch my friends' children moving in and out of jobs. And I am regarded as a pretty independent person. I can only think that whatever capacity for autonomy I had at that time was consumed in the effort of maintaining some independence at home. My mother's needs were unassuageable – I could not meet them, and nothing and nobody else would do. She saw every suggestion of an outing, a holiday, an introduction to other people (or, later, the present of a television set), as an attempt to buy her off. And her worries about financial security, certainly well founded during the difficult years before I started to earn, made her furiously oppose any suggestion of my leaving what was, after all, a secure job. Besides, I didn't know the logistics of leaving one job and finding another.

I did get one rather exciting job offer during this wretched time. I was walking down Villiers Street one day when I saw a man on the other side of the street looking at me. Like a well-brought-up young woman I took no notice, but a few moments later there was a tap on my shoulder. He raised his hat and apologised very courteously for addressing me like this in the street. He said he was sales manager for a firm manufacturing corsets; they employed a troupe of girls who travelled round the country modelling corsets at fashion shows, and they had a vacancy for someone my shape. The salary he suggested was more than twice what I was actually earning. So much money! And travel! But I declined with thanks, saying that I had a good job already. Little did he know how dreadful it actually was. I was laughing all the way home on the tube, seeing visions of myself lashed to a palm tree in Brazil – the other passengers must have thought I was crazy. Today I wish I hadn't been quite so timid, though; I should have explored it at least a little further. Who knows what might have been?

Reality, however, was library enquiries and filing correspondence about library enquiries, and the bottomless filing went on. Sometimes members of ASLIB came to the office for meetings, and one got to know some librarians. That was how, after about a year, I was offered a job in the library of the Royal Institute of International Affairs at Chatham House. It would be a mistake, however, to think that this had anything to do with books on international affairs. What it meant was writing catalogue cards. I even went to evening classes to learn about cataloguing and how to write catalogue cards. It has left me with a useful little skill of printing in a kind of script that gets a lot of letters into a small space. It has also left me troubled every time they change the way the telephone directory is organised, because I thought there were immutable rules about that sort of thing. Who decided that British Gas should be under G for Gas, while British Rail was under B for British? It's very unsettling. Also, I know how to find out how to find things out. But, really, I was very unsuited to being a librarian.

There are some letters I wrote to Alice Jaffé in America at this time, and they tell a very different story. Everything was great, the library job was most interesting, a dream come true, my mother was fine. I don't know whether I wanted to deceive myself or only her. I think that, in my chameleon-like adaptation to all things Anglo-Saxon, I had absorbed a sense that one has a duty to be cheerful. Unhappiness is not only an admission of failure, because it must be your own fault, it is also an embarrassment to others. Rather like curvature of the spine.

In 1950 Fanni died. Politicians spoke at her funeral, and there were warm and loving obituaries. All stressed her goodness and unstinting help for others even during the times when her own life had been so beset by tragedy. A bare six months later, Luis also died. In Karlsbad he had created an exclusive linen store. In London, when he died, there weren't even sheets on his bed. This uncle, who has made me unnecessarily well off in my old age, had nothing to live on in his, and had been selling off clothes and bed-linen in a second-hand shop for cash. When he first became ill I went to the Royal Masonic Hospital, near to where we lived, to ask if they would take him. I knew nothing of Freemasonry, but I knew that he had been a Mason of long standing. But they wouldn't. I think now that I didn't ask at the right level, and allowed myself to be fobbed off by a secretary or receptionist.

So then my mother and I were alone. The only relatives with whom there

94

was any contact were Paul and Alice in Sydney and Trude and Rudl in Calcutta. Air letters were a big event. At the time of Luis's death and funeral I was in hospital undergoing tests. I had started feeling tired and ill and was running mysterious temperatures, for which no cause could be found. I know about psychosomatic symptoms now, but I didn't then, and it was very frightening. Once I collapsed in the street. A short time later I had a fever for five long months. I remember sitting in the window and looking down at the street, promising myself that if I ever got down there again I would never again grumble about anything else. But of course, once I was better, the priorities shifted. When I later learned – and taught – about a psychological theory of the 'hierarchy of needs', which says that when one kind of need is met another will surface, this experience fell into place.

Finally they wrote from Chatham House to say that they were sorry, but they couldn't keep the job open any longer. Then I started to get better. Surprise, surprise.

So once again I had to find work. This time I went to the local labour exchange and asked for any kind of part-time work. This was partly to test if I was now fit enough, and partly to leave time for applications and interviews for 'proper' jobs. I was sent to a small pharmaceutical company on the river at Hammersmith, where they made wheat-germ extract and vitamin pills. I became a factory hand, some of the time working in the addressograph department where envelopes were addressed and stuffed by hand with advertising materials, and some of the time packing pills. To do this you held the handle of a wooden board which had twenty indentations. You dug this into a heap of pills and brushed off the surplus. In this way you had twenty pills, which you funnelled into a bottle.

I started to enjoy myself.

Industry

Getting the hang of the job took about ten minutes. After that it became automatic, and one sat round a table with a group of very pleasant women, chatting all day. The subjects were very like those one had chatted about at college. The language may have been a bit different but the essentials, both topics and ways of thinking about them, were the same: family, friends, men, local intrigues, national news (it was 1952, the year King George VI died). There was a young man who came into the department three or four times a day with packaging materials, bringing empty cartons and taking away full ones. He had been brought up a Christian but was losing his faith, and three or four times a day the threads of this discussion were picked up: was there a God, how did one know there was a God, if there was a God why did he let disasters happen? Just like at university. Other visits could enliven the day: someone making a collection for a wreath or the children's Christmas party, someone selling nylon parachute material which had probably fallen off the back of a lorry. And always these visitors from other departments brought interesting bits of news and gossip. Other excitements were when the river-barge housing the personnel department sank with all the records, which happened fairly regularly.

Once a month there was a one-day induction course for all those who had joined the company during the previous month, from the chief accountant down to the lowliest factory hand. We were told about the company and its products, heads of departments explained what their departments did, and there was a tour of the plant. It was totally fascinating: wheat was bought from Rank Hovis and brought to the factory in barges. The first production process was to extract the wheat-germ from the whole grain. What was left after that was pressed to extract an oil that was rich in Vitamin E. And what was left after that was sold to Heinz for thickening soups, for more than had been paid for the original wheat. Amazing!

The work itself was undemanding, and for the first time I was not so tired after work that I couldn't go out and have some social life as well. After three or four weeks, instead of leaving as I had intended, I changed to working full-time. I stayed for nearly a year, and really had to force myself to think about moving on. People were saying to my mother, 'You make sacrifices to let her go to university and look at her, £5 a week in a factory.' And I too began to think that I should probably not let this way of life go on for ever. However, I certainly did not regard it as an 'experiment', as people since then have sometimes tried to suggest. It was real, and I was a real part of it, not an observer.

Two things have remained with me from that experience. The first is a life-long love affair with industry: it may be kinky, but I am never as happy as when I am in an industrial situation, puzzling out how it all works and fits together – the materials, the customers, the suppliers, the machinery, the people, the relationships, the economics – the sheer life of it. And I am very good at it, organisational diagnosis is probably what I do best. The second is a life-long fascination, not to say obsession, with the question of work satisfaction. Why was working in a factory so pleasant and interesting and alive, when working in a library, *prima facie* a much more suitable job for an educated young woman, had been so miserable? To explain it one has to look at the details, I get cross when journalists and sociologists make broad-brush assumptions and jump to conclusions. For instance, an important element of the pill packing and the envelope stuffing was that it was auto-matic and needed no attention. That was why we could talk and think about other things, develop friendships and get involved in each other's lives. If the work had required some attention without being intrinsically very interesting, such as perhaps work with a sewing-machine, it might have been quite different. An important element of the library work had been that there was virtually no connection between the catalogue cards and the books they represented, or between the office where they were produced and the main library and the work which may have been going on there, let alone the whole organisation. No one had taken the new recruit round Chatham House to explain how that worked, or got any of the scholars who worked there to talk about what they did.

I was reminded of this years later, in the 1970s, when I was doing some work for the National Economic Development Office. In a factory making electrical equipment I came across a woman who was assembling the back half of an electric iron. She had been doing it for fourteen years and longed to know how the front half was made, but did not have the opportunity to find out. What a waste of her interest and intelligence and potential!

Now I knew what I wanted to do. At that stage I was not yet thinking in terms of designing work to suit people, only of people doing jobs that they were suited for. That seemed desperately important, and the route to it was personnel management. I enquired how one trained for that (I knew now how to find things out) and applied to take the personnel course at the London School of Economics. The tutor was Nancy Seear, who was to become a friend. At the interview she said that I should try to get some more industrial experience before the course started. So I went back to the labour exchange, and this time was sent to a small firm of local builders.

The builders were two brothers, who employed a few labourers in an ad hoc sort of way. My job was switchboard operator. I don't know what the brothers did when they were not in the office, but much of the time they were there, sitting at a table behind me, working out and placing bets on horses. They were very nice to me and sometimes included me in the stake: if the horse won, I got my winnings; if it lost, they would fund my part of the stake. There was very little to do, so I brought in some knitting. Mainly I had to answer the phone and say that no one was in, and take messages. The brothers owned some run-down houses, and the only time the switchboard was busy was when it rained and worried tenants called to ask if someone could come and repair a leak. As always, I had to say that no one was in but I would pass on a message. Once, during a heavy rainstorm, a woman who called was quite distraught, crying about her leaking roof. The brothers and I were on friendly terms; I turned round to where they were working on their bets and said couldn't someone go and see to it? One of them looked up in astonishment. 'Good God!' he said, 'You sound like a ruddy socialist!'

The personnel course was a phase of tremendous development for me and made more impact than three undergraduate years had done. The learning content was exciting, and was interspersed with practical assignments and attachments to companies. In a chain of grocers I was used, feeling very uncomfortable about it, as a phoney shopper to test whether staff suggested additional items after the things I had asked for. I also served in one of the shops and learned how to bone sides of bacon, scraping the maggots off first. In a pharmaceutical firm I made two hundred steak-and-kidney puddings in the canteen. One of the tins of meat had gone off, but I was told to mix it in with the good ones; no one noticed, or suffered any consequences.

The course also coincided with our move into the two-roomed flat and with my getting some psychotherapy, which the GP had suggested when no cause could be found for my mysterious fevers. After the course I started applying for personnel jobs and in the meantime worked as secretary to Solly Sachs, the South African trade unionist who was here in exile and whom I had met in the Fabian Society. He wanted to start an affair and when I said no, argued, 'I understand that you want champagne, but what's wrong with cold beer while you're waiting?' It was a flattering offer, especially as much of my work as his assistant had been to fend off enthusiastic ladies.

I became personnel officer for a small factory in Bermondsey which made paint tins for the Metal Box Company. On the morning I set out for my first day in this job I met the postman with a telegram from Solly. He was on holiday in the south of France and wanted me to join him there. I stopped off at a post office at the Elephant and Castle to send a wire back, saying I realised how perverse it must seem to start working in Bermondsey rather than loll about on a beach in the south of France. The post-office clerk was visibly displeased.

The factory at Wilds Rents was part of Metal Box's south London branch, the other part being a few streets away. That contained the main personnel department, with the branch personnel manager who was my boss, and a network of women staff who were all related to each other, and deeply suspicious of anyone who was not local and who had been to university to boot. By contrast my factory manager, Mr Clift, could take such peculiarities in his stride. The Wilds Rents factory had belonged to a family called Boutle before Metal Box bought it, and among the older people was still known as Boutle's. Mr Ernie Boutle still dropped in sometimes for a chat with Mr Clift, who had joined Boutle's as a boy of thirteen. He had now been there over fifty years. He later wrote a little booklet, laboriously typed by the factory secretary, called 'My life in Industry from 1900 – 1954'. I treasure its flavour and the picture it paints, and will indulge myself by putting some extracts into an Appendix (Appendix 3).

I was the only white-collar or 'staff' person in the Wilds Rents factory, which meant that I started work at nine, an hour later than everyone else. Mr Clift delighted in leaning against the door of his office as I walked across the yard, and yelling, 'Good arternoon!' for all to hear. Working with him was a joy.

Of course, I made mistakes. It was October when I first joined, and one of my first jobs was to collect staff orders for company products. In their other factories Metal Box made various household items such as trays, bread bins and cake tins. At Christmas staff could buy these at cost price, and many relied on them for Christmas presents. Two days before Christmas my boss in the parent factory informed me that the goods were not going to arrive until January. I thought that there would be at least a strike, if not a revolution. There was nothing I could do, except let people know as quickly as possible. Some psychologist at the LSE had said that people don't read notice boards so, having printed off a lot of notices, I stuck a notice wherever I could think, including on the way in to the women's lavatories, where it was bound to be seen. Came a deputation of large and menacing Works Council representatives. They were very angry, not about the fact that they were not going to get their bread bins, but because I had put a notice about bread bins near lavatories. It was disgusting, it was indecent, and if I didn't take it down there would be a formal complaint to the Works Council. I took it down.

We had a small print department, since some of the lines we made had designs printed on the body of the can. At one time there were more orders than we normally handled, and we had to organise a night shift for the print department. Now, printers were the élite of the trade union movement and, I had always been told, had to be handled with kid gloves. The question arose how to provide meals for the night shift, since we were not geared to catering at night. It was agreed that the cook would leave food out for the printers and that they would heat it up themselves when they took their break. On the first day of this arrangement I went into the kitchen before leaving for the day, because I was a bit nervous about it. To my horror I found that what had been left out was cold fish and chips left over from lunch. The cook had gone – she usually left by about three – and Mr Clift had also gone for the day. Breaking any number of unwritten rules, I fetched the keys to the larder from his office. In the larder I found a joint of cold roast beef. I am not very good at carving, but I cut slices from this joint and left them out, together with some pickle. Next morning I went in early, to find that the printers had taken the fish and chips and left the beef. Then I had to wait for the arrival of the cook. Luckily she was too astonished at what I had done to be able to muster any other reaction.

Many of the women on the staff were dockers' wives, at a time when there were many dock strikes. Periodically one or other of them would put her head round my door, cast her eyes to heaven, and say ''E's out again!' Once, when a line had stopped, I found a crowd of them dancing a raucous 'Knees up, Mother Brown'. While I was still wondering whether I ought to do anything about this, they had roped me in to take part.

A slightly trickier moral dilemma was how to respond to presents of stolen apples which people brought back from their annual hop-picking break. Many of our staff joined in the annual exodus from south-east London to the hop fields in Kent, and our production schedules were adjusted to allow for it. For people in jobs it meant that they could not accrue pension rights, because their period of service was interrupted every year. But when hop picking became mechanised during the late 1950s, the end of 'hopping' was the end of a much-valued tradition. I accepted the apples with thanks.

Another factory tradition was the annual outing to Southend. Crates of beer were loaded onto the charabanc for the outward journey. Then we spent the day wandering along the beach and the pier, having our fortunes told, riding the bumper cars, looking at what the butler saw, and on the way back we sang, between stopping at pubs.

A pub near the factory also organised outings twice a year, with weekly contributions collected from its regulars. For one old lady on our staff these were her only holidays. Twice a year she had such a good time on the Saturday that the resulting hangover lasted through Monday. Although she was well into her seventies these were the only times she stayed away from work, and each time she explained it by saying that her ceiling at home had fallen down. That ceiling fell down regularly twice a year.

On the fringes of politics

In parallel to starting work I had become involved with the Fabian Society, which after the war was a kind of intellectual home for a lot of Central Europeans. In London there were weekly lecture-and-discussion meetings, nationally there were weekend schools at Easter and the New Year, as well as week-long summer schools. These were especially popular while currency restrictions made foreign travel difficult. Later there were also summer schools abroad. In some ways the Fabian Society became a kind of substitute family, and not only for me. From my first summer school in 1953, where Bill Rodgers taught me how to cheat at croquet, the Fabian Society provided a mix of political discussion, lasting friendships, boyfriends, serious writing, satirical reviews, and some interesting and some odd people. It also contained contradictions. I remember fondly a comment in the pub after one Fabian Annual General Meeting: 'The trouble with Buckingham Palace garden parties is you always meet the same people.'

In that setting I became very involved in questions of industrial organisation and the nature of work. Very few Fabians had experience of industry; they were mostly lawyers, journalists, teachers and social workers. The Labour Party's trade unionists mostly spurned the Fabian Society. Ian Mikardo was a funny, know-it-all, arrogant management consultant, Austen Albu had been an engineering works manager before going into Parliament; there were not many more. Austen collected those few into a dining club, which came to be known as the Austen Albumen. The idea was for young scientists and technologists to meet Members of Parliament occasionally over dinner at the House of Commons. As I walked across St. James's Park to one of these dinners and reflected that I had been accepted by the people in the Bermondsey factory as well, I thought that there might just possibly be a chance of eventually shedding my 'refugee syndrome'.

I didn't realise how much it showed. Austen Albu and his family became my close friends for over forty years. Not long before his death he was reminiscing about that dining club and suddenly began to tease me about my apparently obvious pleasure at being part of it. But then, he could not know what not being part of things means. Austen made me a member of the Reform Club when they allowed women in, but it took many years of membership for it to feel like 'my' club.

For many years I was on the Fabian Society's Schools Committee, and for some years on its Executive. I found that, if I nagged persistently enough on the Schools Committee, they would give way out of sheer weariness about once every two years and agree to either a weekend or a summer school on an industrial topic. Some of these I directed.

The personal turmoil I had experienced about finding meaningful work was not the only reason why getting involved with industry seemed the right way to go. In the politics of those post-war years one of the main hot issues was nationalisation. The steel industry was nationalised, later re-privatised, then re-nationalised, then again re-privatised. It was becoming clear to me, though, that many of the values about working life that were being discussed within the Labour Party, and that were so in tune with the values I had brought with me from pre-war Czechoslovakia and from Fanni's influence, would not be met by a change in ownership alone. Both Fanni and the Labour Party were influenced by the acute and clear-cut privations that working people and the out-of-work suffered before the Second World War. Though some of those problems could be tackled politically, what happened inside organisations seemed to me at least as important in influencing the lives of people at work and could not be tackled in the same way. There may have been good reasons for nationalising key industries, but a machine-paced repetitive job would remain a machine-paced repetitive job, and a boss who did not think to explain how your part contributed to the whole would not be magically changed. This was not a matter of public or private ownership, it was a matter of how things were organised.

Moving into Research

In 1955 Metal Box decided to close the Wilds Rents factory, incorporating it into its sister plant, and Mr Clift decided to retire. It was time to look around. I went to see my former tutor, Nancy Seear, to ask about the job situation in personnel management. She asked whether I had ever thought of doing research. Up to then I hadn't.

I don't know whether Nancy's suggestion was a random one; I know that she had liked the piece of research I had done as part of her course. I also know that her mind was on research at that time, as she had become a member of the Department of Scientific and Industrial Research's Human Relations Committee.

Anyone who wants to understand what is going on in the social sciences needs to look at the funding, who is paying for what. The 1950s were the time of the Marshall Plan, the American programme of support for economic recovery in Europe. Politically there was ambivalence about this American support in Europe, because it clearly had political aims. In any case, however, as part of the Marshall Plan, under the so-called Conditional Aid Scheme, funds had been made available for industrial social research, and there had begun the first broad-based programme of industrial social science research in this country. The problems being tackled were to have some bearing on productivity, and the research carried out was to produce practical results.

It wasn't a new direction. Already in 1947 the Attlee government had set up a Committee on Industrial Productivity to advise on the application of science to the problems of raising productivity, and this committee had included a 'Human Factors Panel' chaired by Sir George Schuster, which had sponsored some psychological and sociological investigations into industrial problems. In 1950 the Schuster Panel dissolved itself, and the Department of Scientific and Industrial Research and the Medical Research Council set about working out how to cover the needs for research in this field. They set up committees to look after three areas: industrial health, individual efficiency, and human relations in industry. The members were academics, senior industrialists and senior trade unionists. With the coming of the Conditional Aid funds these committees now had much greater resources to spend.

The programme was administered by the DSIR. The Secretary of the Human Relations Committee was Ronald Stansfield, a senior civil servant, and Nancy suggested that I should go and see him. Until then the DSIR had been responsible for research in the physical and engineering sciences only. Administering social science research was new to them, and they had decided to locate one of the Conditional Aid projects in their own head-quarters, so as to understand better the issues involved in social research. It was a project on the Human Implications of Work Study, and Stansfield was responsible for that as well as for administering the Human Relations Programme as a whole. I was sitting in his office in Regent Street while he explained some of the history and background, when his phone rang. After listening for a few moments he said, 'Excuse me a minute,' and rushed out of the room. It turned out that a researcher on the work study project had just, that morning, handed in her notice. To cut the story short, they offered me the job and I took it.

So I didn't exactly choose or decide to go into research, there was a lot of coincidence about it. I could just as well – and probably just as happily – have gone on in personnel management. But at that stage I didn't go through a lot of heart-searching about whether this was the right direction to go. My mother had been admitted to a mental hospital for the first time; I just took the job.

Things at home had moved towards a climax during 1955. My mother seemed unrelievedly depressed, always disappointed with me, always angry. One Friday in November I came home from Bermondsey to be met by a fresh onslaught of accusations and upset. I was tired and couldn't face the prospect of this going on for the whole weekend. I said, 'I'm sorry, I've just got to get some peace. I'm going to go away for the weekend, I'll be back on Sunday evening.' I packed a small case, and walked out.

But where to go? On Hammersmith Broadway there was a newsagent's shop with advertisements in the window, and there was a card advertising a cheap room in Shepherd's Bush. I went to the house and rang the doorbell. But the man who answered the door said he was sorry, there was a football match on at Wembley that weekend, with a lot of Irishmen in town, and the room was taken. Up to then I had been mechanically calm and efficient in what I was doing, but now I burst into tears on his doorstep. It startled him considerably and no doubt frightened him as well. Back at the newsagent's I took down another address, this time in Earl's Court, and this time a dingy little room was available. I took it for the weekend, went out to buy some food and some women's magazines, and took both to bed.

On the Saturday there was some kind of Fabian event. I hadn't planned to go but now I went there, just to have somewhere to be. I sat at the back of the hall, hearing the proceedings as from a great distance, through a glass wall. I know now that this can be a danger sign, and think that that weekend was the nearest I have ever come to cracking up. On the Sunday I went back home, and we settled down again.

But two weeks before Christmas I went down with flu. Being at home with my mother all day brought out two things: on the one hand, our relationship was always easier if I was ill, which made me regress to being more a child and gave her a chance to look after me, and also to use her nursing experience. On the other hand, the uninterrupted contact made it impossible for her to hide her frustration, and at last I found out what it was about: she was convinced that I was secretly engaged to be married. Apparently it had to be kept secret because the man's parents were anti-Semitic, but she was deeply hurt and offended that I had not confided in her. She had been telling her friends about this, with a lot of supporting detail, but because it was supposed to be a secret none of them had said anything to me. And this had been going on for months.

I was indeed going out with someone, but there was no engagement and no secrets. No amount of protestation would persuade her of this. The more I tried to convince her, the more upset and angry she became at my unwillingness to confide what she knew to be the real truth, in the end smashing crockery against the kitchen tiles. I didn't know what to do and in despair, as a kind of defence, started to write down what was happening. A few days later I went to the doctor, pretending it was because of the flu, and showed him the notes. He read them and said, 'She is obviously paranoid. I'll give you some pills.' I said that I didn't think pills were the answer, that she needed specialist help. I can still see him in my mind's eye, drawing himself up – he was a very tall man – and saying, 'You came to me for advice. If you don't want my advice there is nothing further I can do.' And I was back out in the street.

But he must have thought better of it, for when I got home he phoned and gave me the name of a psychiatrist. That was the beginning of the end of the nightmare. First, the psychiatrist saw my mother twice. She talked about him as Jesus Christ – from somewhere Christian religious imagery came into the mind of this Jewish atheist – and then he took her into hospital as an emergency and supervised the first of a series of ECT treatments. It was Boxing Day, and his two children were waiting in his car outside – he was in the middle of a divorce and had care of the children over the Christmas holiday.

My mother had ECT again, during two of her later episodes of break-down. I know it is fashionable to despise ECT, but it helped her. For a few days after each series of treatments she had some memory loss, but her memory would come back and I could not detect any deterioration in her intelligence or other capacities. The psychiatrist said, 'To be honest we don't know how this works, but it does.'

Meanwhile she was in hospital for the first time, for three months. I felt very guilty about the relief I experienced, including at having the flat to myself for the first time ever. For the first time too, therefore, at the age of twenty-seven, I was able to indulge my long-felt need to invite friends home spontaneously.

After my mother came home the psychiatrist suggested that she should spend some time at Roffey Park, which was at that time a kind of 'half-way house', to recuperate. However, there she fell into the hands of a psycho-analyst who began an analytic approach quite unsuitable for a woman in her mid-fifties and the fragile kind of person she was. Whatever material he was probing at, it drove her to go out into the grounds and try to cut her wrist with a pair of nail scissors. She told me about it and showed me the scar when I visited; the staff hadn't noticed.

A week or so later she discharged herself, against medical advice. The first I knew about this was a phone call at work, from the police. A porter at South Kensington Underground station had noticed her on the platform, apparently trying to pluck up the courage to jump. He had called the police, who arrested her – attempted suicide was a crime at that time. I phoned the psychiatrist, who met me at the police station and persuaded them to release her into his care. So then she had to be sectioned – it was called 'certified' in those days – and that lasted a few more weeks. It was the first of several times.

She was taken to one of those old, depressing-looking hospitals on the outskirts of London with long, bleak corridors where footsteps made a hollow noise and wards were ugly and large. But the ward sister and the doctor who was in charge of her were both very competent and kind, and took a real interest, and she made good progress. But then my uncle Paul in Australia intervened and wrote telling me to take her away from there and find a private hospital, which he would pay for. I tried to resist, explaining that she was being well cared for, but he insisted. The doctor and the sister were both upset, and so was I. The first thing that happened in the private hospital was that a nurse stole the purse out of my mother's handbag. I didn't dare complain, because I was leaving her there at their mercy.

My mother had several more episodes of a similar illness, at intervals of about two years. But none was as terrible again as the first one. Perhaps the most helpful thing was to discover that this was illness; for ten years I had just seen it as our situation and fate. And now, in any case, there was help available. The psychiatrist also started to look after me. When my mother was settled back at home after the first period in hospital he encouraged me to leave home, which I could never have achieved on my own. I found a furnished room in Chiswick and got ready to move. My mother found the prospect appalling, could not see a reason why one would want to live away from home, cited the young women of her generation who stayed at home until they married. On the morning of the move she seemed on the point of a relapse. She didn't actually mention suicide but I could see it was in her mind, and she had already made two attempts. I phoned the psychiatrist and said I would have to cancel the move. 'I can't go,' I said, 'she will jump off the roof.'

'Yes, it's a real risk,' he answered. 'But you have to take it. If you don't, two lives will be destroyed instead of one. Take your things to your new place, and then come back and have a cup of tea with her.' I did that, and it was all right. And it remained more or less all right from then on.

I had originally tried to get onto a local authority housing list. But in the housing department at Hammersmith town hall, when they discovered that I didn't have a family, the young man taking down the particulars put his pen down and just laughed at me. There was a housing shortage, how could someone with no family have the temerity to want to join the queue! Years later, the director of Shelter gave a lecture at a Fabian summer school, with much pathos about the plight of homeless families. In the question period I asked whether they also dealt with housing for single people. He didn't understand the question. I repeated it. He still didn't understand. I explained again. Then understanding dawned. 'Oh, I see,' he said. 'You mean single mothers!'

Meanwhile, I was starting the new job. However, this appointment meant that I would be joining the Civil Service, and as a foreign national it was necessary to get security clearance. This turned out to take a long time, and there was a gap to fill. The labour exchange held no terrors by now, and I went there to look for a temporary job. It was just after Christmas and there was a vacancy selling programmes in Bertram Mills Circus at Olympia. It was disappointing that by the time I got there the vacancy had been filled, so I spent a less exotic three months supply-teaching, although some of the time it felt very much like a circus.

The school was in East London, and one became instantly involved in staff-room politics. The staff seemed to be divided into two factions: those who discussed education and those who complained about their salaries. My impression was that those who grumbled about salaries were the better teachers. The one thing that united them was hatred of the headmaster, and he did indeed seem a bit of a fool. Once he took me into a room of fourteen-year-old heavies, every one of them bigger than me, and said, 'Boys, this is Miss Klein. She's not an experienced teacher, so be nice to her.' Then he walked out, leaving the boys and me looking at each other. Memory has kindly blanked out what happened next.

One day I came into the staff room laughing about some such happening, and an experienced older teacher looked up from his book and peered at me over his glasses. 'Hm,' he said. 'They're usually in tears.'

At one point the maths master was away with flu. In his classes all I could do was ask how far in their books the children had got with him and, if they said up to page fifty-six, I would suggest that they now tried page fifty-seven. They didn't seem to find this as dreadful a way of proceeding as I did. In a class of eleven-year-olds all was studiousness and quiet until one little boy put his hand up and asked, 'Please, Miss, how many rods to a mile?' I looked out of the window, but there was no answer in the dusty trees. Honesty, I told myself, there's nothing else for it. 'I'm afraid I don't know.' There was a pause, then he said, quite kindly, 'Well, if you could tell me how many furlongs, I think I could work it out.' It is the only time I have wanted to hit a child.

I worked out two lessons that went down quite well, one on how you look for a job, and one on how you would make and sell Maltesers. The question of how to make Maltesers troubled me for a long time: chocolate goes matt if you touch it while it is soft. That is why icing a chocolate cake is difficult, and why chocolates, which are left to dry and harden once they have been coated with molten chocolate, have flat bottoms. So how do they get a chocolate coating onto a round ball in the first place, and how do they get it to stay shiny? This used to keep me awake at night when I had nothing better to think about. I did eventually find out, when I did some work for the Mars company (they are rotated in a large vat, while a film of coating is sprayed on). And I did get one little girl through French O-levels with extra lessons. I was very proud of that.

Research on Work Organisation

I joined the work study project in the DSIR in March 1956. It was just after my mother had come out of hospital and I had moved into my furnished room. There were four of us in the team, three researchers and a secretary. No one in the team had formal qualifications in social science; this made us extra careful about our methods, and we read a lot. One of my colleagues was in process of being psychoanalysed and, although this made him spend a lot of time staring into space, he was also able to alert us to some of the dynamics involved. We developed a habit of noting our personal reactions at the end of interview transcripts, so that they should not interfere with the professional material. At the end of one interview with a young packer in the first firm, he had written 'considerable positive counter-transference'. I gathered that this meant he had fancied her.

The approach was thorough in other ways, too. It was assumed that you can't research something without knowing a bit about it first, so my induction included getting some appreciation of what 'work study' meant[11].

There was at the time an obsessive preoccupation with productivity. It was to be the solution to everything, and it was to remain forever elusive. There was a British Productivity Council with local branches, there were Productivity Teams visiting the United States, new journals, much writing and endless conferences. With little capital available for investment, the emphasis was on techniques. Work study was probably the first of the many management panaceas that were to sweep the country in waves and be the solution to all problems and which now seem to replace each other about every ten minutes (by now they are being recycled: work study has come back as 'business process re-engineering'). It meant a number of different things, and there were fierce ideological debates about what it actually comprised, and whether it was 'scientific'.

I first spent two weeks in the work study department of the food company Crosse and Blackwells. Their office was on the main factory floor, and had

---

[11] The term usually covered some combination of simplifying the way a job was done, and then timing it.

glass walls. Within twenty minutes of my turning up on the first morning, a sequence of conversations had taken place on the other side of the wall:

> First person to second person: 'Who's that?'
> Second to first: 'That's Miss Klein.'
> Third person to first: 'Who's that?'
> First to third: 'That's Miss Heinz.'
> Fourth person to third person: 'Who's that?'
> Third to fourth: 'That's the granddaughter of old Heinz.'

Just as nowadays, some firms got a lot of public relations kudos from their organisational practices. In the 1970s Volvo became as famous for its autonomous work groups as for its cars, in the 60s it was Esso with 'productivity bargaining', in the 50s it was ICI with work study. The ICI work study department periodically ran public demonstrations for a wider audience. The presentation would end with a graph showing flat performance of ICI shares and a sharp upward move coinciding with their work study efforts. The show then ended with a flourish: 'And think what we could have achieved if we had only tried!' This was fine the first time one heard it. By the third time, it sounded a bit unspontaneous.

Lastly, I went on a work study training course organised by the TUC for shop stewards. My function, as the only Londoner and the only woman in the group, was to shop for the presents the members wanted to take home to their wives.

The idea of the project was to do two case studies, one in a firm where work study was being newly introduced by outside consultants, and one in a firm where it had been going for a long time. The first case study was in a medium-sized packaging firm in the Midlands, which we called 'Pakitt Ltd'. The second was in a large engineering company on the outskirts of London, which we called 'Multiproducts Ltd'. At the time I joined the research team, the fieldwork in Pakitt Ltd had been done, and had taken three months. It took us six months to analyse the interviews and write a report. Then it took four years to work the report through with the firm so that it could be published.[12]

The company had a lively and forceful woman managing director, and in the course of these four years she and I had long, tough sessions about the text of the report. During one of these her phone rang. She tore a strip off

---

[12] Stuart Dalziel and Lisl Klein (1960), *The Human Implications of Work Study, the Case of Pakitt Limited*. The Human Sciences Unit D.S.I.R. Warren Spring Laboratory.

whoever it was on the other end and then said impatiently to me, 'Why will they come to me like children, with every little detail?'

I said, 'But look: you expect them to come to you with this; and with this; and with this. How can you be surprised if they also come to you with something small when it happens to be inconvenient?'

She was a person of integrity and intelligence, and there was a long silence while she thought about this. It was my first experience of consultancy, and my first experience of that buzz that tells you a nail has been hit on the head. Getting the text cleared for publication became much easier after that.

I also had a first experience of social science making it possible to predict things. There was a good deal of research on accidents going on at the time. Industrial accidents were classed under two headings, severity and frequency, and the severity rate and frequency rate were thought to have different meanings. At the same time, it had been postulated that every accident is the result of a false hypothesis ('There is no one round that corner'; 'I can reach that kettle'). Putting these two ideas together made me think that in a paternalistic firm, with policies that took good care of workers, there would be a prevailing hypothesis that 'they will take care of me' and there might therefore be a high rate of minor accidents such as falling or dropping things on one's foot.

'Pakitt Ltd' was very paternalistic. There were welfare arrangements far beyond what was required by law, leave for educational activities – provided management approved of the kind of activity – and so on. Accidents were not the reason why we were there, but I ventured a prediction that they would have a high rate of minor accidents. And lo, they did. It was much higher than the national average, and puzzled them greatly. It was exciting to find that one can predict such things, because it also suggested that one might be able to choose policies in knowledge of their outcomes.

The second case study, 'Multiproducts Ltd', was typical of the light engineering industry, manufacturing a range of motor components in batches. There were two machine shops and two assembly shops. Our study was concentrated in the machine shops, and we interviewed operators, supervisors, shop stewards, engineers and managers. For me it was the first experience of intensive fieldwork, and I revelled in it and in the way understanding grew of the way things connected. It also brought surprises: one elderly operator shook his head with concern at the end of his interview and said, 'You poor thing. Have you got to go back and write all that out? Don't you get bored, just interviewing people all day?' And I thought I had such an interesting job.

By the time the interviews were finished my colleagues were leaving the project and I was in charge of writing it up. I got an assistant, and we set about analysing 125 unstructured interviews, from all levels of the firm. We went through a dozen of the interviews to establish what topics people had talked about, and arrived at twenty-six. Then we each went through the interviews separately, dividing the text into the twenty-six categories. If we didn't see a piece of text in the same way, we would force ourselves to argue it through until we reached agreement. It was very laborious, and took two years. No one would fund such rigour nowadays.

Much of the outcome of the two research studies turned on what happens when people's work is closely controlled. In Pakitt, the packaging company, there were a lot of difficulties between the management and the outside work study consultants: management were expecting improved methods, the consultants were hoping to demonstrate gains by time-studying jobs. They concentrated on the area where the various carton designs, having been printed onto sheets of board and partly cut through, were stripped away from the surrounding board; the main change they introduced was that operators had work brought to them by a lower-paid porter instead of going to fetch it themselves. The operators found that they were working more continuously than before, and there was much argument about whether more continuous meant harder. Mainly they were under greater constraint, lost the opportunity to move about and use a different set of muscles occasionally, and also lost the elbow-room and freedom to pick and choose new jobs which they had had with their old, familiar, system. So both management and the operators were upset with the consultants, and the work study application was eventually thrown out.

In Multiproducts familiarity with a long-established system meant that the operators had regained a good deal of elbow-room. They used it to optimise their own resources of time, energy and money. The operator who explained that he always worked very hard on Thursdays, stowed the pieces in his locker overnight and fed them in on Fridays so as not to be too tired for the weekend was, after all, being entirely rational. The research in fact turned out to be largely a study of 'fiddling'. Fiddling, both when jobs were being timed and in the way output was recorded, gave people some control over their own work situation as well as a chance to use intelligence and creativity which the work itself did not provide.

Some of the fiddles were highly sophisticated. Since the work study engineers were well aware of many of these things, and made allowance for them, fiddling actually became essential in order to maintain equilibrium and the balance of power. Those who didn't take part, for instance some foreign workers who did not understand it or who needed to maximise their earnings in the short term rather than optimise them over time, could create problems. For this reason there was some antagonism towards foreigners, which put me in an awkward position. Once I was standing with a group of supervisors who were grumbling about the foreigners (mostly Poles) in the firm, and felt I would have to say something. 'Actually, I'm a foreigner too,' I said, a bit timidly. A foreman turned to me with a smile. 'I know how you feel, love,' he said. 'I come from Manchester myself.'

For a time I reckoned that I was a world authority on fiddling. Certainly the need to establish some control over one's work situation seemed to be universal. It was another example of research making it possible to predict things. Tell me about your control system and I can make a pretty good stab at telling where the fiddles will be. (Doctors currently have financial incentives to keep the blood pressure of older patients to certain levels. I can imagine what this is doing to the records.)

When I gave a lecture on the research to the annual conference of the Deutsche Gewerkschaftsbund (the German TUC) the members fell about laughing, and called out 'How did you know?' – so obviously it was the same there. The session became so uproarious that I interrupted my talk and said, 'Ladies and gentlemen, please, this is not a comic turn!' This appears in the middle of a sentence in the published text. I didn't know that the talk was being recorded and would be published as it stood.

The work study research in fact provided the first occasion when I gave a paper to a professional audience. I asked the hairdresser to do something that would take people's minds off what I was saying.

A major influence and teacher appeared around this time. In 1958 Marie Jahoda, an eminent social psychologist, came over from the US to marry Austen Albu, whose first wife had died. I was close to his son and was introduced to her. She took me out to lunch, and there began a friendship and learning process which lasted until she died in 2001. She was best known for the first ever study of long-term unemployment, carried out in Austria in the early thirties, and for her work in the United States on race relations, which also led to a standard text-book on research methods. I was a very junior research assistant with no qualifications, in my first research job, and very excited about it. One of Mitzi's qualities was to be a life-long educator. As I enthused about our work she asked, 'What is the frame of reference?' So I had to go back to the office to find out what this meant. Some years later, on a train from Leeds to Harrogate, she tried to teach me the chi-square test of statistical significance. It has to count as one of her failures; I still can't do it. I guess the distance between Leeds and Harrogate isn't great enough.

113

One of her qualities was that she managed to combine being a scientist with being a human being with values, including political values, which in the social sciences gets people into terrible muddles. Her formula was straightforward and simple: you can exercise your political values in choosing what to research, and you can exercise them in deciding what to do with the findings – but absolutely not in between.

Mitzi was completely free from illusions. She pointed to the fact that, in all the welter of research on race relations, prejudice and racial integration that had gone on in the United States, nobody had predicted Black Power; and she took it to be a warning to us not to get too uppity about our subject. And she confessed herself to be defeated – that is, scientifically and intellectually defeated – by the phenomenon of fundamentalism.

In 1990, when I founded the Bayswater Institute, she became a founding trustee. When her first stroke robbed her of most of her eyesight she resigned, fearing that she might no longer be able to fulfil the legal obligations. We hurriedly created the role of President, but she distrusted the idea of a merely formal role. 'What does it mean?' she demanded.

'It means you can nag from a position of authority.'

'In that case, I accept.'

And she made full use of the invitation to nag, keeping us straining on our toes for four more years.

In 1958 I gave a Fabian lecture on 'The Meaning of Work'. Detailed interest in the actual content of work seemed a novel idea at the time. The lecture was the first time I brought together what it was about work that was important in human life, fuelled of course by my own early experiences, and supported now by what I had been learning in industry. My mother's work experience also provided examples: the factory she had worked in during the war had once had an order to produce a lot of metal Ds, the letter D stamped out in metal. These were sprayed with paint and left to dry, and then my mother and another woman had the job of turning them over so that they could be sprayed on the other side. Hour after hour and day after day they turned these things over, until one day the foreman, passing through the department, mentioned that these Ds were to label the drinking water for the troops preparing for the second front in Europe. The whole meaning of the work changed.

The lecture happened to coincide with Shirley Williams making her first appearance as General Secretary of the Society, and we became friends. Shirley encouraged me to turn the lecture into a Fabian pamphlet, but the Executive Committee was at first reluctant to publish it. They felt that this was not a proper political topic. A particularly sharp critic was the industrial relations academic Allan Flanders, and Shirley suggested I go to see him in Oxford. In dulcet paternal tones he said, 'You see, I don't want you to look back in ten years' time and feel ashamed of this.' It was my first encounter with the rivalry of academics. A few years later I was short-listed for a lectureship in Oxford. Allan was a member of the selection board, and was clearly anxious on behalf of the other short-listed candidate, whom he was sponsoring. He began by brushing my CV and publications aside with an 'of course, I haven't read any of this stuff'. Then he proceeded to wipe the floor with me, asking unanswerable questions and interrupting responses I made to the other members. By the time I left the room I was literally shaking. Two days later I received a letter of apology about how I had been treated from the Chairman of the board, which must be fairly unusual.

The Fabian pamphlet became my first publication and went into several editions.[13] As late as the mid-eighties someone in Unilever bought forty copies to distribute in his department. He took the red cover off first.

Widening horizons

I didn't realise until much later what luck, and how extraordinary, it was to have landed in the DSIR, from where the whole wide-ranging research programme was being administered. Located in the DSIR headquarters one saw the whole range of what was going on. Researchers came in to discuss their ideas and one got to know them. Their papers and reports were circulated and much discussed. For the new entrant to the profession there was the fascination of what comes out when a social anthropologist (Tom Lupton) does participant observation on the manufacturing shop floor. There was the dilemma of senior civil servants, who would scratch their heads about the high salaries being claimed by people in the Tavistock Institute because they had to pay for psychoanalysis. From the industrial sociologists (Joan Woodward, Tom Burns, George Stalker) came ground-breaking studies about technology, and markets, and how they affected organisation.

The various environments – scientific and technical, economic and commercial, political – featured strongly as influences in these studies. There was the relevance of ergonomics and the relevance of psychoanalysis. There was hearing about the first group relations conference in this country, going there out of curiosity and coming back not much the wiser. There was much

---

[13] The meaning of work. Fabian Society Pamphlet no. 349, 1963.

of what would now be called 'networking': Rosemary Stewart, director of the Acton Society Trust, hosted meetings between researchers and managers. Stansfield would say to a researcher, 'Ah, so-and-so in Bristol is doing something relevant to what you have in mind. It might interest you – I'll introduce you.'

This is the template that the DSIR experience has wired into my head. By chance I had landed right in the centre of this ground-breaking programme, and the perspective that gave me was to stay with me for ever after.

One of the researchers who came into the office to discuss her work was Joan Woodward. She was engaged in research that was to cause a big stir, both in the social science and in the industrial world. It drew attention to the fact that manufacturing organisations functioned best if they organised themselves according to their manufacturing technology, rather than according to general principles. What a surprise. At the time, such 'general principles' were drawn from army experience and included such things as the 'optimum span of control' – i.e. that a manager should not be responsible for more than about seven or eight people, because he (it was usually he) was responsible for their relationships with each other as well as with him. Today it is still hard to persuade people that the best way to organise depends on the particular circumstances you are in. It means you have to think seriously about your situation, while it is so much easier to follow general rules. So the search for the ultimate general rule continues. In a culture of acronyms, bullet points and executive summaries, it is difficult not to get jaded as global 'visions' and total, comprehensive solutions to all problems succeed each other – STS, TQM, BPR, EC, TPM, WCM, CI, ... Since these packages are what gains attention, I have thought of patenting one myself, to be called TATTA (Think. And Then Think Again.)

Joan showed interest in our study and liked my work, and was not fazed by the fact that I had no social science qualifications. So when the others in the team decided to move on, she offered to supervise my writing up the second study. She was joining a newly formed Production Engineering and Management Studies section at Imperial College; through several metamorphoses this eventually became the Business School. Stansfield appreciated the offer and, as the DSIR was about to move out of London, I joined her at Imperial College, still on the payroll of the DSIR, to produce a little book called 'Multiproducts Ltd'.[14]

Stansfield himself was neurotic, sexist and very creative. He was a physicist who had been involved in operational research during the war, when any

---

[14] *Multiproducts Ltd. A case study in the social effects of rationalised production.* HMSO 1964.

and all disciplines were drawn upon to do research on operational problems, paradoxically developing their disciplines as a by-product. This was in tune with the values and approach of the DSIR/MRC committee members and researchers, which were geared towards science and scientific method in the service of problem solving. In the final report of the Schuster Panel, Sir George Schuster had written:

> ... for the better understanding of problems in human relations and human behaviour, the great need is for accurate factual observation of things which are actually happening in industry, for the collection of clinical material – of evidence on the way in which various influences are working – and the proper collation and interpretation of that evidence, so as to ensure that methods and policies can be considered in the light of that evidence and not under the influence of prejudice, hasty generalisations from inadequate data, individual hunches or superficial public opinion. Observational studies of this kind can be regarded as 'scientific' if 'science' is used in the widest sense – the Baconian sense – in which it includes any orderly study of the natural world.

This was the approach taken in the Conditional Aid programme, and this basis of 'accurate factual observation of things that are actually happening' paradoxically produced some major strides in theory. There didn't seem to be any conflict between theory development and practical usefulness.

Several of the studies in the programme were in the general area of how structural factors in an organisation, like its technology or the nature of its markets, affect the view of the world, attitudes and behaviour of the people involved. If maintenance is costed in with production, relationships will be very different than if the two functions are in different cost centres. Tracking such links between structure and behaviour has served me ever since as a way of looking at organisations. I get the most enormous kick out of the detective-story quality of it. When you are new to an organisation you are allowed to ask stupid questions. The excitement comes when you find the questions beginning to be less stupid. When you say to a client, from this basic sense of 'hard' and 'soft' factors interacting, 'If this is the way you describe it over here, does that mean that such-and-such may be happening over there?' and they look a bit surprised and say, 'Yes, I suppose it does!' I feel like Miss Marple and Lord Peter Wimsey rolled into one. And it keeps happening; this is a very robust framework. It is also useful because people can be helped to see how the difficulties or conflicts they experience may have been designed into a situation, and are not all due to their personalities.

At the same time as this organisational research, the links between attitudes, behaviour and technology were being formulated in the Tavistock Institute as 'sociotechnical theory'. It was the same principle, but at the level of the workplace rather than the whole organisation, and it served to put theory round my own experience and understanding about work satisfaction. The work being produced by the Tavistock Institute at that time was very exciting, but it was couched in difficult and mystifying language. I thought of offering my services as translator to the Tavistock Institute.

But the question of language is not as simple as that. In a sense you can't win: if you put something simply, it is 'only common sense'; if you put it technically, it is 'jargon'. Later, when I was in the Tavistock Institute myself, I once ran a course on job design, together with Hugh Murray, for the board of a company. In my introduction I spoke of the importance of leaving options open in the design of production methods, so that operators could work some things out for themselves, and all round the table heads nodded in agreement. Later Hugh gave a talk in which he referred to 'minimum critical specification', which of course means the same thing. They complained about jargon and being 'blinded with science'; but they remembered minimum critical specification, which gives something to refer to, while leaving options open had been too easy to agree with and forget. Nevertheless, much of my effort has been and still is about removing mystique.

Stansfield was difficult to work for, but he had a great gift for putting people in touch with each other – industrialists with researchers, researchers with others who were pursuing a line that might have a bearing. In a paper on 'Current Research on Social Problems in Industry' he had written:

> The most up-to-date information, of course, can only be obtained by personal contact ... moreover, I believe that the most reliable way of finding out what research is in progress bearing on any particular point in which one happens to be particularly interested, is by judicious use of the grape-vine – the important thing is to know a few good people whom one can ask who is likely to have the information one wants. Then one quickly gets passed on to the right people ...

In this way understanding was cumulative and grew in many places. It is a long way from present-day computerised literature searches: young researchers now are not directed to 'good people whom one can ask'; work is not deemed to exist unless it can be retrieved from a computerised database, and it does not get into such a database unless the author has thought of it in terms of 'keywords'. So some creative work does not get into such databases. Neither does work which is more than a very few years old, because the databases cannot cope. Neither does work which crosses the boundaries of academic disciplines. I have published in engineering and anaesthetics journals, but when a social scientist publishes a paper in the journal of another profession, the paper reaches neither database. Under-standing is a long way down the list of what is achieved in this way.

Some of the people involved in the Conditional Aid programme came from fields other than social science. Some had gained their early experience working on problems in the armed forces, and the idea of research in real situations for a purpose was natural to them. By comparison the university professionals sometimes seemed remote from the real world. When we were preparing for our second case study I was sent to consult a very eminent professor of industrial psychology about methods. He suggested that to study the effects of financial incentives we should set up one group of engineering operators who would be working on a bonus system and another group doing the same work but not on bonus. It took courage for a junior research assistant without qualifications (but who had worked in industry) to point out that in a real situation which is not a laboratory you can't play around with people's pay in this way; and even if you could, this method would have told us nothing beyond the difference between these two particular groups.

The professionals could also be bewildering. The first time Stansfield took me to a meeting of the British Sociological Association he introduced me to someone who responded with, 'I believe we have met, but we are only peripheral stimuli.' The next time, on the other hand, when Joan Woodward was giving a paper, Nancy Seear leaned over – I don't know what deep insight I was expecting – and in a penetrating whisper said, 'She needs a new bra!'

If Fanni had been alive at this time I am not sure that she would have liked the direction I was beginning to take. Concern for the quality of people's working experience became focused on the conditions which influence that experience. This had been so for her too, but for her it had meant putting the emphasis on political action, while for me it meant putting the emphasis on organisation. As far as industry was concerned, political action had little impact on people's day-to-day experience, and personnel management was also too restricted. The great excitement lay in discovering and understanding how organisations and technology functioned, and in seeing that understanding put to use. And if this was to be effective, nothing less than honest observation and description would do, wherever that would take one. It could take one to questions of self-deception – of organisations, or their advisers, believing they were doing one thing while the reality was something different. Reality became the most important value of all.

In the 1950s and early 60s these values – of reality and working on problems – seemed to be congruent with each other. Government and science and social science seemed to be together, with many hitches and problems, but engaged in the same enterprise. It seemed to fit me, or I it, like a glove. The Fabian Society was running study groups on science policy. I started editing a volume of Fabian Industrial Essays, though in the end this faltered. But I was in the middle of all this intellectual turmoil, and had practical experience to offer as well. As for our project team, we didn't see research as being primarily for academic publication. It was to understand how things functioned, in order to help them function better and to help policy-makers choose policies in knowledge of their consequences.

But after the mid-sixties this congruency was lost. Some time in the 1970s I gave a talk at a Labour Party supper club in Wellingborough. The local Labour Party had a custom of meeting for supper once a month, with a speaker. Wellingborough is near Corby, where the steelworks had not yet been closed. I talked of work satisfaction, and how jobs can be designed, or redesigned, to make work more meaningful for the people doing it. In the discussion afterwards a woman stood up and said, 'I wish my husband was here. He works at the steelworks, and when he heard that there was a social scientist speaking, he refused to come.'

There is a clue to the reason for this antagonism to social scientists in another experience from around that time. I was giving a seminar about the use and application of social science research to the staff and post-graduate students of a university department. In the discussion period I was strongly attacked, on two counts: helping organisations to function better was helping capitalism to function better and therefore delaying its overthrow; and for my Institute to take fees for such help (I was working at the Tavistock Institute at the time) just showed how they had sold out. Looking round the room I reckoned that I was the only person there who was actually losing a day's pay to be there. The position that money was dirty (unless, of course, it was laundered through the Treasury) was an easy position to take – the reality value was being sacrificed to the superficially humanitarian. It is not altogether surprising that, when Mrs Thatcher came to power a few years later, she was able to tap into reactions to this and swing the pendulum with devastating effect in the other direction.

Of the various voices in my head, Fanni's had been the most dominant (jostling alongside my mother's, to keep me grounded in everyday realities and housekeeping, my father's to make me relax and not take things too

RESEARCH ON WORK ORGANISATION

tragically, and my school's, to assert morality and duty – quite a mix). For Fanni, you fight politically to create better conditions for the poor and deprived, and when you encounter them directly you give them all you have. For me, there was much about working conditions that could not be dealt with politically, although I was to make some attempts. Where these things had their roots in organisation, you had to understand organisation. I cannot say that is why I moved into research, it was much more haphazard than that. But it is why, of the various options around, I stayed with organisation research – it fitted. But it also became important in its own right, just trying to understand how things work, testing that out with the people in the organisation and working on it with them.

Reality came to take first place. That is where I am curious to know what Fanni would have said: if you mind about reality, you may become very passionate about the integrity of research, and about how researchers are trained. That can seem to be some way from the original human impulse, and look as if there is a distance between the two sets of values. I hope she wouldn't think that.

Research on Industrial Organisation

Joan Woodward had been brought into a unit called Production Engineering and Management Studies at the Imperial College of Science and Technology because it was felt that industrial sociology should feature in the education of engineers, particularly production engineers. I was seconded there by the DSIR, who were moving out of London and were glad of this chance of professional supervision during the writing of the book.

Once the writing, and with it the project, was coming to an end, my lack of formal qualifications began to be a problem. I couldn't make progress in the scientific civil service with a degree in languages, and arranged to go back to the London School of Economics to spend a year reading around in psychology, sociology and methods of research, and to take the sociology degree exam. The reason I was able to do this is rather sad. In keeping with the spirit of the times the Nuffield Foundation had instituted a series of Senior Sociological Scholarships, in the hope of attracting mature engineers who wanted to convert to social science. But it was difficult to find suitable ones. The conversion of a linguist was not what they had intended, but there was money left in the scheme and I got one of these scholarships. It was quite generous, because it was assumed that engineers would be earning good salaries. In the meantime Joan was preparing a second major piece of research, and I was to come back after my 'sabbatical' to join her.

At the LSE I was allocated a tutor. I was thirty-two by then, and he didn't really know what to do with me. He gave me essays to write. The first time I turned up at a tutorial to get my essay back, he hadn't read it. When this happened again the next time I said, 'Look, if you're not going to read them, I'm not going to write them.'

He said, 'Yes, I know, I'm so sorry. I don't know what to do. Do you know, at the end of last session I had three hundred unread essays. What on earth can I do?'

'Bloody-well read them,' was the only answer I could give; an undergraduate would probably have found this difficult. I didn't add that he should perhaps spend less time on television appearances. Another lecturer explained that, when marking exam scripts, he only read sample pages. When student rebellion broke out later it was not in the least surprising. The students might have expressed their disaffection in political terms, but I believe that they were simply not being cared for.

My mother and I still had friends among Fanni's circle of political émigrés from around Karlsbad. We sometimes visited them together, or they visited her, always an occasion to bring out the old recipes for open sandwiches and cakes. In various ways people were settling down. Some compensation payments from the German government began to come through, enabling some people to buy homes, and this gave an important impetus to the settling-down process. My mother got a small pension from the German government, making her less dependent on me. But the process itself opened up wounds and triggered off one of her bouts of mental breakdown and hospitalisation.

The émigrés began to die out. There is a café near the Golders Green crematorium where the refugee community tended to congregate after a cremation (they were now too busy with their lives to meet often), to reminisce and catch up on news. It became a ritual during the 1950s and 60s, a kind of sad/nostalgic reunion before everyone went back to their London jobs and homes.

In Joan Woodward's earlier research project she had found that, if you postulated a scale of increasing complexity of production technology – from unit production at the simple end, through batch production and mass production to chemical process production at the complex end – a lot could be predicted about attitudes, behaviour and organisation at the two ends of the scale. In the middle this was not so. Batch production can be organised in a lot of different ways, with different consequences, and the idea developed that here the clue would lie in the control systems – that is, the way in which targets (of quantity, quality, different kinds of cost) were set and actual outcomes measured, and what happened when the two were compared. So this became the subject of her next major research project. The project eventually did not get as much public attention as the earlier one had, but I have always felt that it was more significant, and have certainly found it more usable and useful in practice.

The control systems project began with three researchers working with Joan. We devised a method which we called the 'tracer study'. It involved tracking a product through everything that happened to it, from design and marketing, through production, to sales and distribution, investigating the systems and decisions that impinged on it along the way. It is a splendid way to learn about organisations, and I have often used it since then. I have tracked products through manufacturing processes; letters and telephone enquiries through a bank; patients through a hospital; medical consultants through their hospital ward rounds.

Jeff Rackham tracked a batch of products through an engineering firm. Peter Combey tracked the building of a prototype computer, and ended up with a whole room full of data that nearly overwhelmed him. My 'tracer' was a four-week batch of a brand of household soap. I interviewed everyone who had anything to do with the systems and decisions around it, and then spent four weeks in the plant itself, doing what came to be called a milk-round of all the people involved, from the works manager through the various control engineers to the department operators and the man who swept the department floor (and who was the only person in the department who knew the daily schedule because he dusted the manager's desk). One interview, with a maintenance engineer, stays in my mind and has served me since then as an illustration of the dynamics of work satisfaction. It was the usual kind of unstructured interview in which no specific questions were asked, and for about two hours he talked freely about his job. At first he took a fairly tough line: 'All I'm interested in is the money. This firm pays well, and that's the only reason I stop here. What a working man wants from his job is the pay packet, and don't let anybody kid you about other fancy notions.'

Half an hour later he was talking about the firm, and discussing various things that he thought were wrong with it. I said nothing, but he seemed to think that he was being inconsistent, because he stopped himself. 'Well, you see, when you get a bit older, and you've paid for the house, and your wife's got a washing machine – you don't need money so much any more and you find you start noticing the firm. And by God it can annoy you!'

Half an hour after *that* he said, 'You know, what I really like is when the machine goes wrong and I'm the one who knows how to put it right.'

What one thinks this man's 'real' views were would depend on when the interview closed. Like the skins of an onion, they were all real; the question is which of them gets tapped. In all my years of working in this field I have never met a single person who did not have some of the layers under the surface.

Once the fieldwork was finished, I spent two years analysing the material. There was nothing I didn't know about soap production; I had soap coming out of my ears. That was fine, but one morning towards the end of this time Joan came into the office in great excitement: her eyes were shining, her cheeks were pink, and she said, 'I think we may have a chance to do the Heinz Baked Bean!' I didn't think I could face it. Two or three years buried in baked beans? My earlier longing was certainly coming home to roost.

During this time the first major business schools were being set up in this country, in Manchester and London. The London Business School made much play of the importance of the behavioural sciences in business affairs, and advertised a post to head up a strong behavioural science department. I applied, but heard nothing. Eventually an American, Dean Berry, was appointed. When he had settled in London he got in touch and invited me to lunch. Apparently when he had arrived to take up his post he had found a filing cabinet in his office with more than a hundred job applications from British social scientists, which had never been processed. So he set about contacting these people, to try and smooth their ruffled feathers. That's a lot of lunches. And all the while one had been hearing on radio and seeing on television the director of the London Business School pronouncing that there are no social scientists in this country.

But then something else turned up, which I felt hit the target – of combining research and reality on the one hand, and development and improvement on the other – slap bang in the middle.

Social Science Adviser in Industry – The Esso Years

On the Underground one morning in 1964 an advertisement on the back of someone else's *Times* caught my eye:

Industrial Sociologist

Esso Petroleum Company Ltd is to recruit to its Employee Relations department in London a well-qualified social scientist who will help in the analysis of the social pressures in a large industrial organisation. He will do this by direct investigations of special problems, many of which he will help to define.

The successful candidate will be expected to advise on all aspects of human science research and must therefore have good qualifications in sociology, social anthropology or allied subjects. It is essential that he should also have had experience in the application of social and psychological theory to industrial problems. Wider experience in academic research, in education, or in the clinical and social sciences could be an advantage. An eclectic approach to the human sciences, rather than adherence to one school or one set of methods, would be highly desirable.

This appointment will give considerable scope for advancement and will require high intelligence and initiative. The salary, to be agreed by negotiation, will be commensurate with these requirements. The successful candidate will almost certainly be above 30 years of age, and is most likely to be in the 35–45 age group.

I could not have imagined a job description that fitted better what I felt myself to be about. I spent twopence on a copy of *The Times*, talked it through with Joan, and applied for the job. The Esso people said they had not expected that the new post would be held by a woman, but they appointed me.

There was an unexpected argument with Shirley Williams, who said, 'If you take that job, I'll never speak to you again.' The Vietnam War had started and

Standard Oil, the parent company of Esso Petroleum, was strongly involved. I had to admit that I hadn't thought about this aspect. Once I did, the parent company and its political involvement seemed far away and the link tenuous. I felt that refraining from taking the job would not make a difference to anything, while taking it would perhaps enable me to do some useful things. Above all, it would allow me to learn about how the social sciences can be made useful in practice. I didn't know what that meant in terms of commitment to the parent company, and I remain uncertain about how to draw this kind of boundary. Shirley, of course, did not carry out her threat.

There had been two ventures into making use of research, or consultancy, during my time at Imperial College. The first came via Joan Woodward from the Flax Spinners' Association of Northern Ireland. In spite of the high unemployment in Northern Ireland they found it difficult to recruit staff, and wanted to understand why.

I had visited all twenty-three flax mills in Northern Ireland. It was in 1963, some years before the problems of the Province erupted into overt violence in 1968/69. But everyone warned me to be careful – religious issues affected industrial relations. No one explained exactly how, they just kept telling me to be careful. Very cautiously I asked one mill manager, 'What's the religious situation here?'

'Seventy–thurrty,' he growled.

'Er – which way?'

'The wrong way!'

I left it at that.

I presented the Association with a rather critical report, including a good deal about the situation of the industry as a whole. As for the recruiting problem, physical working conditions were pretty bad in these mills, which were old, dark buildings full of dust and steam. It was not surprising that people didn't want to work there. The industry could not afford to knock down these old, outdated mills and rebuild them. What they could afford, and did to show that they were taking the report seriously, was to build new lavatory blocks alongside some of the old mill buildings. I guess they are the only monuments I shall ever have.

The second foray into consultancy came at the end of the soap production study. A good relationship had developed with the firm, and they asked me to come back as consultant. We discussed an idea for re-thinking the production process in order to make the work more meaningful. A meeting to discuss this went well, until a senior manager asked, 'If we work the way you are suggesting, shall we be freeing up the operators' motivation? Are we likely to get more output?'

I said, 'I don't know; let's try it.'

The whole thing collapsed, almost visibly. I could see disappointment spread through the group because I had said, 'I don't know'. They expected a consultant to be confident; to know. It was clearly impossible to go on.

The company's works manager had very much wanted the project, and was very disappointed. Later, when I was working for Esso, he sometimes came to see me in London, and each time this failure to get a project off the ground came up. Finally one day he thumped my desk and shouted, 'Your bloody integrity!'

Nowadays I would know how to handle that situation, but at the time I didn't have the skill to bring together the two roles of researcher/scientist, who needs to be true to the real state of knowledge, and consultant, who needs to have care for the anxieties of the clients. Simply claiming that of course productivity would improve would be unethical. The fact was that one couldn't know for certain what the effect on productivity would be. One could, however, have made clear to them how the scientific aspects and consulting aspects of the situation created a dilemma, and then join with them in designing the project in phases with review points, so that if things did not go well it could be closed down without damage.

I never set out to be a consultant. What I have wanted has been to find ways of using the methods, concepts and findings of the social sciences because they have a big contribution to make in dealing with industrial and organisational problems. How to get that contribution made was clearly not straightforward, as this experience shows, so one needed to learn consultancy skills. But they were only a means to the end; I have a complete blind spot about why anyone would want to 'be a consultant' as an end in itself.

The Conditional Aid Programme had paid off, in several ways. Because the social sciences had produced creative and valued results, industry had become interested: there were many meetings between industrialists and researchers, and the DSIR commissioned journalists to write short, simple accounts of research reports. The government also set up a committee chaired by Lord Heyworth, the Chairman of Unilever, to look into the organisation of social research and the supply of researchers. As a result a Social Science Research Council was set up, on a par with other research councils, though with nothing like their budgets.

The Secretary of the Heyworth Committee was Albert Cherns, a psychologist who later went on to get one of the first grants from the new SSRC, to start up a Centre for the Utilisation of Social Science Research at Loughborough University. This, and Esso's initiative in taking an industrial sociologist into the company, were the two moves into utilisation.

The usefulness of the social sciences was in the air. C.P. Snow had recently published a lecture on 'The Two Cultures', positing a gulf between the arts and the sciences and pleading for more respect for science and funding for science education. I felt that this missed the point. The cultural dichotomy was not between the arts and the sciences but, in both fields, between the pure – art for art's sake – and the applied. In the social sciences the time to explore usefulness and application had come. The Heyworth Report was suffused with the belief that research in the social sciences was important and valuable, and should be used. It therefore also discussed the issues involved in use:

> In expressing their research needs and in constructing research div-
> isions or units, user organisations must bring social scientists into a
> close working relationship with administrators ... In the physical
> sciences the translation of research findings into practical applications
> is the function of the specially trained development scientist or en-
> gineer, who understands both the relevant scientific discipline and the
> technology of the establishment in which he is employed. In the social
> sciences, even when allowance is made for the difference in the nature
> of applied research, there are very few people whose functions cor-
> respond to the engineering or development function in the physical
> sciences, and nowhere are such people trained. If anything approaching
> the full potential value is to be obtained from research in the social
> sciences, an attempt must be made to define and analyse this function.

This is what I joined Esso to do. The company's employee relations adviser had been one of the people giving evidence to the Heyworth Committee. He was interested in the subject, and he was a friend of Tommy Wilson, a former Chairman of the Tavistock Institute, who had become social sciences adviser to the board of Unilever. He had gone on to persuade the board of Esso Petroleum to create the post of social sciences adviser there as well.

It was not to be like the Unilever post, which was mainly one of education (Tommy spent a large budget every year on books and journals) and of personal advice to the Chairman. Nor was it to be like the post in the Glacier Metal Company, which had been pioneered by Elliott Jaques. He was by training a psychoanalyst and used that as his approach; it seemed to me unlikely that there would be many psychoanalysts who would want to work with an industrial company in this way, or many managing directors who would be as enthusiastic and committed as Wilfred Brown at Glacier. There was no one who had entered into such a situation 'from cold'. If using the social sciences to help with problems was to become widespread, I felt, there would need to be a more ordinary or 'normal' way of doing it, and it was to find out what this could be that I took the job.

There was another argument, this time with a colleague, about the kind of conditions I ought to make before accepting the job. He said that if you arrive in a Rolls-Royce you get treated in a Rolls-Royce fashion, and that I should make tough conditions about the status and the services that were to be made available to me. But arriving in a Rolls-Royce was not my style. I agreed with Esso's ER adviser who said that the new function would need to earn credibility, and I thought it reasonable, and realistic, to start at middle-management level. If the work was found useful, it would spread outward from there. If a high-status, board-level adviser was introduced and imposed on people, that would set up dynamics that would make it impossible to assess the real value of the work. It was nevertheless bad luck that one of the two joint managing directors, who had been the only board member supporting this project with real enthusiasm, was seconded for two years to the newly formed Prices and Incomes Board precisely at this time. Two weeks after I joined the company he toured head office on a round of goodbye visits. He put his head round the door of my office, said, 'Well, Miss Klein, we look to you to change all our thinking' – and disappeared.

The job

We had agreed that the aim was to develop areas of application and use. For over two years, it worked well. A programme of work developed and grew, with the social science function forming something like a medical or legal practice. I never had a large department, though for several years I had a colleague. The pattern that developed was that when a problem or a question arose I, and later he, would go some way towards preliminary work and diagnosis, with people in a range of departments. Once it became clear and agreed what was needed we sometimes did the work ourselves and sometimes it was formulated as a 'project', which would be contracted out to other relevant researchers or consultants. In this way we were able to draw on a number of university departments and research bodies and, in line with the orientation I had acquired in the DSIR, on a wide range of disciplines and experience.

These were not 'social science' projects. They were projects about the organisation of distribution systems, about the work in a pipeline control room, about the relationship between the sales and marketing functions, redesigning the system of refuelling aircraft at London Airport, redesigning the bridge of a small coastal oil tanker, looking at the life and work on large oil-tankers, working with the marine management group on their own relationships and development as a team.

I didn't think in terms of formulae or packaged solutions, I thought of social science methods as adding to the tools that people had available to them, of the concepts as adding to their understanding, of research findings as sometimes having a substantive contribution to make, of concepts and findings as helping to predict what was likely to happen if things were done this way or that way. But always it was about making a contribution to the mainstream activity, never about social science becoming a mainstream activity itself. There was some training for industrial engineers and operational research people, and a good deal of helping people to think through their situations and arrive at their own ways forward. The phrase 'Thanks, I think I know what I want to do next' was very satisfying to hear.

It is the clangers that one remembers with particular piquancy. I was sneaking home early one afternoon and in the lift met the marketing director, who was also sneaking home early. 'I suppose you're off to Wembley,' he said.

'Why?' I asked. 'What's happening at Wembley?' It was the day of the soccer World Cup Final in 1966, which England memorably won against Germany. Ouch.

In trying to understand the realities of the kind of work we were doing I felt there was a danger of using up the present stock of what I knew, and not replenishing it. There was also a certain professional isolation, and I knew that Tommy Wilson in Unilever felt this too. Albert Cherns and I put our heads together and made a list of all the people we could think of who were interested in social science application or utilisation. It now reads like a list of the great and the good among the organisational social scientists of that time: Albert himself, Tom Burns, Joan Woodward, Tommy Wilson, Eric Miller, Sylvia Shimmin, Gurth Higgin, Hugh Murray, Harold Bridger … I invited them to a seminar; they enjoyed it and wanted to meet again. It became a kind of club, which met about three or four times a year to talk shop. The members insisted on keeping it informal, and it came to be known as 'Klein's Mates'.

What we were doing in Esso was attracting attention, and I was 'headhunted' several times during this period. I turned down three invitations to apply for university chairs – it was the time of massive expansion in the universities – and I also turned down an invitation by H.R.F. Catherwood to join the Department of Economic Affairs. Some of these opportunities simply came too soon after I had started the Esso job – we had not yet had enough chance to see how it would turn out. I have of course sometimes wondered whether turning them down was foolish, but I think I would do it again. I was so passionately convinced that what we were doing was important, and committed to testing it to the limit no matter what, that I hung on stubbornly, even later when things began to go wrong.

In a review of the activities to the board, I said:

> ... I shall not feel that this has been effective until the incorporation of social science knowledge and methods becomes an absolutely routine, ordinary, even boring part of what goes on. Every system or gadget that is introduced brings with it social and organisational consequences, whether you like it or not, and it should be completely axiomatic that people take steps to predict these and to cope with them. It is not difficult to persuade middle managers of the sense of this because they know it. But they won't do it until you hold them accountable in this way. When some bright spark comes to you with his pet project, ending up with a flourish that it will save 30 per cent of manpower and the discounted cash flow is ... you should be asking him, 'What are the changes in skills, in demands, in roles and relationships and in organisation that the remaining 70 per cent will be faced with, and what are you doing about that? And what mistakes will the remaining 70 per cent be making as a result of the changes, and how does that affect your DCF calculation?' Do that a few times and this company will be utilising social science very quickly.

And I added:

> But it's more than this. It's not just a case of predicting and meeting the future, you can make the future. You can decide what kind of a society you are going to be involved in and you can create the structure which will produce that society.

Outside the job

Home was now a small flat with a long lease, and I had the kind of social life that many thirty-something people were living in the 1960s. For some years I had a kind of 'salon': open house on Monday evenings, with coffee and cakes, always saw at least six friends, who sometimes brought others, and a lot of good conversation. There was giving and going to dinner parties or cheese and wine parties, which was an easy way of entertaining at that time. There was also getting involved and dis-involved with men, although I won't discuss the important ones. Throughout my life, whenever I got involved with a man I could always tell whether my feelings were really engaged by whether I started to fantasise about showing him round Karlsbad – I have such a deep need to bring the things that are important to me together into some kind of whole. People are often unsure about whether they are really in love, but I had a sure-fire yardstick. There was a brief fling with Tommy Balogh, one of the two Hungarian economic advisers to the Wilson government (without the Karlsbad fantasy). He would sometimes drop in after a meeting at Chequers, his pockets stuffed full of scraps of paper with notes towards his autobiography, which he would pull out: 'Look, darlink, vot zat idiot said!' I have an image of Cabinet meetings during Harold Wilson's premiership, with every single member busily scribbling their memoirs. It would make a nice scene on stage. His explanation of Galbraith's ideas on the Affluent Society was succinct: 'Vot I require from a frigidaire is zat it should be cold, not zat it should be pink.'

My friends were largely Fabians, or present and past colleagues. Sarah Wolton and Roger Broad met at a party of mine and married. We have been close friends ever since, and their children take me for granted as part of their scene. Whenever they squabble, it is of course my fault. I also reconnected with an old friend from King's during this time. Anita Brookner and I met again by chance in a restaurant, and developed a habit of telephoning each other at least once a week. I once calculated that if one were to put these phone calls end-to-end it would, at the time I did this, have added up to about ten months of talk non-stop twenty-four hours a day. It would be extraordinarily repetitive, though the content has changed over the years – from men and our mothers, through the vagaries of our respective analysts, to the peculiarities and new territory of old age.

My mother's cycles of breakdown, hospitalisation and recovery gradually tailed off. I still don't know what it really was, I only know that her last fifteen years were settled and were tolerable for her. Our relationship also was better and more relaxed. She sometimes made the cakes for my coffee evenings and sometimes we made them together. When I was looking for a flat she helped me look and where we differed I gave way on relatively small things because I had gained the important one. So I took the flat she liked, which was near to where she lived, rather than one I had liked better, which was farther away. And I cooked with electricity, which she felt strongly about, though I would have preferred gas. We continued always to have covert tussles about privacy. If I went on holiday she would say, 'Leave me your keys, I'll clean your carpet while you're away,' and I would, as always, not be able to cope with this and get out of it clumsily.

Trude and Rudl, my mother's sister and brother-in-law, had moved to London when Rudl retired from his job with the Indian Oxygen Company. The two sisters had very different temperaments and had led very different lives. As I have said, Trude and Rudl seemed to have picked up some of the habits of the British Raj, while my mother's life had been stringent. But family feeling was strong, and the old pattern of mutual visiting re-established itself and provided material for gossip. The three of them shared memories and jokes from their youth in Neusattl. My mother had been a very good pianist, playing by ear pretty well anything she heard, and there were memories associated with that. One or other of them had only to hum a plonkety-plonk-plonk bar or two of the 'Pavlova' Gavotte by Lenke for grins to spread over all three faces. Somebody had written some German lyrics to this, the silliness of which comprised the joke. Rudl died in 1966.

The Australian relatives travelled a lot, and sometimes came to London. One visit from Alice sticks in my memory. I had the idea of taking the three ladies – my mother, Trude and Alice – to Glyndebourne. I had never been there myself, this was also a sign that our standard of living had improved. (I measure the rise in my standard of living by looking at my friends: there was the first time I knew someone who kept a bottle of sherry at home – kept it anyway, didn't just buy it when visitors were coming. Then there was the first time I knew someone who owned a car. And then I knew someone who had a weekend cottage in Suffolk. Now I have friends who have a second home in France.)

We arranged to meet at Victoria Station at 3.00 to catch the train. I took the afternoon off from Esso and went home to change. Then I got on the underground to Victoria. At Gloucester Road a thought hit me: 'My God, I've left the iron on!' I couldn't risk it. I got out of the train, caught a taxi, and asked the driver to take me back to West Kensington, wait a couple of minutes, and then on to Victoria. Of course I hadn't left the iron on.

It was a brilliant July day, and we would have made it if there hadn't been so much traffic. As we drew up at Victoria, it was just past the hour and the train had gone. The three ladies were standing forlornly outside the station in their finery, and I felt desperate. I asked the driver what it would cost to drive all the way to Glyndebourne. He had to make a guess and quoted £8.00, which says something about inflation in the time since then. I said all right, the three ladies piled into the cab, and we set off. The driver didn't know where Glyndebourne was, I did my best to read the map, and the three ladies tried to make me feel better with remarks like, 'Look at this lovely countryside, we would never have seen this if we'd caught the train!'

Latecomers are not allowed in at Glyndebourne. If we had known for sure that we were late, we could have relaxed and accepted the fact that we were going to miss the first act. But it was touch and go all the way. As we finally drove through Lewes, a church clock struck and then I did relax, knowing that it was too late. But the performance started late that evening, and we got in. I have no idea what we saw. There may be a clue in the fact that I am probably the only person in the Western world who doesn't like *Così fan tutte*.

When I left Esso in 1970 I was given a silver handshake, and spent it on a trip to Australia. On the morning I left there was a telegram from Alice: 'Don't forget to switch the iron off!'

In 1967 I found a small lump in my right breast. It turned out to be benign, but it had to be removed. Joan Woodward came to see me in hospital, and said that my situation had prompted her to examine herself and she, too, had found a lump. Only hers was not benign, and there began the terrible cat-and-mouse game that is breast cancer. You think it has gone, and then it comes back somewhere else. The last time I saw her was one day in 1971 when I visited her in her office at Imperial College, where she was waiting for her husband to take her home. She looked very small behind a desk which suddenly seemed to have grown. I asked, 'Do you want to talk shop, or shall we just gossip?' With a tired smile she said, 'Oh, let's just gossip'. That was how I knew how ill she was – shop talk was always the greatest of pleasures. She died five days later.

My time in Esso coincided with the Labour government of 1964–70, under Harold Wilson. It was trying to come to terms with industrial realities in a way in which previous Labour governments perhaps had not. They had little experience, but were no less confident for that. Two major conferences on industrial productivity were organised, which ended up with carte blanche for management consultancy activities of a kind that progressive industrial companies were leaving behind. Politicians are difficult to influence. I had a meeting with Tony Benn, who was Minister of Technology, and some of his senior civil servants. At the end of it, Tony Benn said that the kind of things I had been talking about were all right in his Ministry 'because I talk to the typists'. I wondered how many of the typists he talked to? What did he talk to them about? How often? And what about people who were not typists? It was hopeless to try to penetrate such armour.

And then there was the Wilson government's wish for the country to be in the forefront of technical developments, with its slogan about the 'white heat of technology'. The phrase was first coined by Harold Wilson in 1963. That summer the Fabian Society organised a series of policy conferences at the Bonnington Hotel in Bloomsbury, one of them intended for young scientists to make their contributions to this discussion. I was at this conference, on a Saturday in July; Harold Wilson was to join it in the afternoon. We sat at long tables. I sat opposite Steven Rose, a young biologist whom I knew slightly. At three, Harold Wilson duly came in and joined the top table. A few minutes later a note was passed down the long table and reached Steven, who turned a fiery red and tiptoed out of the room. Harold Wilson also tiptoed out, and I thought how thrilling it was that young scientists really were now being consulted by the Labour leadership. What he had been consulted about was this: on the following Monday a debate was to be held in the House of Commons about the housing scandal that was being operated at the time in Notting Hill Gate by the notorious property developer Peter Rachman. Sitting tenants were being terrorised into leaving their homes in order to make the houses free from rent control so that they could be either let at higher rents or sold. Wilson coined the term 'Rachmanism' for this kind of activity, and for his speech he needed a good biological technical term to describe the creepy-crawlies you find when you lift up stones. And sure enough, on the following Monday the Leader of the Opposition, committed to science and technology, thundered in Parliament: 'Sometimes one turns over a stone in a garden or field and sees the slimy creatures which live under its protection. This is what has happened in these past weeks. But the photophobic animal world has nothing to compare with the revolting creatures of London's underworld, living there, shunning the light, growing fat by battening on human misery ...'[15]

The professional environment

Harold Bridger – more about him later – used to say that in psychoanalysis all the data is there in the first session, if only one recognised and understood it. The first sign that the Esso experiment was not taking all of the environment into account in fact came on my first day in the company. I was taken out to lunch by Ralph Coverdale, who headed a division which other people thought of as management training, but which called itself 'Management Studies'. He had developed a form of small-group training which claimed to

---

[15] House of Commons Debates, vol. 681, p. 1058.

provide a universally applicable and comprehensive way of solving both work problems and relationship problems and to be an application of 'behavioural science principles'. He was at the time developing his first 'project' at one of the refineries, a project being a programme in which every member of management and supervision went through the training and trainers then went on supporting and coaching them in their management meetings back on the job.

It seemed that the employee relations adviser, whose marvellous job description so matched what I felt needed doing and wanted to try, was at the same time sponsoring all kinds of other things as well, and putting them in competition with each other; Coverdale training was not the only one. His aspirations for me, and for social science, were genuine. But he was a politician, who hedged his bets. If you start enough hares, one of them might get through – then that is the one you back. The books and people from whom I had learned my trade didn't say anything about competition.

The Coverdale programme was to go through parts of the company like a religious movement, with many of the characteristics of fundamentalism. Years later the manager of this particular refinery came to see me when he was retiring, and asked, 'Why didn't you tell me?' At the time, though, one could not have told him anything, he would not have heard it.

Joan Woodward said that if she had known about this she would have told me not to touch the job with a barge-pole. It was my first real encounter with 'Organisation Development', or OD. This was generally some form of project or training activity aimed at changing people's behaviour. It was beginning to spring up all over the place, most often brought in by American consultants. There was a positive invasion of American consultants in Europe during those years, and they generally came to England first because there they did not expect language problems.

This kind of activity also claimed a kind of idealism, in the sense that its proponents were convinced that there is a 'good' way to be and a 'bad' way to be; their aim, and the aim of this version of 'applied behavioural science', was to turn what they considered to be bad guys into good guys; not long ago I heard a consultant talk about his 'hit list for paradigm change'. The difference in approach between that and using social science to understand the fit between different elements of an organisation and between it and its environment has dogged the industrial and social science scene for decades, and I have found myself much involved in the battle. At one point an eminent American social scientist who was visiting me in Esso asked, 'Why do you people buy all this crap from us?' Why indeed.

Eventually 'this crap' hit Esso as well, in a very powerful way. But for the moment both the idea of ideological differences between approaches, and that they compete in a market, were clouds no bigger than a man's hand.

In the academic world quite different things were happening. The 1960s were a time of massive expansion in the number of universities. A whole generation of new incumbents of university chairs, who also now occupied seats on the committees of the Social Science Research Council, overthrew the tradition of social science for application and use – the very purpose for which the SSRC had been created. There was no kudos in building on what had been done, only in doing things that were different. Sociology became very politicised and preoccupied with grand theory, and with feminism; psychology became very preoccupied with methodological detail. 'Usefulness' became a dirty word – both scientifically and politically unacceptable – and was to be rejected by the social science establishment for the next thirty years.

So the late 1960s and 70s were a time of growth in teaching and research in university social science departments, and they were a time of growth in the number of experiments and projects in industry. But the most important thing about this was that these were entirely separate, and different, developments. The 'organisational change' or 'organisational development' programmes in industry were not research-based, and academic research was not intended for use. An enormous gulf grew between them, and I think that for a long time I was probably the only person in the country actively spanning it. The preoccupations that so fired 'Klein's Mates' became less and less central either to what was going on in industry or to thinking in the social sciences of the time. The book I later published putting some of my work together is called *Working across the gap*[16].

More about the job

In the course of my third year on the job, two things happened. The first was that the ER adviser who had engaged me retired. His successor was not interested in this activity, and I learned what I have experienced many times since then: people don't like inheriting things, they like to initiate things of their own.

The second thing that happened was that Standard Oil, New Jersey, decentralised its activities, setting up regional boards around the world, including one for Europe. The headquarters of Esso Europe were in

[16] London, Karnac, 2005.

London, and there appeared an employee relations manager for Europe, whose general approach was that the natives needed enlightening. Europe needed to be brought out of the dark ages.

Esso was about to have a new Chairman, and he spent the three months between being appointed and taking up his post in Esso Europe. He discussed with the employee relations manager the organisational problems that were awaiting him, and the ER manager suggested getting some social science help. He arranged for the Chairman to meet Rensis Likert, who headed the Institute of Social Research in Michigan, and when the new Chairman arrived to take up his post he brought with him a $300,000 project to be undertaken by the ISR Michigan. With considerable pride and excitement he was about to introduce social science to Esso.

Our policy of starting quietly at middle levels of the company and working outward from there had proved politically disastrous. My original sponsor was on the point of retiring and didn't intervene, and his successor aligned himself behind the Esso Europe ER manager.

The proposed Michigan project was to be led by Likert's successor, Dr Stan Seashore, and was along classic American 'Organisation Development' lines. It was about trying to change people's behaviour, and was therefore fundamentally different from what we had been doing. In a selected part of the company they would first diagnose the prevalent behavioural styles of managers by means of a detailed questionnaire; they would then introduce a 'change agent' who would set out to change the managers' behaviour by means of various interventions; and then behavioural styles would be measured again.

I drafted a memo to the Chairman, explaining that there was already some social science going on in the company and asking, if he was prepared to support such activities, that the precise form of new work should, in the first instance, be left open for discussion. I hoped that it could be related to what was already going on. The new ER manager categorically forbade me to send the memo. I considered sending it anyway, over his head, but decided that it would create an impossible situation for the Chairman, and for me, if I did. Meanwhile he didn't know that I existed, and there was no way of letting him know.

The two years that followed were horrible, taken up with a battle in which territorial conflict and conflict about theory and values could never be properly disentangled. At one point I visited the team in their institute in Michigan. On the wall of their office was a map of the world with red pins marking the places where they had projects. Just like the old British Empire. And at the same time, on that same trip to the United States, I had visited people in the operational department of Standard Oil who dealt with distribution systems and who were very interested in what we were doing, once they had reassured themselves that we were not out to manipulate their behaviour. In my resentment I saw many parallels between American and British imperialism. The British version had had a military wing, a commercial wing and a missionary wing. In the 1960s we saw the American military adventure of Vietnam; the commercial wing was represented by its multinational companies; and the missionaries were the management consultants, especially the 'behavioural science' consultants. In one heated argument with the Esso Europe ER manager I said, 'The trouble is, you don't really have a role. So you want mine. You're competing for the job of social sciences adviser to Esso Petroleum.' He thought about this for a moment. Then he said, 'Yeah, honey, that's right.' I later wrote a book about the Esso work,[17] and when the then Chairman of the Social Science Research Council reviewed it he described this as 'very high indeed on my list of best male chauvinist pig remarks of the year'.

In the end both sides in the battle foundered. The marketing department, where the Michigan project was intended to take place, turned it down. That was perhaps some vindication of my policy of working from the ground upwards rather than in a way that is imposed from above. But the in-house social science activities also wound down. The battle had used up too much of the available energy, and there was now no support from the new ER manager.

Some years later, when the dust had settled, I met Stan Seashore at a conference in Toronto. Standing talking with a group of colleagues I told them that we had spent two years fighting each other. 'It would have been more fun if she hadn't been right,' said Seashore. It was gracious, but it didn't undo the damage.

In the course of those two difficult years I became a client for consultancy myself. Someone in the 'Klein's Mates' group suggested that I should talk to Harold Bridger, who was said to be particularly good at helping with this kind of situation.

Harold had been one of the founders of the Tavistock Institute of Human Relations. He was a mathematician turned psychoanalyst turned organisational consultant. He had a unique blend of on the one hand identifying with the client – not just listening with a non-judgemental expression on his face, as so many do, but really entering into the experience to understand it, what he called 'starting where they are' – and at the same time

---

[17] *A Social Scientist in Industry.* London, Gower Press, 1976.

conceptualising what is going on so that it can move forward. I started working with him around the Esso situation in 1968, and it was the beginning of a friendship and colleague relationship that was strong and solid until his death in 2005. For nearly forty years he gave me a sense of being completely understood and completely endorsed. It has been a tremendous, unwavering and unsurpassable gift. At the same time I learned a great deal from him, much of it about the dynamics – often the unconscious dynamics – of the situations I have worked with and been in. Although I still think that having an analysis is important for professionals in this field and helps to protect their clients, I in fact learned more from working with Harold than from my own analysis. But it was the endorsement that has mattered most.

I also, in turn, made a contribution to Harold's work. He designed and developed a learning model known as a Working Conference, which is used all over the world. It is one of the two models of group relations training that were developed in the Tavistock Institute. Since I have been associated with it, the emphasis has gradually shifted from being primarily about understanding groups to being more about understanding organisations. The seeds of this were already there; it is the relative emphasis that I have influenced. In recent years I directed the Working Conference in this country but Harold was still, at nearly ninety, a loved *éminence grise* at the workshops. Nobody minded if he occasionally fell asleep. I have been very lucky in my teachers.

When things were winding down in Esso, Harold was one of several people who encouraged me to join the Tavistock Institute. It seemed a natural kind of move.

BOOK THREE

For the next nineteen years I was in the Tavistock Institute of Human Relations.

The Tavistock Years

When I joined the Tavistock Institute in 1971 it was in the grip of 1968-style youth rebellion and radicalism, and probably in the most difficult phase of its existence. I was told that its representative on the committee which arranged joint monthly scientific meetings with the Tavistock Clinic was demanding that scientific lectures should be given by the porters. This is the way that the radical chic of the time is sometimes caricatured; here it was apparently really happening.

As a matter of fact, 'scientific lectures' *were* sometimes given by 'Lofty', the head porter. There was a series of films about small children in hospital, made by Dr James Robertson and his wife from the Clinic, which became very influential and which were shown to audiences of doctors and medical administrators from all over the world. The vivid, heart-breaking scenes of distress and regression among these children led to the policy of allowing mothers to stay in hospital with their small children, which is now widespread. Lofty had worked the film projector and heard the accompanying commentary so often that he knew it all by heart, and he sometimes entertained his friends from the local police station with them in the bar. I never heard Lofty lecture on maternal deprivation myself, but it must have been a treat.

The Tavistock Institute had originally grown out of the Tavistock Clinic. The Clinic was founded in 1920, but had its origins in the First World War, when a number of psychiatrists had given their services free of charge to soldiers who were suffering from battle fatigue, or shell-shock, or whatever label got attached to collapse under the terrible battle conditions of that war. How one got labelled was important: if a soldier could no longer cope, for instance could not face going back to the trenches after being on leave, he could be court-martialled and shot for cowardice.

Psychotherapy on a strongly Freudian basis continued in the Clinic between the wars, but from quite early on there was also an interest in social psychology and in the functioning of groups. There was said to be an early paper – this may be apocryphal, I haven't been able to trace it – showing that

144

army units with so-called 'high' morale produced fewer casualties than army units with 'low' morale (whatever morale was taken to mean at that time). In other words, it was not only the personality of the soldier and the conditions of the war that were important, but also the kind of social support around him.

In the Second World War, members of the Tavistock Clinic joined the Royal Army Medical Corps in a range of senior roles and its medical director became consultant psychiatrist for the army. Actual battle conditions were not as horrific as they had been in 1914–18, and the approach of the psychiatrists led to a number of other activities where clinical and social understanding combined. For instance, preoccupation with problems of morale led to an interest in leadership and therefore in selecting officers for qualities of leadership. The Tavistock people helped to devise selection tests based on group methods, which were administered by the War Office Selection Boards; these methods were later adopted by the civil service and by some industrial companies. They also did work on re-settling and rehabilitating prisoners of war, in a situation where the prisoner in his camp had sometimes been safer than his family at home. They also got involved with the development of therapeutic communities, treating a hospital not just as a container for patients while they undergo psychotherapy, but as a therapeutic setting, where every aspect of daily living contributes to and is part of the treatment.

After the war the Tavistock staff went on engaging in activities of this kind, which aimed to link psychoanalytic understanding with other forms of social science in a highly integrative approach and use it in non-clinical situations. But when the National Health Service was being set up in 1947 there was a problem: the Tavistock Clinic could go into the NHS, but these organisational activities did not fit into something designed to be a medical/ health service. To accommodate them the Tavistock Institute was founded, with a start-up grant from the Rockefeller Foundation. It was first a branch of the Tavistock Clinic and then incorporated separately.

For many years the two organisations shared the same building, but over time the links between them became weaker and antagonisms developed. Therapists who were not interested in the context of the patient's life joined the Clinic, and social scientists who were not interested in psychodynamics joined the Institute. In the early days of the Institute, having a personal analysis had been more or less a condition of employment. By the time I joined in 1971 perhaps a third of its members were or had been in analysis ('those who didn't go off to their analysts went off to the pub'); by the time I left in 1989 I was one of only three.

There had been two earlier explorations about my joining the 'Tavi'. The first was towards the end of my sabbatical year at LSE, before I re-joined Joan Woodward. We thought that, before committing myself to this, it would be worth exploring whether I should join the Tavistock Institute instead. I was seen there by three of its luminaries, Eric Trist, Fred Emery and Harold Bridger. Afterwards I had a letter from Eric Trist saying that they felt I should opt for Imperial College, as they 'would not want to deprive Joan Woodward of my very valuable services'.

Later, when this trio were my friends, Eric said that the real problem had been that Fred couldn't cope with senior women colleagues. Fred said that the real problem had been that Eric couldn't cope with senior women colleagues. And Harold denied having been involved in the process at all.

The second time was while I was with Esso. I met two Tavistock people, Hans van Beinum and Gurth Higgin, at a group relations conference and they suggested I should join the Institute. I was in great awe of the theoretical writings of the Tavi, and said that I couldn't aspire to that level of abstraction. 'Oh, but you have theory in the guts!' said Hans. It is one of the nicest compliments I have ever had.

À propos theoretical writings: one of the best-known Tavistock theoreticians was Philip Herbst (who later changed his name to David). By the time I joined the Institute he had left to live in Norway, but he was really a citizen of the world, turning up now in India, now in Gibraltar, now in Israel, now in Algeria. In the mid-1980s, after a long absence, he turned up in London, wanting to reconnect with old friends and colleagues. It happened that there was a small flat available in the house I was living in, and I got this for him, so that for some weeks we were living under the same roof.

David was eager to re-establish old links, and I suggested we might give a joint party. Wonderful! But, he said, we really needed two parties – no, three, there was this category of person and that category of person (categories, a higher level of abstraction than people) – no, what we really needed was four parties. I managed to negotiate this down to two.

The first party was for Tavistock colleagues and went well. We then started to plan for the second party and, as the list of people to invite got longer and longer, I realised that I wouldn't be able to cope and suggested that we should get a caterer to provide the food. David agreed, but then came the question of drinks. I didn't have enough glasses. The caterer said we could hire glasses from him at 10p per glass, and forty glasses at 10p each did not seem so terrible to me. David, however, saw it as money wasted. If I were to buy cheap glasses, he said, it wouldn't cost much more, and then I would have the glasses, whereas hiring them was throwing money away.

This became a big argument. From his point of view, buying was in the long run more economical than hiring. From my point of view, I didn't need forty glasses; I didn't have room to store them; in order to find and buy them I would have to take half a day off work, losing half a day's income; and I would have to bring them home in a taxi, I couldn't carry forty glasses on a bus – David himself was not a person who did such practical things. The taxi fare alone would wipe out the economic advantage. None of this made any impact – the argument went on for seven solid, exhausting, hours and remained unresolved. There was no way the operational realities could be brought to bear on the theoretical concept. The practical problem was eventually solved because we found a caterer who let us borrow glasses for no charge. But my view of high-level theory has been permanently affected.

There were several reasons why I had wanted to join the Tavi. First, I wanted to be somewhere where I could go on learning. I knew several of the people there, and found them stimulating and mind-expanding. The prox-imity of the Clinic, and its history, also seemed to be an opportunity for learning, particularly about the links between psychodynamics and organ-isation, which I had found fascinating to read about but mysterious. This fascination is, I think, shared by many people, and is what originally gave the Tavistock enterprise – Clinic and Institute – its attraction. The spur for me was a simple one – I don't like mysteries, I need to tease at them until I understand. I wanted to learn more about these connections and am still exploring and working at them. It was sad to discover that the link, both between the two institutions and in the work, had largely been abandoned.

Second, it was at that time the only place in the country where action research – that is, using research to work on problems and involving the people in the situation actively with that rather than regarding them as just the passive subjects of research – was intellectually respectable. In the history of the Institute this followed naturally from the origins in psychiatry, which by definition means doing clinical work. It was therefore the only place where I could go on exploring the questions that had sent me to the Esso job. University social science departments were at that stage strongly opposed to action research or applied work of any kind, regarding it as unscientific in method and subversive in values. Management consultancies, on the other hand, were not concerned with research. There was nowhere other than the Tavistock Institute where one could pursue both research and development, and examine the combination, without a sense of making concessions.

And third, it was the place where what they called 'sociotechnical theory' had been formulated. This, too, was very close to where I was coming from.

As part of the Conditional Aid programme, the Tavistock Institute had studied technical change in coal mining. They had concluded that a work system is not just a technical system, as engineers see it, nor is it just a human system, as some behavioural scientists see it. The technology and the people influenced each other, in both directions, and the term 'sociotechnical' had been coined to describe that. It had shown up clearly in my own research, but I hadn't conceptualised it. They were particularly impressed by the way in which groups of miners were able to manage themselves and their work where the technology permitted it.

There was a lot of argument in academic circles about whether these findings amounted to 'theory'. I didn't, and don't, care. They made sense of so much of my own experience. Technical and social factors affect each other: in the work study research, the way in which work was organised and sub-divided affected the operators' view of the world, how they saw things. People talked about 'good' and 'bad' jobs'. A 'good' job was one that had an easy price, was not subject to tool trouble, and had a sufficiently long production run to make bonus. An operator said, 'When I say it's a good job I mean they're clean and easy, they've been well inspected. The last lot I had, they hadn't been properly inspected, so they won't go onto the jig and that stops you making bonus.' It is not the usual definition of a good job. In Esso an operational research engineer thought that the ideal system for distributing fuel oil would be one where a truck driver would arrive at the distribution terminal in the morning, find his route and instructions in the cab of his truck and drive off, without any contact with anyone in the plant. And at the same time, everyone connected with distribution worried about why truck drivers were not 'motivated'! Sociotechnical theory put a conceptual framework round the things that I had been discovering and working on.

The obvious corollary is that you can also design technical systems to have benign effects, and that you can contribute this understanding to the education of the engineers who design such systems. Marx, I think, made only one mistake: he attributed the problems he saw working people having to cope with to ownership of the 'means of production' and did not take seriously the part played by design and the models of man in the minds of engineering designers. His chapter on Machinery and Modern Industry in *Das Kapital* is full of descriptions of how technology and behaviour affect each other. For the sheer pleasure of the detective-story chain of cause-and-effect, from technology to behaviour and back again, I enjoy citing them. For example:

In the English letter-press printing trade, for example, there existed formerly a system corresponding to that in manufactures and handicrafts, of advancing the apprentices from easy to more and more difficult work. They went through a course of teaching till they were finished printers. To be able to read and write was for every one of them a requirement of their trade. All this was changed by the printing machine. It employs two sorts of labourers, one grown up, tenters, and the other, boys mostly from 11 to 17 years of age whose sole business is either to spread the sheets of paper under the machine, or to take from it the printed sheets ... A great part of them cannot read, and they are, as a rule, utter savages and very extraordinary creatures. To qualify them for the work they have to do, they require no intellectual training; there is little room in it for skill, and less for judgement; their wages, though rather high for boys, do not increase proportionately as they grow up, and the majority of them cannot look for advancement to the better paid and more responsible post of machine minder, because while each machine has but one minder, it has a least two and often four boys attached to it. As soon as they get too old for such child's work, that is about 17 at the latest, they are discharged from the printing establishments. They become recruits of crime. Several attempts to procure them employment elsewhere, were rendered of no avail by their ignorance and brutality ...[18]

(I also got a great kick out of using examples like this from Karl Marx in a lecture to the board of AT&T in New Jersey. What's more, they loved it. That visit, in the 1980s, was also when I met my cousin Walter again for the first time since childhood.)

What the Tavistock Institute did was, first, to give a name to this interaction – 'sociotechnical' – and second to take it down from the societal level, where you can't do anything about it unless you overturn the world, to the work system level, where you can. Work systems can be redesigned.[19] Also, since most of those early Tavistock researchers had some clinical

---

[18] Marx, K. (1887) *Capital* (English translation 1958) London: Lawrence & Wishart.
[19] Overturning the world didn't do the trick, either. I met a Soviet sociologist who had done a study in a car plant outside Leningrad. The method of production was the same short-cycle, repetitive assembly tasks as in Western car plants. He found that older workers, who had little education, were quite content with their work, but younger workers, who were better educated and therefore had higher capacities and expectations, were bored and depressed by their routine, repetitive tasks. When he reported on this to the local political committee, the response was, 'Nonsense, our workers are happy'. But he elaborated on his findings, which were convincing, and then the response was, 'In that case, we must abolish assembly lines'.

background, they made it scientifically respectable for feelings, relationships and experiences to be part of the data when work is being studied.

But there were also shortcomings. The early years of the Tavistock Institute are often seen through a rosy glow which, for some people, invested the very name with magic and prevented them from looking coolly at what it was and what it was not. The early work shows a creativity which was both brilliant and at the same time flawed and I find to my own surprise, as I write and reflect on all this, that I am angry with those early pioneers – not because of their contribution but because of the way the guru culture they encouraged has inhibited further development. In both areas, the sociotechnical and the psychodynamic, creative and exciting work seems to have brought with it a sense of omnipotence, which can mean that you find it less and less necessary to check your hunches, to continue developing the field systemically, and to take on board the work of others.

On the sociotechnical side, instead of using the interaction between social and technical aspects of work systems as the starting point and going on to explore wherever that took one, the autonomous work groups which had been found in the Durham coal fields came to be seen as the answer to everything. First taken up in Norway, sociotechnical theory came to be identified with industrial democracy, and industrial democracy with autonomy on the shop floor. With the second of these I have much sympathy. It was a great step forward to recognise that forms of industrial democracy in which representatives are elected to governing bodies (as, for instance, in Germany) don't necessarily make much difference to the daily working experience of the people on the shop floor. (Though you can't leave it at that. For instance, increased shop floor autonomy would mean less need for supervision. I was once discussing with Fred Emery that, when making such changes, one should consider the whole system and not merely throw supervisors out. He brushed this aside with an impatient 'Oh, they've had power for too long!')

But the first of these propositions does not hold. In the climate of fervour surrounding autonomous work groups it has been very difficult to argue that in some situations they might not be the answer, that there might be other things about work organisation that were equally or more relevant, and that there were problems in group working too. How can you argue against autonomy?

And then there was the question of embedding these concepts into institutions such as the education of engineers, the funding of research and development, methods of design. 'Projects' may be exciting, but the difference they make is limited; no amount of project work can counteract the assumptions about work roles that are built into capital appropriations, technology design or software engineering before the consultants turn up.

The psychoanalytic work also did not seem to be susceptible to testing. You announce an insight – such as that organisational arrangements can be an unconscious defence against anxiety – and that's it, end of story. It was indeed a brilliant insight. But you need to be willing to explain why you see a situation that way. And you have to work out when it applies and when it doesn't, and why it may apply in some situations and not in others. Instead of that, there was a tendency to interpret any doubts or questions as 'resistance'.

I first encountered this bullying way of using psychodynamic understanding during the process of joining the Institute (beginnings again!). There was a series of interviews and selection tests, and then I heard nothing for three months. So I phoned to ask what was happening. 'Ah, you're getting anxious, are you?' said the voice on the other end of the line.

Lack of rigour was a chink in the armour of the early Tavistock generations, which opened the way to rebellion and reaction in the next one. Eric Trist and Fred Emery left the Institute at the end of the sixties, Eric to work in the United States and Fred to return to his native Australia. Before they left, four new young people had been recruited, who were to dominate the Institute for the next decade and more. Those of them who had some social science training were critical of the science of the early work; those who didn't rebelled anyway. So the early work was not continued or developed further.

Youth rebellion was not unique to the Tavistock Institute; during those years it was happening in academic institutions all over the Western world. And how can you argue against youth? Older people found themselves in the trap of either being 'in' by subscribing to any or all kinds of trendy political correctness, or being 'out' and considered reactionary.

During the year before I left Esso, the employee relations manager and I had pursued the idea that I should go on working for Esso, but from outside the company rather than from inside. We had explored a number of social science institutions, and this would have constituted a major contract for someone. Among others we had talked to the Tavistock Institute, and three of its senior staff – Fred Emery, Hugh Murray and Hans van Beinum – came to see us. The discussion went well, and then the ER manager said, 'Well, that's probably as far as we can go today. I'll get in touch with you. Who shall I write to?'

They looked at each other, then one of them said, 'You can write to anybody.'

151

'Yes, all right,' he said, 'but who shall I write to?'

'You can write to anybody.'

That was 'democracy', what someone has called 'perverse democracy'. They could not risk a concession in the direction of what might be seen as élitism, even to the extent of giving a potential client a name to write to. Of course, there was no contract.

Idealism could also provide a cover for other things. It is understandable that, standing in the shadows of giant world figures who had not taken trouble about their induction and development, the only way for the next generation of the Tavistock Institute to achieve some identity for themselves was to do something different. They began by doing large-scale attitude surveys. These were not in any of the Tavistock traditions, but they brought income. And, since the Institute was chronically short of money after the ending of the Rockefeller grant, with income came power.

But as I try to understand and explain how these things came about, I also realise that this can be a defence that cushions your reactions. Because what it felt like was tyranny and obscurantism; the effect within the Institute, for a good many years, was not far short of a reign of terror. It was as if no one else but the rebel group could be allowed to have ideals and ideas. When they wanted to do something, this was autonomy; when others wanted to do something, 'there is a need for control'. For those who were fiercest in denying any kind of power to others, of course regarded power for them-selves as being their democratic due. Teaching or mutual training was considered élitist, so there was none. One doesn't like to grudge so many young people of the 1960s their apotheosis; but for many others there was a bitter downside.

(The genuine idealism of those years was also strangely a-historical. I am reminded of a lecture about the early days of the Fabian Society given at a summer school by Margaret Cole, the widow of G.D.H. Cole. She was at the time not just an old lady, but a very old old lady. In her quavering, breathless, throaty voice she said, 'The young people of today. Seem to think that they have invented. Sex. I remember at a Fabian summer school in about 1930. Coming across a group of young men. In the nude. Sitting on a bench. Having a competition. About who could get the best erection. By the power of thought alone.')

The internal organisational upheavals were painful, time-consuming and at this distance are too tedious to recount. At the same time I also saw the Institute's struggles as a healthier way of dealing with the problem of organising oneself than could be seen in some more structured and bureaucratic academic places. So, for that matter, was the need to earn one's keep, though it meant a constant worry about the supply of work, which played a part in the problems and power struggles. My contract of employment stipulated a salary, 'provided that your work generates enough income to cover it and the associated overheads'. I saw nothing wrong with that, nor with the fact that there was a month when a note came from the Finance Office, saying 'sorry, there's not enough in your account for a salary this month'. I didn't consider that the world owed social scientists a living, and we all thought that universities were feather-bedded. If one was not able to demonstrate credibility to some funding agency or client, why should one be entitled to income without question? Later, when stringency hit the universities too, anyone who had been through the hard school of an independent research institute like this one was at a distinct advantage.

Over the years, through the painful feuds and rifts and crises of the organisation, it probably generated envy that my solid colleague relationship with Harold was unassailable. Because of the break in tradition and values, Harold was actually more unhappy than I was. I sometimes said to him that, if I started to feel as badly as he did, I would leave. We made a few attempts to move out and attach ourselves to other institutions but they came to nothing. His position was, 'Why should I leave? I founded the place. It is they who have left me.' But he gradually began to spend more and more time in Australia.

The amount of energy that was consumed in power struggles was amazing. One Christmas the Royal Opera House put on *Die Fledermaus*, with a mixed Austrian and English cast, and mixed German and English language. A visit to Covent Garden was very rare for me, and this one was really special. I love *Die Fledermaus*, this was a wonderful production and, on top of that, to find the mixture of English and German the official language, and to be able to enter into both the English and the German jokes, for once made me feel really at home. I came home drunk with pleasure, to receive a phone call from one of the young radicals, canvassing my vote for the coming management elections. On Boxing Day. It helped me, however, to recover a sense of proportion, for in the broader scheme of things this was just ridiculous.

The way to survive was to keep one's head down and not seek a high profile. In age I was between the pioneers on the one hand and the new young group on the other. In approach I felt critical of aspects of the early work, but thought that an immensely valuable baby was being perversely thrown out with the bathwater. Fred Emery once referred to the Tavistock Institute as 'the hole in the doughnut', meaning that the work that had created its reputation was being pursued everywhere except there. That hurt, because it was largely true. But in important ways it was also not true. For one thing, some of the work that was going on in the 'doughnut' was merely sycophantic. For another, there was relevant work going on and my own work was all on the original core dimensions. Luckily there were good opportunities, and these were to take the sociotechnical approach into the directions of design and of policy. I also went on exploring the contribution psychodynamic understanding could make towards organisational social science. Almost the only remaining link between the Clinic and the Institute was a monthly scientific meeting organised across the institutions in the building. A committee of people from the different institutions organised these meetings, and I chaired it for about fifteen years. Planning the scientific meetings was easy, and the Scientific Committee spent much of its time on scientific discussions. Apart from the work and friendship with Harold, those discussions with professionals from the Clinic were probably the most enjoyable part of my life in the Institute.

It was a difficult place to be in, but it was a good place to work from.

The Work

The work that came my way was varied and exciting, and I enjoyed the mix of consulting and research. There were quite a lot of consulting assignments, and there is probably a whiff of the old refugee syndrome in the pleasure I got from looking out of the window of a train as it passed factories and office buildings, and thinking, 'I know them'; 'I know them'; 'I know them'. There were also assignments of various kinds abroad, in Israel, China, India and Germany.

On making use of the social sciences

First came writing up the Esso experience, and to do that I brought with me a grant from the Social Science Research Council; bringing funding in had been a condition of joining. Esso staff and directors were generous about clearing the text for publication, including the bits they didn't like, and came to a very nice launch party for the book. The Michigan people also cleared the text for publication. One publisher had turned the manuscript down on the grounds that it was not clear whether this was social science or autobiography, and Marie Jahoda made play with this in her preface. The reviews were very pleasing.

On organisation

Banking

My first organisational consultancy was with one of the four British clearing banks and it taught me a difficult lesson about the relationship between research and consulting.

At a conference I had met the bank's personnel director by chance. A few weeks later he got in touch because he had been considering for some time

155

how to get a contribution from the social sciences to the work of the bank. He didn't have a specific problem in mind, more a general sense that there might be something useful here. After some exploratory work that gained the confidence of the personnel division, the question was how to use the new resource.

A few weeks later the bank set up a 'customer service working party' which I was asked to join. Management felt that, in the course of a merger between three constituent banks and massive computerisation, customer service might have slipped. The question was how to improve it. To this question I answered that I needed first to understand more about how banking functioned. A study of the work and life of a branch was commissioned jointly by the personnel division and the customer service working party. A team of five researchers spent a week in each of four branches and produced a report. It was a very rich report (which my own branch manager thirty years later said was still relevant) and it contained a mix of observations and suggestions. What's more, it only took three months to produce, which for a major piece of research is not bad. But during those three months the customer service working party was disbanded, and I was too engrossed in the study to take this as seriously as I should have done. I needed not only to do a good piece of diagnostic research, but also to maintain and develop the relationships and institutions necessary for making use of the diagnosis afterwards. When the report was ready, its main client had disappeared.

The consultancy relationship lasted for another seven years. Although in a direct sense the report was not as effective as it might have been, it served as a kind of passport to a whole range of other things, demonstrating our bona fides and the fact that we did now understand – had, as it were, entered into – the world of our client.

Ken Eason was part of the team and did some work with the bank's organisation and methods department. At one point they wanted to talk with him and asked him to lunch. Afterwards I asked how it had gone. 'As far as I remember,' he said, 'it went sherry, hock, burgundy, port, brandy ...' Ah, those were the days.

I've mentioned clangers before. The bank's personnel division held an annual conference, which would end with a formal dinner and an invited after-dinner speaker. One year I found myself sitting at the top table next to that year's speaker, the director of the London Business School. The problem about the top table is that you have no one opposite you; if conversation doesn't work with your neighbour, you are in trouble. Jim Ball and I tried, but it wasn't working: 'Do you know so-and-so?' 'No, I'm afraid not. Do you know so-and-so?' 'No, I'm afraid not.' ...

156

At last we hit on someone we both knew, Nancy Seear. I relaxed with relief and said, 'Oh, I've known Nancy for years. Last time we had supper together, she was giving me advice about the menopause.' The silence that followed was profound. Not another word was spoken for the rest of the dinner, and I have spent many an idle moment since then wondering what the poor man might have said.

Hospital anaesthetists

There was a small but very interesting study of hospital anaesthetists. It included spending time in operating theatres, where the surgeons had their own brand of fun. When everyone is togged up with caps, masks and gowns, you can't always be sure who is there. At one point I heard the surgeon's voice say, 'Is Miss Klein here?' I identified myself, and he went on, 'Come and look at this: have you ever seen a vasectomy tube?' An iron determination not to give him the satisfaction of seeing me flustered made me able to take a long look and comment calmly, 'That's really interesting!'

The anaesthetist's job was often compared with that of a pilot: busy and hazardous at the beginning and the end, boring in between. 'Dr X goes in for fast landings,' said the theatre nurse.

It was a case study of the Division of Anaesthesia in a district general hospital, and it turned out to show in a very useful way how structure and dynamics interact. (Incidentally, the process of getting their agreement to the study also showed it. The anaesthetists generally met over sandwiches and coffee once a week for professional discussions, and I was invited to one of these meetings. I put the case for the study, and then they explained how they worked: They serviced the hospital's general operating lists, as well as providing a service for dentistry, obstetrics, and psychiatry. But the general operating lists had priority – however short-staffed they might be, 'if you are scheduled to have an operation, you will have your operation'. I asked whether this meant that I might come across an obstetrician in the hospital grumbling that 'you can never get hold of an anaesthetist when you need one!' One of the consultants frowned into his coffee for some lengthy moments and then said, in a surprised and thoughtful voice, 'Yes. I suppose you might.' One gets so used to thinking in a detective-story way about organisation, that my prediction just seemed like common sense. But to them it was not 'mere' common sense; it showed that there was some scientific underpinning to a social scientist's approach. They agreed to the study.)

I had by that time worked out a model of how personal factors, group factors and structural factors of a situation interacted (structural meaning things that are given and which can't be changed in the short term). This study provided a nice example: Open interviews were held with the fourteen anaesthetists, two consultant surgeons and a senior nursing officer, and I spent about fifteen hours in theatre, observing the work. This kind of research yields very rich data. But the richer the material, the less easy it is to analyse. I spent a long time soaking myself in the material. It was the usual painful process of feeling confused and overwhelmed by the richness and forcing myself to stay with it – *'wo wohn' ich in Paris?'*. Eventually I had to say to myself, 'You've got a framework – use it!' So I searched through the material for things that were given, and found three: the fact that an anaesthetic is a relatively bounded, short-cycle event; the fact that a patient comes into hospital for surgery and not for an anaesthetic; and the scientific and technical content of anaesthetics and the way in which this had developed. These three all had the quality of being given, at least in the short term. It then turned out that much of the material fell into place behind these structural facts.

Take the scientific and technical content of anaesthetics: enormous strides had been made in recent years in the development of new drugs, new methods, and new equipment. These developments had had several consequences:

Greater professional standing for anaesthetists. At the same time as leading to greater separation from surgery, the distinctive nature of the scientific and technical content of anaesthetics had brought a sense of independent professionalism for anaesthetists, as well as high status, expressed in consultant posts. This had led to a more complex relationship with surgeons, both at the level of the profession in general, and at working level. When GPs had done anaesthetic sessions in local hospitals, the question of competition for leadership would not have arisen, nor would the surgeon's right to dominate the scene and make the rules have been questioned.

Greater separation from surgery. In the 'old days' surgeons had known about anaesthetics and sometimes administered anaesthetics themselves. But the knowledge and methods, at the same time as growing, had established themselves as clearly different in kind from those of the surgeon. An operation used to be a single undertaking, it was now two distinct undertakings: 'There was a partnership between the surgeon and the anaesthetist. You were looking after that patient together, you would exchange ideas about the patient. Now it's different; you are looking after different ends of the patient.' A surgeon said, 'Anaesthetic technique has left me behind. I don't really understand now, if he tells me what he's doing ... and I'm not really interested.'

Changes in surgery. In turn, developments in anaesthetics had meant that more complex and difficult surgery could be carried out: 'We can keep the patient alive while they do those fantastic things.' It also meant that routine surgery had become easier: 'They don't need such dexterity any more, because with improvements in anaesthetics we can keep the patient under for six to eight hours while the surgeon fumbles about ...', 'I've anaes-thetised for simple hernia, which should take forty-five minutes, and I've sat for three or four hours because the surgeon's not very good.'

More patients could be anaesthetised. Not only could more types of operation be performed, but they could be performed on more types of patient. Patients with various kinds of ill health, either connected with or indepen-dent of the reason for operation, could be successfully anaesthetised. However, there was a cost in worry for the anaesthetist: one of the people interviewed said he was worried the whole time. A second was in two minds whether to give up the job for this reason. A third, recently qualified, said that although with time the anxiety was getting less, 'I still wake up in the night imagining procedures. I wake up and think the oxygen's run out or something.' A fourth said, 'Sometimes I see a patient who's going to be operated on Monday morning, and I can worry all weekend about that patient.'

It was medical policy that the pre-operative examination of patients should be carried out by those anaesthetists who were going to treat them, so that they could know what to expect and prepare their strategy. In this hospital this policy was carried out, but many of the anaesthetists referred to other hospitals where it was not. It seemed at least possible that, where anaesthetists don't make a practice of doing the pre-operative assessment, this may be a defence against the anxiety involved: '[Where I come from] the consultants don't go to the pre-med, because if there's a problem they wouldn't sleep.'

So why was the policy sustained in this particular hospital? The operating theatre complex, although old, was well designed. Apart from an accident and emergency theatre and the obstetric theatre, all the theatres were cen-trally located in one place, opening onto a common concourse. From this also opened the recovery room, and coffee and changing rooms. The advantages of this arrangement were often stressed: 'It's not so at the Y where I do some sessions. I feel very cut off there, and isolated.' It meant that, first, it was easy to continue teaching junior staff, since it was easy for senior staff to be there when needed and to slip out and leave juniors on

159

their own when things were routine. Second, one could easily ask a colleague to stand by for a while if something was complicated. The anaesthetists recalled an earlier time when one theatre had been located in another block and a registrar would be on his own there, no matter what happened. Moreover, doctors had almost certainly also gone home directly from that building, again no matter what had happened. For a third consequence of this layout was that it provided the opportunity to discuss technical issues with colleagues both before and after operations, and therefore also to work through some of the anxiety. On a day when a difficult case was expected in the afternoon, the consultant concerned spent the whole morning in the coffee room, discussing it with the colleagues who came and went. So the layout of the operating theatre complex created the conditions for a form of social support among the anaesthetists, which was important in helping them manage some of the more difficult personal aspects of their role. It seems very likely that this was what made it possible to sustain the policy of examining patients pre-operatively. It is also very unlikely that suggesting purposely set up support groups would cut much ice with these professionals.

When a draft report on the study was sent to the Association of Anaesthetists' research and education committee one of its members, who was head of the division of anaesthesia in a large teaching hospital, phoned me. In his hospital the operating theatres all opened onto a long corridor. He said, 'You know, this is interesting. This morning I had a woman patient I was worried about. But I'm the boss, I'm not supposed to get worried. I have one woman colleague I don't mind admitting it to. But she was working at the other end of the corridor, and going all that way for help would have been a big deal. Anyway, I couldn't leave the patient that long.'

So the scientific and technical developments in anaesthetics, while bringing great advances, had created situations and relationships that affected the roles involved. In particular, they had brought some personal consequences for anaesthetists in the form of anxiety. The architecture of the building made it possible to work through this anxiety by making it possible to get professional support from colleagues. This in turn made it possible to sustain medical policy.

Now that's what I call a good detective story.

On how work is organised

Several opportunities to get involved in work organisation and the design of jobs came my way during the 1970s. Two of them involved contracts in Germany, two involved contributing to the design of factories, and one involved technology design – although that one didn't work out too well. In the seventies issues of sociotechnical systems and work design came very much onto the agenda all over Europe. To quite a large extent I believe that this was triggered by work done in Volvo in Sweden, and the attendant publicity. The Volvo work at least meant that when one was struggling to explain what one was trying to do, one could collapse and say, 'You know, like Volvo' – and people would get a sense of what you were trying to say.

Research – The Commission for Economic and Social Change in Germany

One day Nancy Seear asked me to chair a meeting at the London School of Economics. A German professor, Burkhard Lutz, was to give a lecture and she thought he might have problems with English. He didn't, but this formed the beginning of a major stream of working relations and work. After the lecture I took him to dinner, and then we were to have coffee with Nancy, who was by then in the House of Lords. My first impression of Burkhard Lutz was awkward. He stood at the edge of the terrace of the 'Prospect of Whitby' inn, looked out over the Thames, and said that the scene was like an office at the end of the day before the cleaners have come. I could take that kind of remark, might even privately agree with it, but at that time had difficulty taking it from a German.

We talked shop, and he showed a great deal of interest in the question of work satisfaction. I told him a bit about my work and later sent him my Fabian pamphlet. It turned out that he was a member of the Commission for Economic and Social Change which had been set up in 1971 by Chancellor Willy Brandt to advise the German government on what research was needed to underpin an informed social policy. They had set about it in a most thorough and systematic fashion. The first thing they did was to commission a 'system study' to map the areas that were relevant to an informed social policy. There was a mural in the entrance hall of their office, showing the results of this system study. It was a complicated network of blobs and lines, the blobs representing topics that needed to be researched and the lines how they were connected.

One of the blobs was called 'work satisfaction', and that research they commissioned from me. At the time there was no experience of this topic in Germany. One of the Commissioners expressed this in characteristic fashion when he asked, 'Is it true that everyone else is cooking with wine and only we are cooking with water?' Although foreign, I had the advantage of speaking German, though my German wasn't very good at that stage. I remember sitting in a committee meeting next to Burkhard Lutz and whispering to him, 'What is "perception" in German?' In a loud stage whisper he answered, '*Perzeption!*'

The more I learned about Brandt's Commission, the more I came to admire the way policy development was being tackled. When the documents for my contract arrived at the Institute, it was Project No. 57! Research as a basis for policy, and on such a scale, was unthinkable in this country. I later wrote up and published the story of the Commission for Economic and Social Change, in the hope of kindling some efforts at emulation, but things don't work like that.[20]

Envy, I discovered, went in both directions. The first time I went to Germany to discuss the project I visited the Commission in their office in Bad Godesberg, a suburb of Bonn. After the meeting, over lunch, they explained how to get back to Bonn. There were about five trains per hour, so I said, 'Well, if I miss the one you're suggesting, I'll get the next one.' With real envy one of the Trade Union members said, 'How wonderfully pragmatic!'

However, things didn't quite work out the way it had been intended. By the time the Commission finished its work and was ready to report, Willy Brandt had resigned from office. His successor, Helmut Schmidt, was not interested. The Chairman of the Commission told me that, after much delay, they eventually sent a note to the Chancellor saying that the Commission's report would be handed over on a certain date, 'if only to the porter'. It was then received formally by two Ministers, but not by the Chancellor himself. This is not to say that there was no outcome; there were some important consequences and in any case consequences are often indirect and difficult to trace. But the loss of the central impulse when the sponsor disappears is exactly what had happened to me in Esso and what happens in many other forms of project, irrespective of level or country. The waste involved is incalculable.

The studies that were being commissioned were not intended to do basic research but to gather together the current state of knowledge. For me it was

---

[20] The work of the Commission for Economic and Social Change in Germany. In: Martin Bulmer (ed) (1987). Social science research and government. Cambridge University Press.

a wonderful opportunity to catch up with reading, and with what was happening in the area of work organisation both in this country and in Europe. I visited Holland, Norway and Sweden, where most of the action was at the time. It was a chance to be rather more systematic about this stuff that I had been plunging into, and the outcome was a book published first in German, and then in English, under the title *New Forms of Work Organisation*.[21]

In Norway, Einar Thorsrud and David Herbst met me at the dock (I went by sea, because I get very frightened flying) and took me to visit a project. 'We have now moved into banking,' they said, and we visited a branch of a bank in the mountains, where some work was going on. At the time I was consulting to a bank with 3500 branches, but I would not have talked of myself or of the Tavistock Institute as having 'now moved into banking'. It is a continuing thread that I find it very difficult to come to terms with such self-confidence, but know at the same time that people take you at your own valuation; if you don't make a noise you are not heard.

Consulting the 'Humanising Life at Work' programme in Germany

The 1970s were an optimistic time, there was a lot going on. One of the German civil servants I met later wrote about how the industrialised nations 'had just begun to permit themselves the luxury of talking about the quality of life' before they were hit by the Arab oil embargo. In 1974 the German government launched a major programme to 'humanise life at work'. I cannot remotely claim that this was a consequence of my work on new forms of work organisation for the Brandt Commission; rather they both arose from the same common impulse, in which the German metalworkers' union (IG Metall) had played a major part. But I think my study may have influenced the people who set up the programme. The programme was enormous. Having come late to this topic – though it was certainly not true that everyone else was 'cooking with wine' – they now approached it on a larger scale and more systematically than anyone else in Europe, indeed in the world.

Companies that were prepared to do something to 'humanise' their work, in whatever way, were invited to formulate their plans and estimate the costs, and could then apply to the government for financial support. Their project

---

[21] *Neue Formen der Arbeitsorganisation.* Verlag Otto Schwartz & Co. Göttingen, 1975; *New Forms of Work Organisation.* Cambridge University Press, 1976.

plans had to have the agreement of their elected Works Council, and they had to allow the project to be researched. So companies would approach the funding system hand-in-hand with researchers; if the project was approved, the companies would get half their costs and the research organisations the whole of theirs.

A committee was set up to process these applications. It consisted of civil servants, employers' representatives, trade union representatives and academics. I was invited to join, in the role of '*Gutachter*', a kind of cross between expert consultant and monitor. The function was two-fold: to be part of the decision process for awarding the grants, and to monitor the projects once they started. Together with one of the German academics I became monitor for the first of the projects, which was a very large one in Bosch AG, who made electrical goods, and later, on my own, for a small firm called Peine which manufactured screws and bolts.

So during the next seven years I spent a lot of time in Germany. The landscape and architecture in parts of Germany are very reminiscent of Czechoslovakia, and there were many shocks of recognition and pangs of homesickness. Yet I never made a detour to Czechoslovakia on one of these trips, although it would have been quite easy. It was the time of the 'iron curtain', and it seems to me now that there was a kind of iron curtain inside my own head. It protected me from the homesickness becoming unbearable, and allowed me to get on with a life on this side of it.

While my cousin Sue, whose husband sometimes went to Germany on business, refused to set foot there, I saw this as an opportunity to try to face and deal with things German, and with myself in relation to them. More importantly, I saw the programme itself as an attempt on the part of Germany to deal with issues of democracy and human development and dignity, and felt grateful for the opportunity to play a part in that. As the only foreigner to be involved I felt not only very honoured but also very much on show, needing to demonstrate the values that were being introduced into work organisation in my own behaviour, not only in any substantive contribution I might make.

When I had first started to visit Germany I had found myself quite instinctively guessing the age of anyone I met. If they were, at that time, under about fifty, there was no problem. If they were older there was a quite automatic reaction of 'and where were you?'. Most of the people I encountered in the Humanisation Programme were on the comfortable side of this boundary, and I formed good and lasting friendships. I still exchange Christmas cards with the chief production engineer of Bosch, who has of course long since retired. Also, one of the administrators of the Programme has remained a friend. He recently quoted at me a limerick I had doodled during a committee meeting, and which I had forgotten:

A semi-autonomous Turk
Said, 'This change agent chap is a jerk.
I would much rather sit,
Chew tobacco, and spit.
Make my other half happy at work!'

Then I, in turn, remembered the complicated discussion we had had about whether one should use the more usual English formulation of 'my better half', given the gender politics of the time, and that this was about Germany's Turkish guest workers. Once I wrote one of my reports on Bosch in doggerel verse.

There was one difficult exception to these friendly relationships. For the work in Bosch I was paired off with an elderly professor of ergonomics who had learned his ergonomics and *Arbeitswissenschaft* ('science of work') in the German air force during the war, and had no inhibitions about reminiscing about those days. Some of the time he had been stationed in Russia, and he was eloquent about how uncivilised Russian people were and how bug-infested their houses. Indignantly he recounted how he had given up the unequal struggle against bugs and decided to sleep in his car. The thought that he had no business to be in a Russian house at all did not occur to him, either at the time or later. The administrators of the programme saw the difficulty that had been created, but once the arrangements were in place couldn't quite see how to change them.

I had to deal with a certain amount of envy within myself, both because of the great opportunity that was opening up in Germany for the things I thought important, and because of the sheer scale of the resources being applied. People with no experience in the subject were being awarded salaries two or three times what anyone in my own Institute was paid. One of the research institutes involved in the first project included in its estimates money for a new truck to carry equipment around. 'Why do you need a new truck?' asked one committee member. 'Because the present one is getting worn out,' said the director of the institute without batting an eyelid. He got his truck.

That first proposal was for the Bosch project, and it was very large and cumbersome – seven production plants, five research institutes, and an eventual cost of twenty-six million Deutschmark. There were many criticisms of the plans, but eventually the committee chairman, from the

Ministry of Research and Technology, faced us with a difficult question: 'If we don't fund this, what are we going to do?'

The problem, however, lay not so much in the Bosch project as in the fact that it established a pattern. If that was the way to get funding, people reasoned, we must do it the same way. So the immense problems and effort and waste involved in trying to coordinate the work of multiple sites and many research teams became the norm. The programme eventually ran into political difficulties, and this was one of the reasons. By that time, however, it had also set the pattern for others. I don't know whether the design of the European Commission's research programmes was directly influenced by this German pattern, but they are on similar lines and suffer from similar problems.

While the Germans were new to the topic of work organisation they brought to it approaches that, in turn, were new to me. These approaches 'spoke to' something in me. I formulated it in a lecture at the Tavistock in terms of a marker buoy somewhere in the Channel: every time I passed it, in either direction, my attitude about a whole range of things changed.

For one thing, they did things by law. An enthusiast in the Ministry of Labour had managed to get a clause inserted in company law to the effect that 'scientific findings about the workplace must be applied'. If one said this to a British audience they tended to laugh. Most of the things we were talking about were not 'scientifically proven'; you cannot 'prove' in that sense that people need opportunities for learning and decision making in order to develop. And yet there were many things contributing to the working environment to which such a law could apply, and because of it working conditions in Germany were likely to become progressively better than in Britain. Not only my central European background, but my experience of personnel management told me that.

Again, it was not social scientists but production engineers who, once they had taken the idea of job satisfaction on board, developed methods for incorporating operators' preferences into the design of production systems.[22] They were equipped for this while the social scientists, just like British ones, were only equipped for researching it, not for taking it into design.

Did I mention clangers? It is dangerous to make jokes if you are not completely at home in a culture. One day the committee had before it the project application of a large industrial group. We had read the documents (always very heavy) and were now to discuss the proposal with the

---

[22] Metzger, H., Warnecke, H.J. and Zippe, H. (1975). Neue Formen der Arbeitsstrukturierung im Produktionsbereich. Z. ind. Fertig. 65, 665–670.

applicants. The atmosphere was tense, about thirty people were standing around in the committee room dressed rather formally for the occasion and speaking in hushed voices. One couldn't be sure who was an industrialist, who a researcher, who a civil servant. As we took our seats I thought I might break the tension and announced, 'Well, I'm open to bribes!' There was total silence, which seemed to me to last for about three weeks. Not a murmur, not a smile. Then the Chairman said, 'Now, item one on the agenda ...'

Design

In England I had three opportunities to get into questions of design. Two were about taking part in the design of new factories, in companies that wanted a contribution about the design of jobs. These were exciting opportunities. I had long felt that it was necessary to consider the nature of the work that was being created at the stage of plant design, because after that many options are already closed. Most sociotechnical projects were about redesign, where the possibilities were already quite limited. The philosophy in redesign was about involving operators in contributing their experience to the design of the jobs, but in the design of a new plant the operator doesn't exist yet. So it was quite a different situation, and a case of inventing and adapting methods.

The first company was Trebor Sharp, the confectionery firm, whose directors were planning to build a new plant for making mints. In the course of the Esso work I had learned about simulation methods. In Trebor I adapted the idea, the first time right at the beginning, when I tried to understand the production process by talking my way through it as if I were the raw material and the product. The second time was when the management team had reached the stage of a tentative layout, which they had set up with the use of Lego bricks. They had spent a weekend doing this, and then asked me to comment on it. I said, 'I can't really think my way into this. What is actually happening down there? Suppose it's seven-thirty in the morning, what is going on?' One of them said, 'All right, I'll be a press operator.' Another said, 'We don't know if we're going to have press operators.' Gradually they took on roles according to the work that needed to be done, and then someone said, 'OK, it's seven-thirty in the morning, the bell's gone and the doors are open ...' He was interrupted – 'What do you mean, bell? Are we going to have bells?' And there followed a long discussion about clocking-in and time-clocks.

By mid-day we had, in this way, worked our way through the start-up and first hour or so of production. In the process a number of things in the layout were changed and it was interesting to see how difficult this was to do, even with Lego bricks, given the hard work that had gone into the original arrangement.

The second company was building a vegetable canning plant. Here I was not able to persuade them to make a model, though once the plant was up and they found some places hard to reach for maintenance, they wished they had.

In Germany I had learned about a method of getting people to articulate what they felt was important in a job, allocating priorities to those qualities, and then getting them designed into the job. I adapted this for the canning plant. We had set up a job design committee, which included management, engineers, and representatives from three trade unions. That was possible because the company already had some other production activities on the new site. At one point I presented this job design committee with a list of possible characteristics that a job might have, and got them to put these in order of priority. There were many differences, not only between management and unions but between the different unions and between individuals. I thought it important that they should experience some success in job design, so rather than spend a lot of energy on these differences we decided to work on a characteristic that was fairly well agreed and which had fairly high priority – 'being able to influence one's own pace of work'. We then explored this with the engineers: they took us through the proposed production layout systematically, only from this point of view of machine pacing. It turned out that, at the point where lids were to be put on the cans, an operator was going to be locked into a twenty-second job cycle. We collected ideas about alternative methods and compared them systematically on capital costs, labour costs and job design qualities. At some capital cost an arrangement involving a twelve-minute cycle was selected and installed. It may not have been an ideal solution, but the job design group had experienced that design does not come from God but can be influenced.

The company had had some previous experience of the Tavistock Institute. When I first met them the project manager was unexpectedly frosty. It turned out that, some twenty years earlier, people from the Tavistock Institute had been at work there, and this engineer had been declared 'not material for promotion'. The pain and resentment were still there, and I had to work hard to overcome them.

I had my own problems when I first met the board. I had prepared a presentation about job design, but the Chairman had other concerns: 'What do you think of [a ready-made food product]?' he asked.

'I'm afraid I don't know it,' I had to admit.

'Well, what do you think of [another one]?'

'I'm afraid I don't know it.' This went on, embarrassingly, and eventually I tried to explain my ignorance: 'It's just that – I'm afraid – I rather like cooking.'

'Oh. One of those!' was his verdict.

Two days later a large parcel of samples arrived at the Institute. We were awash in fast foods.

In both companies I learned a lot about the problem of phasing. The computer engineers in the canning company became very interested and supportive about the idea of designing satisfying jobs. 'But,' they said to the job design committee, 'please decide what you want before the floors are laid. Once the concrete is laid, with channels for the cables, we can't change it.' At that stage the committee was simply not able to express a view, there was too much new technology to take on board. It was, after all, new to the engineers as well.

At Trebor a project group at board level had been formed, and when I first met this group a site had been acquired and planning permission for the new factory obtained. They were beginning to discuss the choice of architects and the general shape of the building. Two concepts were being debated: the idea of a large, hangar-like structure within which there would be freedom to arrange and rearrange things, and the idea of a 'village street', with small production units as well as shops, a bank, a post office. Within a few minutes of joining them, I was confronted with the question, 'What do you think – large hangar or village street?'

Of course, I had no idea. The problem was that the company felt that they could not even begin to talk to architects until they had some idea of the basic shape of the building they wanted; one couldn't sensibly discuss the shape of the building without some idea of the production layout; and I couldn't contribute to discussion about the layout without some socio-technical analysis of the production process, which needed time. At that stage I hadn't even seen it. That was when I broke the deadlock by saying, 'Look – I'm a piece of sugar, I've just been delivered. What happens to me? – and then talking my way through the whole production process.

Although it was exciting to be involved at such early stages, I discovered that in many ways it was already late. The capital appropriation which the canning company had obtained from its parent company already had built into it assumptions about the kinds of job that would be involved. And a good deal of equipment, in both companies, would be bought off the shelf, allowing no opportunity for change. But working with such problems, and getting them understood and even partly resolved, was endlessly interesting and very satisfying.

The third opportunity was a chance to get involved in the design of equipment. Howard Rosenbrock was Professor of Control Engineering at the University of Manchester Institute of Science and Technology. He was one of the few senior engineers who was interested in the sociotechnical ideas and in job design, and he got a research grant to design a 'Flexible Manufacturing System' such that the operator should stay in control. An FMS is an automated system incorporating many manufacturing operations that would previously have been done on separate machines. He put together a research team and a steering committee. The research team consisted of an engineer, a computer scientist and a social scientist; I was a member of the steering committee.

It was a stimulating group, which engaged in endless philosophical discussions about the nature of work and of manufacturing. Possibly the most rewarding part of the experience for me was travelling to Manchester and back with Mike Cooley. Mike was a brilliant, articulate design engineer who first attracted public attention as founder member of the Lucas Aerospace Combine Shop Stewards' Committee, which worked out a 'Plan for Socially Useful Production'. The ideas were both about the kind of products that modern technology should help to create and about methods of production that should support and develop human capacities instead of suppressing them. Lucas couldn't cope with him.

But in some ways I am not very happy about that work. Howard wanted the project steering group to make a major contribution to the research itself, and in this he found me ineffective. I have always needed to get some understanding of the technology I am dealing with before I can make a serious contribution, and for that a few steering group meetings per year were not enough. There were in fact two technologies to absorb: the technology of metal cutting, and computer technology. On the first, I used a week of my holiday and asked UMIST to give me some concentrated teaching, treating me like a first-year engineering student. In this way I learned enough at least to understand what the researchers were dealing with. The teaching included a video, in the course of which two things happened: first, the actual engineering content was very fascinating. And second, within the first minutes the operator was mentioned as a cost and was never mentioned again. The unspoken implication was that, if he or she was skilled that would be a high cost, if unskilled a low cost, and if they could be eliminated altogether that would be best of all. And this would of course set a young engineering student's attitude for life, so that the likes of me would be running after them for ever after, saying 'Yes, but ...'

The computing side I never mastered well enough. It was my first serious contact with computing, and the project constituted far too deep a deep end to be thrown into without some systematic training.

Howard was rather ambivalent about social scientists; he saw them as always criticising engineers but never making a contribution themselves. He gave the young social science researcher whom we appointed quite a hard time, and he seemed to like putting me on the spot. Once, when I mentioned leaving options open for the operator, he took a piece of paper, made a quick calculation, and said, 'I reckon there are about four billion options. Which ones do you mean?'

The main outcome of the project was that Howard and Mike Cooley obtained a grant under one of the European Commission's research pro-grammes to develop a 'human-centred' manufacturing system. And the main outcome of *that* was that for many years the European Commission felt it had done its duty by human aspects of manufacturing. It became impossible to get human considerations taken account of in any of its other projects.

On working with groups

This was different from my other engagements with Tavistock traditions. It was at first more alien for me, less natural a development from where I was already. In 1956 I had heard a lecture by someone who had been to the United States and had been swept off his feet by something called group dynamics. It had been the most wonderful experience of his life, he said, which couldn't possibly be put into words. I decided to find out what this was about: if there was anything there worthwhile and real, I felt, it must be possible to find words for it. So when the Tavistock Institute announced its own first Group Relations Conference at Leicester in 1957, I went. I went there 95% sceptical, and came away 90% sceptical.

It was a two-week event, and during the weekend in the middle they showed the film *Twelve Angry Men*, which is about a jury trying to arrive at a verdict. Afterwards Harold Bridger, one of the consultants, gave a com-mentary in terms of the dynamics going on within the group of jurors. The trouble was he got some of the facts wrong. He would say, 'You remember when A got up and went to the window . . .', only it hadn't been A, it had been someone else. I felt some sense of outrage and protested, followed by others. If one couldn't trust these people to get a few simple facts right, how could one trust them about this mysterious, intangible stuff? (Interpretations about 'pairing' when three of us had been prevented from attending one of the sessions because someone's car broke down had not helped). Later the staff wrote an account of the conference and sent a draft round to the participants. The 'mid-term rebellion' had very fanciful interpretations attached to it. I wrote to explain why and how the rebellion had actually come about, and they had the integrity to change the draft.

I didn't meet Harold again for some years, but it is to this episode that the roots of mutual respect may be traced. When I later learned from him and worked with him, it was this integrity in relation to reality that formed the bridge between a scientific and a dynamic framework. I never saw him make a dogmatic interpretation, or hide behind mystique, or drop unexplained hints about 'unconscious forces' in order to put the other person at a disadvantage.

As for group relations, I went on trying. Every few years I would muster the courage to have another go, hoping that this time perhaps I might find out what a group is. I learned much, but the central core continued to evade me. A group as a setting, a vehicle for exploring many things, certainly; but a group as an entity in its own right or even, heaven forfend, an 'organism' – I simply couldn't see it. When I began to work with Harold as a consultant in the training and development event he called a Working Conference, he observed that I was working with the dynamics of the content of a group's work, while he was working with the dynamics of the group itself. Once, when he had made an intervention that 'the group is splitting the task', I said that I knew what he meant, having seen the same events, but didn't know whether, with such a comment, he was giving the group a scientific observation or a piece of poetry. That sparked off a two-hour discussion, all the way from Stratford to Hammersmith, of which I still remember the exhilaration.

This division of labour between the dynamics of the content and the dynamics of the group was quite satisfactory as long as I was working with colleagues who had a greater sense of 'the group as such' than I. Then one day I found myself working with someone who was looking to me to provide the understanding of 'the group'. Me! Who still wasn't sure whether there was such a thing as a group!

There is nothing like responsibility to speed up the learning process. It was all right. For the first time, I worked with things that I had relied on others to work with. I found myself able to say 'The group is ...' and not have my fingers metaphorically crossed behind my back. It had only taken thirty-two years.

More about the use of the social sciences

If the Esso experience could be seen as a detailed case study of using the social sciences, it seemed important to follow it up with some comparisons. I wanted to collect accounts of other such experiences, and for this I joined up with Ken Eason, from Loughborough University. It was difficult to get funding: we applied to the Social Science Research Council but at the time this had set its face against applied work, the academics on its committees finding the idea of usefulness both scientifically and politically unacceptable. Those were also the politically correct days when having a reputation as a centre of excellence was a reason for *not* getting funding. Under the Thatcher government the SSRC was almost abolished; it was saved by the skin of its teeth and re-emerged as the Economic and Social Research Council, or ESRC.

Eventually we did get our research funded, by the Anglo-German Foundation. In the course of that project I experienced a phase of personal poverty, which felt much tougher than when I was young and my mother and I had been really poor. Ken was seconded to the Tavistock Institute half-time for the project, which took three years. So the Institute had to pay Loughborough University half his salary, for which I was responsible. His canny professor had pitched it at a level where they could replace half of Ken with a whole junior lecturer. Inflation was very high during this time, but the Anglo-German Foundation had built only the German rate of inflation into its grant, not the British. On top of that, the universities had for some years fallen behind the rest of the country with pay rises, and chose this period to catch up. Ken's salary went up by far more than the grant allowed, and I would have to find the difference.

I needed to think quickly of ways to economise. My first shock reaction, when I discovered the deficit in my Institute account, was, 'Well, I can use tea-bags twice.' Not very useful. I cut my salary, gave up having a secretary in the Institute and a cleaner at home, bought no clothes and had no holidays that year, gave up taxis (a habit developed in Esso; I have never had a car) and economised stringently on food. Between Christmas and Easter that year I bought meat once. Of course none of this is real hardship, the constant gnawing worry was that it was not enough to make a significant difference; for that I would have to move house – sell my flat and move to a cheaper part of London. It didn't come to that, but I discovered some of the problems of middle-class poverty. One of them is that people don't believe you. When I told Marie Jahoda about it, she burst out laughing, saying, 'Oh come on – not you!'

At the same time I was fighting a very unpleasant battle in the Institute to get them to approach the Anglo-German Foundation about the problem. They refused; they didn't want to risk upsetting a potential grant-giver. It shows the inconsistency in the organisational model: members of staff were in some sense autonomous, as if they were employers, and in some sense dependent, as employees. Wearing the autonomy hat, I was responsible for generating the income. But I was not allowed to defend the income, I had to let my employers do that, and they wouldn't. This battle went on for several months, but eventually the management group changed its mind and agreed to write to the Foundation. A cheque came by return of post; the Foundation must have been prepared for this all along. The research took a long time to do, then to write up and to publish; the book finally came out in 1991.[23]

In 1993 the research councils were required, in a White Paper on Science, Engineering and Technology, to relate to the users of research. It misses a point: there is a difference between 'relating to users' and being useful. 'Relating to users' is too short-term. When you are doing research you often can't know what particular 'user' may benefit from it, and those who do genuinely long-term work will be discouraged and alienated. Research that is useful and usable can be translated for many specific users. Research that is aimed at specific users stops there.

Still, for the social sciences it was better than what had been before. No doubt against the inclination of many of the people involved, the climate slowly began to change. In 1996, when I was in the Bayswater Institute almost twenty years after our failure with the SSRC, I was commissioned by the ESRC to look at the relations between researchers and users in one of their programmes. In 1999 I was at a workshop they organised about the general issue of relations between researchers and users. Someone said that it would be a good idea to collect case studies of applied social science. Our 1991 book was, of course, out of print by then. I should have called this memoir *Bad Timing*.

More about the fringes of politics

In the 1970s work satisfaction had come onto the public agenda. As I've said, it was probably because the Volvo car company in Sweden reorganised production at their Kalmar plant into autonomous group working, and

---

[23] Lisl Klein and Ken Eason. *Putting Social Science to Work*. Cambridge University Press.

generated a lot of publicity about it. In Britain the *Financial Times* carried articles about it and Conservative MPs wrote to Maurice Macmillan, the Minister of Labour, to ask whether we should be doing something like this. It is an abiding puzzle to me why the Labour Party, which after all has the word 'labour' even in its title, has never shown any interest in how working people actually spend their time at work. It was under a Conservative government that a small Work Research Unit was set up within the Ministry of Labour.

Even *Coronation Street*, a sure-fire barometer of currently live topics, had people discussing job satisfaction in the bar of the Rovers Return. I am devoted to *Coronation Street*. In 1978 I went to India for a month, followed by a second visit to Australia. (Alice met me at the airport. A big hug, a kiss, then she held me at arms' length: 'Darling, I will take you to have your eyebrows dyed!') When I got back to England, Minnie Caldwell had disappeared from Coronation Street. I have not been able to find out what happened to her, my friends don't share my taste in television viewing.

The Fabian Society has always had the function of providing a channel for those who were not directly in the hurly-burly of politics to contribute ideas. I didn't want to go into politics professionally. James Callaghan once offered to find me a parliamentary seat, and I thought seriously about it but decided against it. First, I doubted whether I had the energy. Shirley Williams once said that the main quality a politician needs is stamina, and I believe her. I didn't think I could cope with the late nights and the rushing around. The second reason was that, while I thought I could do the job, I did not think I had what it takes to fight an election to get there. There were two or three fields I knew about, but in an election campaign you have to pretend to know about everything. You have to have answers and opinions, and you have to have them instantly, you are not allowed to say, 'I don't know,' or 'I'll try and find out about that and come back to you.' It seemed to me that the qualities needed to get the job and the qualities needed to do it were in conflict. Once during a slightly drunken party Shirley, who was contesting the parliamentary seat she won, having failed the first time, said, 'If I get in this time, I'll see you get a peerage.' She must have forgotten.

My concern with questions of work satisfaction and job design was known, and there was support for it. But experience of actually changing the nature of work was mostly through projects at the level of individual organisations, it was difficult to translate into a broader policy. The work in Germany in the seventies was giving me ideas of how this might be done. I could see both the value and the problems of what they were doing in Germany, and had ideas about how it could be adapted to be both more realistic and more suited to a British background and British ways of thinking and working. I wrote a paper for the Fabian Society outlining a policy for tackling the problem of satisfaction in work. They liked it, and arranged two opportunities for me to present it at policy levels in the Labour Party. The first involved a meeting with Michael Foot, who was for a short period in the mid-seventies Secretary of State for Employment. Job satisfaction was not something in which he was personally interested, but he did the proper thing and sent the paper to the relevant civil servants in his department. Unfortunately the 'relevant civil servant' turned out to be Gilbert Jessup, the Director of the Work Research Unit. He was a Civil Service psychologist, with no knowledge of the topic or experience of industry, and was soon to be replaced. He was discovering the excitement of contact with industrial organisations. Policy was not nearly so exciting, and his response to Michael Foot was, 'If my staff had to administer policy, they would not have time to do projects.' I thought, and still think, that this was wicked.

The second opportunity was to present the paper to the Labour Party's Home Affairs Committee. They liked it, apart from one member, Tony Benn, (not yet at that time chairman of the Committee). His objection was that it was 'blinding workers with science'. 'I hold meetings with workers at factory gates,' he said, 'that's the way to involve them.'

'You hold meetings at factory gates when something dramatic has happened in a place,' I answered. 'I'm talking about the times in between.'

The chairman summarised the feeling of the meeting as being very positive. They decided that the paper should go next to the joint Labour Party/TUC Liaison Committee, which had been formed both to prevent the PR disasters of clashes between them and to work on an economic and industrial policy which would be acceptable both to unions and the Party. The paper never reached the Liaison Committee, and I can only speculate about how that came about.

That was when I left the Labour Party. It was some time before Roy Jenkins, David Owen, Bill Rodgers and Shirley Williams left it and formed the Social Democrat Party, and not for the same reasons. I then joined the SDP and, sadly, it meant having to leave the Fabian Society. They were prepared to have members of the Social Democrats as 'associate members', but after so many years and so much involvement I was not willing to be a second-class citizen. There was a very emotional and stormy meeting in the House of Commons, at which I said, 'If you change your minds, let me know,' and left.

The Social Democrats had a number of committees working on areas of policy, among them one on participation in industry, chaired by Michael Shanks. I presented my policy paper to this group, who welcomed it and said it was just the kind of thing they were looking for. I left it in their hands and was very upset to find, when the policy 'Green Papers' later came out, that these ideas were not included. I tried to find out why, but nobody seemed to know. The best suggestion that someone came up with was, 'I expect the girls in Cowley Street didn't understand it when they were putting the papers together and left it out.' I later left the Social Democrats, or Liberal Democrats, too. It is painful that someone who is as political as I am cannot find a party to identify with. I know that I am not alone in this.

When the Blair government came into power, I tried again. By now this was probably perverse, and more a matter of curiosity than anything else. I wrote to David Blunkett, then the Secretary of State for Education and Employment, and after many weeks got a charming and silly letter from a junior civil servant telling me not to worry my head about these things, they were all being taken care of. Through an acquaintance in the department I tried to find out more. There was to be a Green Paper on Lifelong Learning, with a consultative element incorporated. A section of the paper invited readers to submit ideas, and I was assured that this would be the best way to get ideas heard. I found that hard to believe, but tried it anyway. When I later enquired, the information was that there had been three thousand submissions from individuals and two thousand from institutions, and staff in the department were engaged in trying to 'summarise' them. Bless their cotton socks, they were probably the younger brothers and sisters of the girls in Cowley Street.

Is it boring to be consistent? Already in Esso, in the mid-sixties, I had felt that the logical development of what we were doing would be to get a contribution on human and social aspects of the business out of 'project mode' and built into what was happening, as normal a part of technical and organisational thinking as economic aspects. By the mid-eighties I was desperate that there were no signs of this happening, not so much in Esso, which I had left by then, but anywhere. By then there had been many projects, in many parts of the world, and I had myself been involved in a good number. But each time one began to work with engineers, and managers, and trade unionists, one had to begin again from scratch explaining and persuading; and each time a member of a project team or steering group moved on and was replaced, one had to start from scratch again.

In 1986 an opportunity to further such integration presented itself. I was invited to give evidence to a Committee of the European Parliament, and included in this evidence a suggestion which should go some way towards dealing with this problem of institutionalisation: it was that technologists applying for development grants from the European Commission should be required, as part of their grant applications, to say what effects they expected their project to have on a number of categories to do with people and organisation. Not that one would expect such predictions to be accurate, but technologists would be forced to give thought to these matters and that, in turn, might feed back into the education system where the separation had its roots. Some of the MEPs liked this idea. They modified the categories to include some others which they considered important, and in November 1986 the Parliament passed a resolution stating that:

The European Parliament ...
Believes that applicants for financial support under community technology and research schemes should be required to state what effect they expect the new technology to have on employment, the nature of the work, skills, health and safety at work and older workers for whom retraining is no longer possible ...
(Doc A2-142/86)

I really thought that something important had been achieved. I was particularly pleased at having demonstrated, or so I thought, that all this was not mere empire building on the part of the social sciences, for in such a framework an explicit contribution from the social sciences would become redundant.

The resolution has never been implemented. Indeed, when I enquired about it, Commission staff seemed to be unaware of its existence. I had this naïve assumption that the civil service is subject to the Parliament, but in the European Union it is not so. This was very depressing. However, something must have happened. The European Commission's research activities are organised into 'Framework Programmes', that is five-year plans and budgets, and in the literature for the fifth Framework Programme, starting in 1999, human, social and organisational considerations permeate the text. And then the application forms came out and it was there! It was thirteen years after my paper and the parliamentary resolution. Of course I don't know what the process of influence has been. And even now concern for these factors is not structured in – it is not mandatory. But it is meant to feature in the evaluation of proposals; we will have to see how that works out.

During my time in the Tavistock Institute I made two attempts to get involved in one of these programmes. At a conference of the Collège International pour la Recherche en Production (CIRP), a kind of club of prestigious production engineers, I had been asked what research was nee-ded to make people more willing to work with production systems. I had answered that there had been an enormous amount of research already; the problem was that it didn't get used. If more research was needed, it was about the decision processes when new production systems were being designed and implemented; but that this should be done in an action research frame, with social scientists accompanying the process and making whatever contribution from research and experience they could. The members of CIRP liked this idea, and it developed into an application to the European Commission's ESPRIT programme, sponsored by CIRP. It was rejected, with a strong recommendation to re-submit, and then rejected again. (Fifteen years later, the Bayswater Institute which I founded in fact became engaged in such a project. You just have to live long enough.)

I did, however, learn something about creative accounting. There were two ways of getting research funding from the European Commission: one was aimed at a hypothetical industrial situation and assumed that industry would get commercial benefits from the work and should therefore con-tribute half the costs; so under this system you added up your costs and received a grant for half that sum. The other system was aimed at a hypothetical university situation and assumed that anyone in a university was being paid for already; so you could claim the whole costs of anyone who had to be taken on extra for the work, but the costs of the member of staff who would be leading the project, or anyone else already in the organisation, could not be paid.

Neither of these methods was in fact viable or realistic, so corruption was inevitably built into the system. The Department of Trade and Industry retained the services of a consultant accountant to help British applicants formulate their costings, so that the UK could claw back its share of research funds, and I was introduced to him. We arranged to meet, and he asked if I would mind meeting near his home, which was north of London. I don't remember the reason; I think someone in his family was ill. The place he suggested was a so-called 'Business Centre' in a motorway service station on the M1. So the Tavistock's finance officer and I found ourselves belting along the M1 to this service station. The 'Business Centre' turned out to be a large room, with semi-circular niches around the edge, giving a kind of scalloped effect. Each niche consisted of comfortable chairs arranged round a coffee table. Coffee, tea and mineral water were liberally available, and these arrangements could be hired by the hour. Like a brothel. Several of them were occupied when we arrived, and I was very curious to know what was being transacted there.

Our consultant turned out to be pleasant and intelligent. He said that in our circumstances the 50% method was the only possibility, we would have to state costs that were so high that getting only half of them would serve. That, apparently, was usual. He quizzed the finance officer about the Institute's accounting methods and costs, and then he came up with an idea: the building in which we worked belonged to the National Health Service. It housed the Tavistock Clinic, which was part of the Health Service, and space was rented to the Institute. The Institute had a thirty-year lease, which was nearing its end, so the rent was relatively low. It had been economic when the lease was first issued, but twenty-five years later it was cheap. The consultant said we should get an estate agent to give us a letter certifying what economic rents for office space in that part of London really were, and that we should then claim that level. The difference was substantial, enough to make us able to use the 50% method, so that is what we did.

I had to remind myself that this was, as it were, official government advice, since it came from an official government adviser. And presumably similar consultations were going on in similar motorway service stations all over Europe. Never mind Plato and Aristotle, Beethoven and Shakespeare, Botticelli and Vermeer; the pan-European culture now was ingenious creative accounting.

Changes

In 1975, on my return from one of the German trips, I found that my mother was ill. She had been complaining of indigestion and constipation, but nothing had been found wrong. Now she said that she had been vomiting and couldn't understand why. It was a Friday, and I stayed with her over the weekend. I am endlessly thankful that I did that, for in the middle of Sunday night a slight sound from her bedroom woke me up. She had fallen to the floor and was unconscious. The emergency doctor I called said she had had a stroke, and had her admitted to Charing Cross Hospital.

She died there forty-two hours later. It troubles me immensely that I was not actually with her when she died. I had gone down to the hospital shop to buy cigarettes for one of the other patients and, I have to admit, to have a break from my vigil. When I came back upstairs she was dead. Next morning the young houseman who had admitted her was himself very upset. He had not expected her to die and had talked to me quite optimistically about rehabilitation from strokes. Because she had not been expected to die there was an autopsy, and she was found to have bowel cancer. Because she was a heavy smoker, the GP had only had her chest investigated, and had ignored her complaints about digestive problems.

Among my mother's friends expressions of sympathy took some odd forms. Tablets of Valium came through the post, carefully wrapped in tissue paper. Even at her funeral somebody leaned over and whispered loudly, 'Would you like a Valium?' Her funeral was a sign of the times in other ways, too. A few days before her death, while I was away in Germany, a young policeman had been shot in a street near my home. A house-to-house search had uncovered an IRA bomb-factory in my own street, I think the first to be found in London. When it came to arranging my mother's funeral, it turned out that the young policeman was to be cremated at Mortlake on the day we had in mind, and for security reasons no other cremations were to be allowed there that day. So my mother had to wait.

I asked the crematorium if my mother's ashes could be scattered at the same place as my father's had been. They said of course, and an official came into the garden with me to do it. Some time later, on impulse, I enquired about this. On the phone a different official said that they didn't have records going back that far, they couldn't have known where my father's ashes were. Why does that shoddy, uncaring little deception hurt so much?

And so my mother was not around six years later, when I moved house. I had begun to feel that I was outgrowing my little flat and looked for something a bit nearer work and big enough to put up visitors. In 1981 I moved into a lovely flat in a beautiful part of Bayswater. I don't know what she would have thought; she could not but have liked it, but would probably have drawn the line at some rather poncy-looking cornices, with a sharp, 'What *do* you think you're doing?' Actually, I don't like them either, but removing them would have cost too much.

My flat is opposite a church and near a synagogue. Being near both but belonging to neither somehow suits me. It is also near the Greek Orthodox Cathedral, and there was a wonderful Sunday when there was a wedding at the Greek church and a wedding at the synagogue, and the guests were getting mixed up. Taxis were putting these very elegant people down in the wrong place, and I stood in the window watching them running up and down the street.

Soon after I moved in, the vicar of the church put a note through every door in the street, saying that the rabbi from the synagogue was retiring and the church wanted to give him a party. I was so charmed by this that I went to the party, saying that I didn't know which way I was facing and felt a bit hypocritical in both directions. That was the beginning of a friendship with the vicar and his family, which has now lasted for thirty years. In its early years one of the children would sometimes phone and ask, 'Are you all right? Haven't seen your light for a while.' After the vicar's wife died the children drew closer, and I became a kind of proxy aunt to them. Later they brought their various partners to introduce and to inspect me, and now they bring their babies; so now I'm a proxy granny.

Not all the vicar's ideas were as brilliant as the party for the rabbi, though many were original. One Christmas he asked for volunteers to do a 'parish walk'. There were many homeless people in Bayswater, some sleeping rough. There were also, he said, prostitutes in the area who get turned out of their lodgings over the holiday. He asked for volunteers to walk a designated route for an hour each on Christmas day, with sandwiches and a flask of coffee; I offered to take the hour from nine to ten in the morning.

It had seemed a good idea, but it faltered in the execution. When you see a pretty girl outside Queensway tube station at half-past nine in the morning, you can't really go up to her and say, 'Excuse me, are you a prostitute and would you like a sandwich?' I did pluck up the courage to approach one man who looked a likely prospect. He thanked me courteously and explained that he was taking his dog for a walk. My sandwiches and coffee came home untouched.

I have read the solemn final lesson in the Christmas carol service (the vicar said, 'Treat it like poetry – I do') and I have acted as consultant to the Parochial Church Council (I asked if that was all right for a Jewish agnostic. The vicar said, 'Don't tell them'; but I did, and they didn't seem to mind). And I strongly suspect that they prayed for me when I had a bout of cancer. It is the only possible explanation for the big smile and kiss I get from one of the churchwardens whenever he catches sight of me – I am proof that it worked.

Getting sacked

And then I got sacked. There have been various greater or lesser vicissitudes in my life, but they have usually not come out of the blue, one had been able to see them coming. Now, at a time when I thought that my life was relatively settled, I was suddenly sacked by the Tavistock Institute at what in terms of the experience was a fortnight's notice, though technically it wasn't. Here is how it came about:

In 1988 I turned sixty. In the Tavistock Institute that was the formal retirement age, but one didn't have to retire. One could go on working or stop, take one's pension or defer it, as long as one did not cost the Institute more than one brought in. I decided to take no salary for a time and live on

Above:
Directing a Fabian School
on industry, 1963. With
Shirley Williams and Lord
Alf Robens, Chairman of
the National Coal Board.
Left:
At the Salzburg Seminar in
American Studies, 1965.

Top: At the Esso Milford Haven Refinery.
Below: Back at the Richmond Park-Hotel in 1994: the state company's Christmas party before handing over. I am sitting with Dr Dolina, Ing. Mikeš and Ing. Věra Koubská. I think the man standing is the Deputy Minister for Privatisation, with his wife.

My own house party in 1995: some of the guests went to Marienbad.
Johnny Hirsch came home!

Top: Harold Bridger (right) with staff of the Bayswater Working Conference.
Below: The Bayswater Institute in 2007.

my pension, because there was a lot of unpaid work I needed to do. Mainly the book on applied social science was not finished and the funding had long run out.

During those months some other unpaid jobs turned up: a colleague left, and I took on the job of winding up his project on shipping accidents. I discovered that Harold would turn eighty in 1989, and edited a collection of papers for his birthday. My own paper in it summarised where I had arrived at:

In an autobiographical introduction to his book 'The Informed Heart' Bruno Bettelheim describes the dilemma he experienced as a young man after the first world war, trying to decide where to focus his energies: was it more important to work towards the reform of society, or to change individuals? It was his personal version of the old nature/nurture controversy: 'In order to create the good society, was it of first importance to change society radically enough for all persons to achieve full self realization? In this case psychoanalysis could be discarded ... Or was this the wrong approach to the problem and could only persons who had achieved full personal liberation and integration by being psychoanalysed create such a 'good' society? In the latter case the correct thing was to forget for the time being any social or economic revolution and to concentrate instead on pushing psychoanalysis; the hope was that, once the vast majority of men had profited from its inner liberation, they would almost automatically create the good society for themselves and all others.'...[24]

Marx or Freud, then? Structure or dynamics? From outside or from inside? ... I know now, with more confidence than I have about anything, that in this dilemma of structure or dynamics, the sociological or the psychological, it is essential to attend to both. What is more, you have to attend to them simultaneously. It's no good thinking that you can postpone the one while you deal with the other, because the dealing with is unending, so the postponing becomes unending. Also, working on the one produces a frame of mind that is not conducive to working on the other ...[25]

---

[24] Bettelheim, B. (1960). *The Informed Heart: Autonomy in a Mass Age*, The Free Press, Glencoe, Ill.
[25] 'Inside and outside; a struggle for integration' in: *Working with organisations: papers to celebrate the 80th birthday of Harold Bridger*. London, Tavistock Institute of Human Relations, 1989.

During this time I was also in the process of organising a training course on sociotechnical design, again without pay. The post-Trist/Emery generation had rejected that stream of work, but I detected a renewed interest in the next generation after that. The Institute was by that time too weak in the subject to mount a training course, and I did a deal with an American consultant who had a training course he wanted to offer in Europe: the Institute would host his course, in return for some free places on it for younger Tavistock people. The course left the Institute with a small group of people taking a renewed interest in the subject.

Meanwhile I began to think about retirement. My thoughts were to go on working but do less, and develop some other things that I had long been neglecting. I started to take piano lessons, having always felt a sadness at missing out on music because of the war. I also started to go to evening classes in playwriting. My own ambitions to act were a distant memory, but I had a strong feeling for the stage, and have long felt that the things one had been writing about as research would make much better impact as drama. I knew of no English playwright who took working life seriously, except perhaps Arnold Wesker in his play *The Kitchen*, and I wanted to have a go.

But what with all the unpaid work I was doing, by March 1989 my account in the Institute was in deficit. Although I was not taking a salary, other costs such as the rent of my office and other overheads had of course continued. In previous years there had been some bad experiences of people letting their accounts go into the red and then leaving, and we had put some safeguards in place. The main one was a system of 'precautionary notice': accounts would be monitored and anyone whose account went into the red would be given notice, but if things came right the notice would be withdrawn. If they did not come right, this method would limit the damage to the Institute.

So in March I was given precautionary notice. I didn't object. It was handled professionally and properly, and I had consented to the precautionary notice strategy itself. I was, after all, part of the system that had devised it.

My account was reviewed at the end of May, by which time new paid work was coming in. Mainly an old client, the clearing bank, had come back with new work. And as a safeguard, Harold had issued a guarantee underwriting my 'overdraft'; the Institute's administrators had helped him to draft it in a way that would deal with the concerns of the Finance and Administration Committee. I therefore told the FAC that I thought the situation would be all right now, and they could withdraw the precautionary notice. But the new work had not by that time yielded any actual cash – which always comes in a bit later – and the deficit had grown (to £4500, the worst it ever was; not exactly such a big deal). Instead of withdrawing the notice they renewed it till October. I didn't mind too much, though I was a bit annoyed, and just got on with working, more or less forgetting that I was under notice. The deficit began to reduce by about £500 per month. Then, in the middle of October, I had a letter from the Institute Secretary saying that I had to be out at the end of the month.

It was a shattering bolt out of the blue. It was also completely baffling: the deficit was down to £1500 and would have been cleared by the end of the year. We went into a hectic phase of protest and discussion, but none of it made any difference and none of it made sense or threw any real light on what, to me, was a mystery; and none of it changed the decision.

On the day before I got this letter there had been a staff meeting to discuss what to do about the dangerously small size to which the Institute had shrunk. At least six of the people in the room must have known about the letter that was on its way to me, while I didn't. I was a member of the Management Group, but they had been meeting in secret without me to draft it. At one point I turned to its Chairman, sitting next to me. We had been discussing the possibility of having Associates of the Institute. 'Since you and I seem to be the people most interested in this,' I asked, 'should we form a working party to look at it?'

'Yes, right,' he answered, knowing that I would be out in two weeks. It is something I couldn't do if my life depended on it.

Harold was desperately upset. He was in Australia at the time, and I remember him weeping on the phone. He then blasted off a furious fax to the Institute and some members of Council, with phrases like 'The Tavistock Institute is psychodynamically re-enacting the evils of the Nazi regime.' That must have gone down a treat. In any case no one responded, as no one responded to my own letter of protest. Harold was also angry with me for not fighting at a formal level and going to law. But I cannot fight when I don't understand what it is I am fighting, and in a very basic sense I could not understand what had happened. Being sacked for a deficit of £1500, which was likely to be cleared within three months, just didn't make sense. Harold and I argued for the rest of his life about how far the disaster was due to envy and how far to incompetence.

The first real clue came in about March 1990, some months after I had left. I had lunch with two Institute colleagues who had remained friendly, and of course we talked about what had happened. I repeated for the umpteenth time that I didn't understand it. One of them burst out, 'The trouble was, nobody believed that you really had work.' That was news to me, and very strange. I was known to be, if anything, obsessively honest, no one had ever accused me of lying. I was also known to be very conservative in my estimates about work, never daring to count chickens before they were hatched.

Soon after this I ran into a young colleague who provided the second clue. He had been on the Finance and Administration Committee at the time, and now I asked him point-blank if they had doubted my word. He said that one member had persuaded the committee that my claim to have work was untrue, repeatedly pushing the question, 'Where's the documentary evidence?'

He was talking about an American woman who had joined the Institute a few years previously. The Institute had created a 'Development Fund' from money raised by the sale of its share of the library, and some of this money was used to fund a fellowship. Because she was being funded from something called a Development Fund, she argued that it was her mission to develop the Institute. When I turned sixty this woman had organised some birthday parties for me; there was an Institute-wide tea party, and a smaller dinner party. But she had invited people to 'Lisl's retirement party', and I thought then that this was a bit ominous and I might be in trouble – A.T.M. Wilson, the Tavistock Institute's first Chairman, used to say that some people's unconscious is not very unconscious!

The FAC at that time consisted of a Chairman, three further members of staff, and two administrators. The two younger staff members were persuaded that my claim to have work was untrue. But in the autumn of 1989 I had unwittingly created a problem for one of them: I had drawn him into the work with the bank. So there he was, having subscribed to the myth that this work did not exist, and actually taking part in it. He felt bad about this and, when confronted with the direct question, told me what had happened in the committee and apologised for having allowed himself to be used.

The administrators, on the other hand, had other problems. For some reason it had been decided to consult the Institute's solicitor. I didn't know why – it may have been because of a recent history concerning someone else who had been made redundant and who had threatened legal action. But from the solicitor they had learned something quite unexpected: he said that you cannot have someone under notice for so long – it had been six months – because that might be construed as 'harassment'. And if the notice was withdrawn, it would be virtually impossible to put me under notice again because that too – the on/off/on aspect – could be construed as harassment.

In the culture and circumstances of the Tavistock Institute that was pretty far-fetched and injudicious advice. But there it was. They were in a legal fix, or thought they were, and the only way they could think of to get out of it was to go through with the dismissal, irrespective of the actual situation.

They wrote to the body of senior staff, the 'College', with copies to some members of Council, that 'in spite of strenuous efforts to obtain further external funded work ... she remains in deficit and this is likely to remain so. After taking legal advice, we have been advised that there is no alternative but to terminate her existing contract ...'. One would not gather from this phrasing that amateurishness in management had got the Institute into an untenable legal situation, and that was what the legal advice had been about.

I had known nothing about any of this. If anyone had talked to me about the legal problem, it could have been solved easily. I would have undertaken not to sue for harassment and we could all have had a laugh. But that would have meant admitting that the Institute had made a mistake with its precautionary notice policy, and that required more guts than were available.

In these circumstances the myth that had been created, that the work I claimed did not in fact exist, became very convenient because it helped the Institute out of this hole. In other circumstances it would probably have been challenged.

So after nineteen years I was sacked because of a deficit of £1500, which would in any case have been wiped out by the end of the year. Some three years earlier I had, on behalf of the management group, helped organise the affairs of a colleague with an £11,000 deficit in such a way that he would not be forced to leave. Now this same man, a world figure in the field, was Chairman of the management group which, out of sheer incompetence as much as anything else, was sacking me. At Christmas, he and his wife sent a Christmas card signed 'with love' – it was incomprehensible. I had some reputation, had contributed substantially to the reputation of the Institute. Perhaps that was the trouble. But there it was – I had been sacked. One of the many difficult things about it was that people had difficulty believing it. One or two said, 'But you *are* the Institute!' 'Surely you mean you've retired,' said others. I had to insist – no, I had been sacked.

At the time all this happened, I was involved on behalf of the Institute in a consortium that was making a second attempt at applying to the European Commission for a research grant (the one with the creative accounting). The deadline was January 1990, and it was agreed that I should stay on the books till January, but only for the purpose of working on this application. It was lucky that we didn't get the grant; I don't know how we would have handled it. But so it came that I was in a hotel bedroom in Aachen in November, still representing the Institute, to see on television the amazing scenes of the

Berlin wall coming down and the dignified and moving proceedings in the Bonn Parliament, and to watch and listen to the wonderful spontaneous speech made there by the German Foreign Minister, Dietrich Genscher. It was also that night in that hotel bedroom that the force of what had happened hit me with some kind of delayed shock. As always, emotional turmoil took physical form. I felt very ill, but knew myself well enough to realise that it was likely to be psychosomatic.

Some three-and-a-half years later I received an invitation to a Tavistock Lecture given by Nancy Seear. When the time came I found I couldn't bring myself to go. There was so much that was unresolved between the Institute and me that I didn't know how to deal with a social occasion, and thought that members of the Institute, too, would find it difficult and embarrassing. I wrote a letter, saying that I wanted to make one more attempt at working through. I had made several attempts before I left, but there had never been any response and I had said that things which are not worked through hang around. This had proved to be the case. I set out my picture – now more complete – of what had happened, and asked if they could now find it possible to make an apology: 'I don't want reinstatement, I don't want compensation, I don't want lawsuits. What I need is psychological closure, and I believe you need it too ...'

The response said everything except that they had made a mistake: they all regretted that I was left feeling aggrieved; it was clear in retrospect that the management committee of the time had been very clumsy in its handling of the situation and had caused me avoidable distress; their clumsiness was compounded by legal advice about the possible consequences of further extending the precautionary notice, to which they had responded by acting legalistically; they deeply regretted that the way they had acted had caused me so much pain; they placed a high value on the work I had done on behalf of the Institute; and they hoped that we could rebuild a positive relationship.

Talking with another former member of the Institute, I wondered why it was that such storms had blown up around me. The answer was simple and surprising: 'It's because you stayed. You felt a commitment to the Institute's original values that made you stay. All the other people who couldn't bear it left.'

BOOK FOUR

My mother used to say, '*Erstens kommt es anders, zweitens als man denkt.*' (First of all it will be different, secondly from what you expect). It doesn't translate well, but it is apt. At a time when I thought my life was settled, there had been a big shock. But there were two more big surprises to come, and they were of a different order. I can recommend old age – if you live long enough before you actually fall apart, there is a chance for some earlier gaps to be filled, for a little confidence to finally get a foothold, for life to deal a few more cards, as if it needed a chance to make up for earlier shortcomings; perhaps for surviving to be finally expiated. Because, frankly, since I passed sixty-three I've been having a ball.

The Bayswater Institute

The Bayswater Institute was born over a pot of Earl Grey tea in the Waldorf Hotel in London. It was some months after I had left the Tavistock Institute, and I was working freelance. I had reached pension age; one day's consulting fee per week doubled my pension, and I had never had so much income, or so much free time, in my life. But I am not by nature a freelance consultant. I am very institutional, and a large part of me is a researcher. Research is an institutional, not a freelance, activity.

John Marks had been Chairman of Trebor Sharp, the confectionary company. It was a family firm, which in 1988 had been sold to Cadburys. As a result the family had money, and John had put a large sum into a venture that was beginning to go wrong. During my time in the Tavistock I had worked with Trebor on their new factory in Colchester, and now John got in touch because he wanted to talk about the problem he was experiencing. I didn't have an office, and thought I should not see a client at home. John didn't want to talk in his office, because that was where the problem was. As we pondered about this on the phone, I asked, 'Could we meet for a cup of tea somewhere?'

'Good idea!' said John, 'What about the Waldorf?'

The Waldorf Hotel is not the first place I think of when I wonder where to meet someone for a cup of tea. But we got into the habit of meeting there about once a month, John talking about his situation and me talking about mine. I discovered later that he carefully arranged these meetings on days when the Waldorf did not have tea dances.

Long before I left the Tavi I had sometimes thought about starting a new institute, to work with problems of organisation, making use of the social sciences in the broadest sense. At a conference in Toronto in 1981 I had talked about this with Professor Federico Butera, who had founded the IRSO (Istituto di ricerca intervento sui sistemi organizzativi) in Italy. 'Trouble is,' he had said, 'now you think about ideas and work. If you start a new institute, you will think about furniture and tax.' How right he turned out to be!

190

John Marks now made setting up the new institute possible, because – still over tea at the Waldorf – he offered some start-up money. Having had his fingers burned he was never going to put a lot of money into something again, but he offered £20,000 a year for two years. I said that something that was not viable within two years should probably close down anyway, and on that basis we started.

There were other people involved: Harold Bridger was very disenchanted with the Tavistock Institute; he and I had made some attempts to move out together. Now he supported the embryonic new institute with enthusiasm. Penny Jones was another former Tavistock colleague, who had become Director of the Peper Harow Therapeutic Community. She, like me, lived in Bayswater and we had talked of perhaps starting an institute together. Eventually her life took a different direction, but in the meantime she, Harold and I formed a kind of planning group. Harold, who as a psycho-analyst had made a specialty of working with family firms, had worked over a number of years with John and his family. I am sure that John used to go and see him sometimes for reassurance – 'Is she all right?'

Marie Jahoda and Brian Shackel were friends with whom I always dis-cussed everything. They were both world figures in their own fields and, although they and their fields were very different from each other – she was an eminent social psychologist and professor at Sussex University, and he an ergonomist who had founded the HUSAT Research Centre in Lough-borough – they shared my sense of how important it was to make use of the social sciences in the practical world of organisations. Together with John Marks they became the Institute's founding trustees. They were soon fol-lowed by Sylvia Shimmin, an occupational psychologist who had founded the Department of Behaviour in Organisations in Lancaster University, and who shared the same view. Marie Jahoda later became the Institute's President.

Penny located offices in the basement of No. 9 Orme Court, a building belonging to Spike Milligan and Eric Sykes, which added some theatrical spice to the Institute's working life. Eric Sykes still had his office there, and we would sometimes run into each other. He was almost blind, but managed it so well that one couldn't be sure what he saw and what he didn't. When I said hello, and added an explanatory, 'It's the little one from downstairs,' he would answer, 'I know that!'

Harold gave the new institute his Working Conference to run. We called it the 'Harold Bridger Working Conference', and at first he directed it. That was why he could not become a trustee – you can't pay trustees for work. But he attended trustee meetings, in the role of consultant. Then I directed the Conference for some years, and then he said, 'It's about time you called this the "Bayswater Working Conference" '; now Derek Raffaelli directs it. Harold also cajoled Martin Wright, a former finance officer of the Tavistock Institute, into becoming our Company Secretary.

We recruited a part-time secretary, who brought with her a second-hand computer from her previous employer. She and I bought furniture and there was a serious discussion about whether it would be irresponsible to buy more than one waste paper basket (shades of Federico!); and I designed some stationery. Nowadays I behave like an old-world housewife, complaining to profligate younger spenders that we don't need two photocopiers and three printers.

We wanted it to be non-profit and I was introduced to a wonderful charity lawyer, Fiona Middleton, who set us up. She explained that the most economical way to start a new company is to buy an already existing one off the shelf and change its name. We did that, but discovered that to call an organisation an 'Institute' requires strong and prestigious academic references, as well as references from public sector clients – the Department of Health, for instance, not a mere hospital. Organising that takes time; we started work in October 1990, but did not formally become an Institute until August 1992; then we got recognition as an independent research institute from the ESRC.

Just before leaving the Tavistock I had been approached by a consultant physician from Greenwich District Hospital. He had been on Harold's Working Conference and wanted to talk with someone about hospital organisation. Harold told him to talk to me, and we had had some exploratory sessions. There were several possibilities: one of them was through a project they were just beginning, of implementing a large, comprehensive Hospital Information Support System, for which they had won funding from the National Health Service, and that was the one we picked. From my point of view sociotechnical work was less unfamiliar than just launching into the organisational problems of a hospital. I knew nothing about hospitals, all my experience until then had been in industry and banking. From his point of view, the information system (or HISS – one was moving into a world of acronyms which I still find unnatural) was going to be pervasive and would lead into all aspects of hospital organisation. With hindsight I think the real reason was that he was able to squeeze a budget for consultancy out of the HISS project, whereas it would have been difficult to find the money anywhere else. In any case that was the beginning of many years of consultancy and research in hospitals, and later in the broader NHS.

That first programme, with Greenwich District Hospital, was the first work of the Institute, and lasted four years. One of the activities it involved was a study tracking patients through the hospital before, and again after, the introduction of the Information Support System. For this we gave a contract to Sheila Scott, so now we had to work out a model for contracting work. The model got refined later, when Alan Dale wanted us to provide a base for a project he was doing with the new British Library, and for which he needed some professional feedback and discussion. It worked very well, and the condition that such projects had to be congruent with our mission of making use of the social sciences and had to be linked by professional review was well understood.

Sheila was originally a research sociologist who had also trained as a child psychotherapist. That includes training in infant observation, and she added observation to the core skills of the Institute. A second set of projects came from Lucas Engineering, funded by the DTI and involving action research in a motor components factory in Coventry. For this we recruited our first young professional colleague, Joanna Buckingham. The secretary said, 'We're going to have to have payslips,' and designed one. I began to feel as if I was running ICI – the paraphernalia is not all that different.

The selection process for Joanna had included asking the finalist candidates to present a piece of work to each other and discuss it with the group. At the end of the day they said, 'Never mind about the job, can we do this again?' And we did, twice. Some time later John Marks came into the office and said, 'I was sitting next to the Duke of Edinburgh at lunch yesterday [a splendid opening line!], and he was worried about finding a new director for the World Wildlife Fund. So I said he ought to use the Bayswater Institute.' I couldn't persuade him that we were not actually experts in recruitment, and spent two days drafting a proposal, which was duly delivered at Buckingham Palace. The only outcome was that we have a file marked HRH. I don't know whether HRH has a file marked Bayswater Institute.

Marie Jahoda came up once a week from Sussex to give Joanna tutorials. Since trustees cannot be paid for work we took her out to lunch, eating our way systematically down the length of Queensway at a different restaurant every week.

In 1993 I had a bout of ill health and was out of action for five months. Sheila and Joanna went on working at Greenwich and Coventry, Harold went on preparing for the next Working Conference, the trustees went on meeting, the books went on being balanced. That was when I realised that this might perhaps be not just Lisl's hobby, but an institution.

I still wanted to try the idea of accompanying a technical development and making social science contributions to it along the way. The European Commission's project officer had liked it, and when I met him by chance at some event he undertook to try to facilitate another attempt. This time it worked, and that became the second major piece of work for the Institute, involving companies in the construction industry in Finland, Germany and the UK.

In 1995 Harold died. With two of his children and some colleagues who were his close friends I set up a planning group to organise a memorial event. The Tavistock Institute had at that time, for the first time, a director in Phil Swann. I invited him to join this group, and he said he really enjoyed the collaboration. It seemed important that he and I should be seen to be doing this together and should, literally, be on a platform together to honour Harold. Afterwards Phil developed a habit of dropping in at the Bayswater Institute from time to time for a drink and a chat. I think he liked to talk with someone who knew the Tavistock but was not part of it. In turn, he invited me to take part in some work discussions in the Tavistock Institute.

For my seventieth birthday in 1998, John Marks had the Dvorsky sheet music which I had brought with me from Karlsbad orchestrated and turned into a CD.

In 2001 I stepped down from being director, to be followed by Ken Eason and later by Simon Bell and Willy Coupar.

And now, suddenly, we are twenty years old. We are low profile, which sometimes irritates John, who would like us to save the world more quickly, but we do interesting and useful work and we have a growing reputation. Before all this happened I had, as I have said, been thinking about retiring and started to take classes in music and playwriting. That is what the suddenness of being sacked really did – it cut off this process of gradual retirement and trying out something different.

But the Bayswater Institute has been a full-time job, for twenty years. I don't know where the time has gone, but it has been the most satisfying and creative phase of my life. That is the first of the two surprises. Institution building is a bit like cooking – a bit more of this, a bit less of that; now stir, now let it simmer; separate, amalgamate, shape, mix. Although I have stopped being director I am still taking part in the work. I don't know what I was expecting, but here we are, a recognised Institute with a good reputation, debating about whether to celebrate our anniversary. I am cautious about that – I have taken part in anniversary celebrations of two other institutes, one a fiftieth and one a thirtieth, and both collapsed soon afterwards. Among the celebrations we were considering was doing something in the Czech Republic. Because there was another surprise still to come.

The Czech Republic

When the Velvet Revolution came in Czechoslovakia at the end of 1989, I sat in front of the television set in tears. I envied everyone who had some links remaining and a reason for visiting. In particular I remember my painful envy of Tomas Bata, the shoe manufacturer who had taken the first available plane from Canada where he had settled and was being greeted at Prague airport with flowers, saying into the camera, also with tears streaming down his face, 'Now we will build up a shoe industry in Czechoslovakia.'

Czechs kept writing in the press and saying on television that they needed help and advice. But there seemed to be no way of getting an offer heard. I couldn't afford just to take off and go, like Tomas Bata, and would not have known what to do anyway, since I had no contacts; I could not bear just to be a tourist. I wrote to the office of the Občanství Forum, the dissident organisation that was now forming an interim government and whose members were making all these appeals. After a long time there was a reply saying that offers of help were being coordinated by Mrs Havlová, the President's sister-in-law. I wrote a very carefully constructed letter to her, and received an empty, routine, cyclostyled thank you. I mobilised whatever friends I could, to try and establish contacts. One of them introduced me to a journalist who had knowledge of the situation, and he in turn suggested a woman journalist in Prague for me to visit. Just as this was about to happen, she was made ambassador to the United States and left for Washington. Then in April I heard about a management conference being organised in Prague for October. Going to conferences was something I knew how to do: it was late to be offering a paper, so I would have to phone the organiser. The act of picking up a phone and simply dialling Prague was something completely outside my power to imagine. It took three days to come to terms with the idea and muster the courage to do it.

The iron curtain had proved to be a very useful defence. It served to put all that part of my life out of reach, so that I could get on with living on this side of it. Of course, it was not in fact as iron as all that for ordinary citizens.

195

It would have been perfectly possible to visit Czechoslovakia in the intervening years, but I never did.

With the vanishing of the iron curtain there was no longer any defence. But I didn't know where to start. The first contact I managed to get was with a young woman sociology lecturer from Bratislava, who was in England on a studentship. She came and stayed with me, and invited me to come and stay with her in Bratislava. In London she wanted help in finding a birthday present for her ten-year-old daughter. I took her to Marks and Spencer, where she saw a dress that she liked. But they had it in red and they had it in blue, and the choice was too difficult. She was so unused to having choices that she simply could not manage it that time, and left the shop without the dress.

Iveta got me invited to give some lectures in Bratislava, and from this beginning other invitations could be engineered, in Brno and Prague. I didn't want the contact to be academic, I desperately wanted to do something more practical, but a lecture tour was the easiest to arrange. Roger and Sarah Broad, who knew me well, realised that I would not be able to take this tremendous step on my own, and offered to come with me. We planned to visit Karlsbad first, then Prague, then to drive through the country until they delivered me in Bratislava for the lecture tour, which would end with the conference and some appointments in Prague.

In the meantime I had seen a travel agency tour advertised, which offered three days in Prague and five in Karlsbad, now called by its Czech name Karlovy Vary. It seemed tailor-made for my aunt Trude and me, and I offered to take her. She was very hesitant at first but finally agreed. So I went twice that summer and autumn, the first time with Trude; being out of regular work had its advantages.

There are advantages in an organised tour, too. It saves hassles about booking and luggage, and it helps to contain the experience. There was an elderly father with his daughter on the same trip, on a similar mission of rediscovery. I think every plane-load around that time had its quota of émigrés coming back, only just managing to stop themselves from kissing the ground. By three years later I was grumbling about the way they handled luggage at Prague airport, like anyone else. Had it come to this, all that longing, all that nostalgia? Was it like romantic love, fuelled by absence and the being out of reach?

Trude was well over eighty, and I worried about her. But she coped well. We were sitting on a bench at the bottom of Wenceslas Square when she suddenly turned to a young woman on her other side, and said, 'They've got the wrong name up over that shop over there!' The young woman fled.

Arriving in Karlovy Vary was momentous: the tantalising familiarity of buildings and configuration of trees, light and shadow, alongside the absence of familiar people. I stood on one of the little bridges over the Tepl, the tears pouring down my face. It was the same when I walked round the park at the Richmond Hotel. The erstwhile manicured lawns and flowerbeds were neglected, but the rough, unkempt plants and pathways had their own beauty. I didn't dare go into the building, which was now functioning more as a sanatorium than a hotel. After the war it had been used for Russian officers convalescing from war wounds, and this medical component had continued. So it didn't feature in travel agents' lists of hotels, and I didn't think one could go in. Other Karlsbad friends who began to go back for visits around that time were not so inhibited and talked of having gone in quite normally to have a cup of coffee.

We went to the Jewish cemetery, where both my grandfathers are buried. Grandfather Emil Robitschek's grave was where it had been, the tombstone a little crooked and overgrown. But grandfather Wilhelm Klein's grave had been moved, I was quite sure. Not the grave, perhaps, but certainly the stone, which used to be on the right of the entrance and is now quite a long way down on the left.

Trude wanted to visit Neusattl, and we hired a taxi. When we got there, she at first couldn't get her bearings. She didn't recognise what she was seeing, and began to be distressed. The taxi driver wanted to be helpful and asked what her name had been before she married. Then he went over to a group of men working on a building site on the other side of the road, to enquire. 'Oh, yes,' said one immediately, 'it's round that corner. It's the house with a telephone kiosk outside it.' We walked round the corner and Trude gave a little yelp. It was the right house. I didn't have my wits about me enough to enquire how that man could possibly have known. True, her father had been the village doctor, but he had died sixty years before and his widow had moved away soon after.

Karlovy Vary has a beautiful little rococo-style theatre, and we wanted to go there. But what they were showing was Agatha Christie's *The Mouse Trap*. In Czech. Our nostalgia did not extend to wanting to see a whodunnit we had managed to avoid for years in London, and in a language we didn't understand well enough to find out who did it anyway.

In Bratislava I stayed with Iveta and her family. One afternoon I came back to the house to find her puzzling over the instructions to Monopoly. She had brought a travel set of the game for her daughter, but the instructions are complicated. I spent the evening teaching them how to play, not at all sure that I was doing the right thing. But it was certainly appreciated. The little girl, in particular, became an instant capitalist. In high excitement she would shout, 'It is mine! It is mine! You must pay me rent!' whenever anyone landed on her property. No gradual dawning or transition, it was instantaneous.

Iveta's husband worked in radio and had a satirical show that was recorded live on Wednesdays, then edited, and then broadcast on Saturdays. So one Wednesday afternoon I attended the making of this programme, and for the first time in over fifty years I listened to primitive anti-Semitic jokes about 'people with long noses'. They were cut from what was later sent out, but they had been in the original material.

It was only possible for both parents to work because Iveta's mother helped with the housekeeping. Food was not exactly in short supply, but distribution was difficult and gathering together enough food took much time. One day there would be news that cauliflowers had been delivered, so people had to drop whatever they were doing and queue for cauliflowers. Another day it would be eggs. Iveta's mother did this food gathering and helped in many other ways. At Christmas she would bake the traditional cakes and sweetmeats for the family. But she couldn't do it at home, in her own kitchen, and take them to the young people's house. She had to do the baking in their house, because her son-in-law wanted to have the smell of baking in his house at Christmas. I made a mental review of my friends and their in-laws, and wondered how this would go down.

I gradually discovered a great separation between academic and practical life, not specifically Czech, more Central European, so the talks and seminars I gave on using research knowledge for practical life were very apposite. Academics I met were hungry for contact and travel, and had already travelled much. One, who had been to Canada, China, Holland, England, seemed quite overwhelmed by the possibilities that were opening up; I had a distinct impression of indigestion brought on by so much food so quickly.

In Prague I got the same feeling from the people I met, of too many offers on the table, no way of discriminating between them, and exhaustion. I had the opportunity of doing a seminar in the Ministry of Labour, and a meeting with the Deputy Minister. Her own background was sociology, and she was most courteous and friendly, even though she was visibly tired and was due to fly to Vietnam the following day, for the day. For the day?? Yes. There were many Vietnamese guest workers in Czechoslovakia. With the change to a market economy there was expected to be unemployment, and she had to negotiate for these guest workers to return home. And she couldn't be spared for more than a day.

I also had an introduction to the deputy rector of the Economic High

School in Prague. He was only able to see me because a trip to Japan had been cancelled: his boss, the Minister, had discovered that he was planning to go, and had decided to go himself instead. Looking at his weary face I thought it was probably a blessing, but he clearly didn't think so.

In his office were a desk and a table, and both were piled high with business cards from visiting academics and consultants. He explained what the School was doing: to their usual academic degrees they were about to add a PhD in management, and short courses for managers. For these they would use the various offers they had had from abroad: there was the Dutch Project, the French Project, the Canadian Project, the British Project ... I asked him to explain the British project, for example, and he reeled off about ten British universities, colleges and technical colleges which were to be involved. He was quite happy to add me to this list, but I didn't want to be part of such a circus, which seemed doomed to fail. A British civil servant whom I got to know, on loan from the British government to the Czech Ministry of Labour, confirmed my view, saying that since research and educational funds were short in the West, Eastern Europe was full of Western academics trying to get a slice of the Know-How Fund. The jaded appetites of academics and consultants had found something new to feed on.

I learned later that the students of these 'projects' were very dissatisfied and the programme was abandoned, making way for something more organic and integrated. But at the time I gradually realised that for these over-stretched and exhausted people an offer of help was merely another burden to cope with. I also realised – and it was a painful realisation – that the interval from 1938 to 1991 had been just too long. I was in a very narrow age-band of people who were both old enough to remember how it had been before, and young enough to want to do something to help now. Most people were too young to know what it was that might be regained. There were pictures of President Masaryk on walls and lamp-posts, but people didn't actually know what he had been about. When I complained about this to one of my new friends, he explained that recent Czech history had not been taught in schools. That meshes with a strange experience in Karlovy Vary. On that first visit I went to look at the local museum. It was well designed and interesting, but the period between 1918 and 1938 was blank. Nothing.

I came back to London and got on with developing the Bayswater Institute. It felt almost like being exiled all over again; if you live long enough to make comparisons, you realise that there is not just one exile, there are many. The one simply provides the standard.

But all was not over. There is an unexpected coda to all this, almost too neat a rounding off. When you get to be over sixty, you have a fairly settled idea of what your life is about. Mine had important things missing from it, and had involved much difficulty and a crushing setback. But I knew what I was about and was comfortable with that; I had wonderful friends, and I had re-established a basis for doing worthwhile and interesting work that expressed what I was about, in an organisation that was, if less high profile than before, good and solid as a base. Its reputation was growing, its clients liked us, its trustees were supportive and creative, and its working colleagues had integrity and were kinder and more generous and gentle than I had been used to.

And then something happened that was totally out of kilter with all that and which produced, for the next three years, a bizarre mix of the normal and the ... well ... bizarre. I became the owner of the Richmond Hotel. That was the third of the surprises.

Karlovy Vary

It began with letters from my cousin Walter in New York and from family friends, suggesting I should try to get restitution of Luis's property. I was at first reluctant: I still felt very Czech, I didn't want their money. I was financially comfortable; I had no children. But then people sent some newspaper cuttings about a Swiss hotel consortium that was proposing to revive the tourist trade in Karlovy Vary, with the Richmond as their 'flag-ship'. That made me feel different – I didn't mind the Czechs having it, but I didn't see why a Swiss hotel consortium should have it without a fight. I didn't realise until much later that I had completely misunderstood the government's wishes and intentions. They didn't want property at that time, they wanted it privatised as quickly as possible. The only issue was who would achieve privatisation, not whether it should happen.

I thought long and hard about the decision. In the nature of my psyche, I saw it in terms of whether I would feel worse if I tried and failed or if I didn't try. Almost as a matter of therapy, I decided that I would feel worse if I didn't try. That such a claim could succeed did not for one moment occur to me.

I found a lawyer in Prague, Pavel Hrdina. In his will Luis had left me a 30% share in his property, with four other legatees. I was in touch with two of them, and asked if they wanted to join in. One was by then in an old people's home and said no. She died in 1992. The second was John Mait-land-Gordon, the English – or rather Scottish – friend who had lent Fanni and Luis his flat while he was in the army. He said yes, but Dr Hrdina said he would not be eligible as he was British, and claimants had to be Czech. Probably the best thing about this whole process for me was discovering that I had never lost my Czech nationality. I would have shared any proceeds with John but he also died, in 1994. I didn't know about the other two; neither of them was Czech.

I was still concerned not just to be grabbing money. What I still wanted was to find a way to do some work over there. So my instructions to Dr Hrdina were that I was prepared to give up any rights I might have, in return for conference facilities in the Richmond. The opportunity to hold a conference there once a year would have met my values. He thought I was batty, but that is what he requested for me. In the summer of 1993 there was a court hearing, and this request was turned down. Dr Hrdina attended and said he thought the real reason was that there were still a number of what he called 'old-fashioned Communists' on the board of the state company running the hotel, who simply didn't want privatisation to happen. If my request had been granted, the way would have been clear for privatisation; as long as my claim was unresolved they kept their jobs. I now think there is another possibility: the state wanted to privatise – that is, to sell. This would have been more difficult with my conditions attached.

But then all this went out of my head, because in the summer of 1993 I found I had endometrial cancer. I had a hysterectomy, followed by radiotherapy, and during this time Dr Hrdina put in a revised claim, for 30% of the property. I cannot for the life of me remember whether I agreed to this; he had power of attorney, anyway.

In February 1994 this claim was also turned down. I felt that honour had been served. In terms of my own psychology this was a good result: I had tried and failed, what more could anyone ask?

So I said to the solicitor, let's forget it. But he said 'No, no! Now we have to appeal. And we have to challenge the way the law is being administered, it is very inconsistent. And anyway, there is new legislation coming through which makes it easier. And while we're about it, let's be cheeky and try for 100%, since no other claims have been lodged by the due date.'

I didn't know what to do, so I did nothing and just let it drift. Since it was clear by then that the other legatees had not come forward, or would be eligible if they did, the solicitor put in two variants, for 30% as in the will, and for 100%. Then in May he got in touch, saying that there was a Belgian businessman who very much wanted to talk to me. He had fallen in love with the Richmond and terribly wanted to buy it. Dr Hrdina had not given him my telephone number but would give me his, if I wanted to respond. And so began a truly bizarre episode in what was already becoming a pretty bizarre phase of my life.

Mr Kaszirer was a diamond merchant who lived in Antwerp. When I phoned he was most enthusiastic, very much wanted to talk to me, very sorry that he couldn't come to London that weekend but he had to go to Israel on Sunday, to Prague on Tuesday and to New York on Thursday. In London it was the Bank Holiday weekend and I had no particular plans, so I said I could come and see him if he wanted. 'Wonderful! We will arrange the plane ticket, my driver will meet you at Brussels airport and drive you to Antwerp. And afterwards he will bring you back to the airport.' I was still not fully fit after the radiotherapy; I said that I hadn't been well and could not manage there and back on the same day. Fine, he said, we will arrange a hotel for you.

So I went to Antwerp, to the narrow, twisted streets of the diamond quarter, and met this old gentleman in his cramped, littered office, his son, his business manager and his English son-in-law. One of his daughters had married an English rabbi, and Jeremy Rosen and I were to become friends. He had children in England from his first marriage, and he came to London to see them. On those occasions I was sometimes invited to a Sabbath meal, which was awkward because I was not familiar with the rituals. The first time I played table-tennis with his ten-year-old son I was quite out of practice and was beaten ignominiously. He was very gentlemanly about it, though, calling out frequently, 'Oh, good shot!' The next time we played I was a bit more in practice. He still beat me, but not quite so easily, and I heard him mutter, 'Just shows, you can't judge a book by its covers.'

Mr Kaszirer was in his seventies and immensely wealthy. His son now more or less ran the diamond business, and Mr Kaszirer himself had time and huge energy left for what he called 'projects'. There was one in New York (something to do with real estate), one in Israel, and Karlovy Vary. Apparently his wife, who had had liver disease, had been there several times, had felt well there and liked the place, and said he ought to put money into it because it was so run down. Then in November she had died, so now it was a kind of mission for him. Not just hotels, he wanted to redevelop the whole town, build up tourism, extend the airport, develop the golf course and other sporting facilities, already had a contract to develop the casino, was buying a plot of land opposite the Richmond, was in frequent contact with the town's mayor – 'She was sitting right there in that chair, where you are sitting now' – had hired the town's former engineer as a consultant. And he wanted the Richmond, badly. So he wanted to help me get it, so that he could then buy it from me. Like many things I at first did not understand this, thinking that if I didn't get it he could buy it from the state. I think the issue may have been speed and simplicity.

This whole scene was so different from anything I had experienced before, and I was so astonished by it, that I treated it more as theatre than as real life. That was a mistake. Perhaps I was not used to responding to a fast-changing situation as someone who is part of it and not an observer. Also, I didn't remotely think the claim could succeed, especially after two rejections. Anyway, I did the second most stupid thing I have ever done in my life and signed a piece of paper saying that, if I got the Richmond, I would give Mr Kaszirer first refusal to buy it. Then he left for the airport, leaving his son-in-law to play host to me, and shouting abuse which could be heard all over the office about some family feud from his mobile phone all the way to Brussels; the whole episode had taken less than twenty minutes.

Jeremy Rosen took me into the next office and asked, 'Would you like to see some diamonds?' Of course I would. So he went to a safe, placed himself carefully between me and it like they do in the movies, and worked the combination. I don't think it was that he didn't trust me, it was just automatic. In the safe were many shelves, and on each shelf were trays with rows of small brown envelopes. He took one out, showed me the diamonds in it, and explained how to detect a flaw. The value of the stone, it seems, depends on a combination of its weight and purity. Having seen how tiny a flaw was, I said, 'To be honest, I don't see what difference it makes.' He answered, 'To be honest, neither do I.' He looked thoughtfully at the safe and said, 'I suppose there's about twenty-five million dollars' worth in there.'

'And how many safes do you have?'

'Five'.

He took me for a short drive round Antwerp, which I had not seen before, and then he brought me to my hotel. By that time I was very tired, and slept for a couple of hours. Then I had time to spare, and wondered what Belgian television had to offer. I switched on, and it was a little while before I realised that I was watching pornography. You can't be sure these days. Only then did I see the notice on the wall, which said that the first three channels were pay television. My God, this was going on my bill, and my bill was going to Mr Kaszirer! I raced down the stairs to the reception desk and said, 'I've just realised that I have been watching pornography. Please don't put it on my bill, I'll pay cash!' But it hadn't registered yet, apparently you get the first few minutes free.

In a letter to Walter that summer I said:

The Czechs, I think, have never seen money like this, or even maybe energy like this, and anyway I think it possible that his rather oriental methods of doing things are more suited to the current Czech culture than my very British ones, or indeed the solicitor's, who was trained in Germany.

He says things like 'I don't bother with underlings, I go straight to the Minister, the Minister is my friend, we are like brothers, I will introduce you to him if you like.' In June he said with glee, 'Now we've got Karlsbad, now we go and get Marienbad!', which makes me think his wife is serving as something of a rationalisation ...

Claims had to be put in anew by the beginning of July, and during the summer rumours began to circulate. Not being on the spot I didn't really understand what was happening; if I had been there I would probably not have understood it either. It was just that Pavel Hrdina said that he was suddenly being taken seriously and received with respect. And there was an article in the local paper about 'the mysterious owner, a world-famous work-sociologist, whom nobody ever gets to see'.

Because of these rumours I had a conversation with Mr Kaszirer about what we would do if the restitution did come about. For instance, what kind of guarantees would be given to the staff? 'They all have to go. They are no good,' was his answer. That was the first indication I had that all was not well here, and that I might have made a bad mistake. Not just the harshness, but the arbitrary and global judgement. He knew nothing about the staff.

At the end of September came the decision: the restitution was granted, the state company conceded my rights – 100%, not 30%. There still had to be a ratification process, with a contract specifying exactly what was to be handed over, but from some date in November I would be the owner of the Richmond hotel.

The various hotels and spa facilities in Karlovy Vary were run by two state companies, devolved down from the State Spa Organisation, which came under the Ministry of Health. One of them operated all the hotels and facilities at the southern end of the town, including the Richmond, and was charged with the task of privatising them. The Richmond was almost the last, apart from a building called Bath VI, which was to be a complicating factor during the next three years. The director of the company was Ing Mikeš, a somewhat dour and formal but totally straight and honourable civil servant. Our relationship started as one of mutual respect rather than anything warmer, but over time he relaxed and softened, and by 1997 we were sharing jokes, to widespread applause. (When I visited Karlovy Vary in 2000, the problem of Bath VI had still not been solved: Ing Mikeš and I hatched a plot about turning it into a lucrative brothel.) He was in turn responsible to the Ministry of Health. Running the hotel itself was Věra Koubská; she was not a manager in the Western sense, more an administrator, because she had to refer major decisions upwards to Ing Mikeš. By training she was a civil engineer. The hotel had not been run as an individual entity, but as part of the group and apparently did not have separate accounts. Surpluses were siphoned off to wherever in the group they were needed; on the other hand, the money for essential investments was also found centrally.

The Richmond was run at a modest standard, but had a loyal clientele.

The first time I went there after the restitution, there was a party for an old Austrian lady in her eighties who was celebrating her fiftieth visit. This lady was quite a character: I was, of course, the subject of much speculation and gossip among the guests. The first time she spotted me she came up, and in a ferocious Austrian accent, and without the slightest inhibition, announced, *'Gnä Frau, Sie schaffen's net. Sie san zu alt'*. *'Gnä Frau'* is the colloquial abbreviation of *'gnädige Frau'*, a rather old-fashioned and courtly way of saying 'Madame'. What she was saying was, 'Madame, you can't do it. You're too old'. Through all the ups and downs of the next two-and-a-half years, with all the possibilities and variations that were considered, I remembered her verdict and knew she was right.

That first visit in my new role was in October 1994. Roger and Sarah came with me, I felt the need for support. A few days before the trip, I was having dinner in a restaurant with a friend when I started to feel chest pains. After a while I couldn't ignore them, and asked Johnny to take me to the A&E department of St. Mary's Hospital. It turned out to be nothing, and as I was waiting for the formalities to be completed before going home, I apologised to the registrar for wasting their time. 'It's probably stress,' I said, 'I've just become a millionaire.'

He didn't bat an eyelid. Slowly he said, 'Well, that's unusual.'

We were met at the airport by Dr Dolina, the senior of the two resident doctors, the 'Primarius'. He put Roger and Sarah in the back of his car and me in the front, and instantly began to complain about his woman colleague, Dr Sárova. The drive from Prague to Karlovy Vary takes two hours, and by the time we got there I had had good practice in staying out of internal staff politics. In fact, of all the staff, these two doctors were the only ones I came to dislike. In due course their rivalry extended to me: they practically fought over my body, it would have been a coup to get me into their hands – literally – as a patient. Many months later I eventually managed to fend off Dr Dolina. We were sitting round the lunch table with about a dozen people, and he was once again insisting on what he could do for me as a patient. I decided this had to be dealt with. I asked, quite loudly, if it was true that his job before coming to the Richmond had been as head of a military hospital. Yes, it was. Then he would not have encountered many cases of cancer of the uterus? I never managed to put a stop to Dr Sárova's efforts, even in the middle of management meetings, to capture me as a patient.

But back to that first visit. It was comforting in such a strange situation to have old friends with me. Sarah and Roger and I met for meals, and in between they did tourist-type things while I went through a series of meetings.

206

Friday was spent in a meeting with the management and Ing Mikeš. I think that some people in the state company had been preparing a privatisation arrangement. In view of this now being frustrated, I was surprised by the great warmth and excitement with which I was welcomed. It was very emotional and moving. It may be that they realised that they would have been taking on more than they could handle. Certainly they seemed to be looking to me as a kind of fairy godmother who would solve things for them and lead them. In return, they said, they would look after me when I got too old.

I don't have much Czech, although more surfaced from early schooling than I realised I had. I do have a good pronunciation, which can be a problem because it leads people to expect more than I can actually produce. But I did manage to start speaking in Czech and only lapse into German after one or two sentences, which showed that I was trying. After that, someone had to translate for me. I said that I could make no promises; this whole thing had only happened to me three weeks before, and one cannot make important plans in such a short time. I told them about the history of the hotel, the family, my own childhood in the place and my wish to stay linked with it if possible. Everyone knew of Mr Kaszirer's interest. His wife had stayed there last year, they had liked her, but they were afraid of his intentions. I didn't mention the paper I had signed, which was beginning to worry me, though it is possible that they knew about it. (In my solicitor it engendered a conviction that I shouldn't be allowed out on my own. Walter, too, who really didn't want to get involved in any of this, only ever had one piece of advice to give, and he gave it consistently: 'Don't sign anything!')

There was much to learn, and I had to learn fast: the building was 'protected', the equivalent of a listed building in England. However, it was thought that vandalous developers could get round that with bribes, and there was much anxiety about that. There were 66 rooms with 101 beds. Some rooms had no bath or WC, which is not acceptable to modern tourists. I learned later that these were the rooms reserved in pre-war days for the servants that guests brought with them! Now these poorer-quality rooms generally went to patients sent by the Czech National Insurance, which paid uneconomic prices. Foreigners and Czech private patients paid more and subsidised the others, but they still paid less than they would in, say, Baden-Baden, which was one factor that gave us the edge. Prices needed to be raised, but not beyond the point where this advantage was lost or beyond which the present clientele, which was very loyal and kept coming back, was discouraged. Capital was needed for eighteen new bathrooms. And there was a debate about whether the contract with the National Insurance Company was worth having. Politically yes, economically no.

Second, the central heating needed to be replaced, as did the ancient wiring.

And the other major immediate problem was that from some date in November I would own the grounds and the building but not the contents; it was obviously impossible to ascertain whether anything movable had belonged to and was taken away from Alois Klein. So I was expected to buy the inventory, which in the long run might not be what one wanted anyway.

There had been some expressions of interest from potential buyers. All of us undertook to collect as many options and possibilities as possible and meet again in a month to look at them. I promised to make no decisions without at least discussing them fully first.

Towards the end of the meeting I asked half-jokingly if Ing Mikeš might not be prepared to lend me the inventory for a bit, and to my utter surprise he said well, not for more than six months. I considered that to be a considerable diplomatic coup. He also turned up on the following Monday, having tried to negotiate a more economic rate for National Insurance patients; the insurance company was willing to pay 15% more. This still did not cover the real cost, but there was important learning from it: the Chief Medical Officer had assured me absolutely that they would not be willing to pay any more at all. History had brought out a certain passivity in some of the people, and I was beginning to get the hang of which was which.

It was in everyone's interest to delay the actual handover until the end of the year. For me it would be a chance to get over the shock and think about strategy. For them it was a chance to close the books properly. And we were of the same mind that the main aim of any strategy was continuity – continuity of the business and continuity of employment for the staff. So we ended up agreeing to make a short lease from the time of the formal restitution to the end of the year, under which the company would continue to pay the running costs in exchange for paying no rent; and thinking that it might be best to continue such an arrangement for another three or six months. For that, Ing Mikeš would need to get the agreement of the Ministry of Health.

On Monday I met the trade union committee. The Chairman first took me through the collective agreement they were working under, which runs annually from 1st June. Then, again starting in Czech but collapsing into German, I said my piece about how this had all happened very suddenly; I would hope not to have to sell, but might not be able to manage it; if the worst came to the worst and anyone lost their jobs, I would increase by two months' wages the redundancy money that people get from the state; and I simply didn't know yet what was going to happen; I could only promise to keep them in the picture, they would know what was happening as soon as I did.

Then there was an awkward pause during which nobody knew what to say. I began to think I should suggest closing the meeting, when the Chairman said, 'Have you got any pictures of how it used to be?' I said yes, and went to my room to fetch them. The people were fascinated. I offered to have some copies made, and asked which ones they wanted. They found that difficult, in the end they said 'all of them'.

And then a lady stood up and began very formally: 'In the name of the trade union . . .', which frightened me badly. But: 'In the name of the trade union, we want to say that we like you very much. We would enjoy working with you and would like you to be the one who runs the Richmond; and we want to wish you well in your coming endeavours, however it turns out, because we trust you.' By that time I was in tears. And Ing Mikeš, who was present, found that he could produce a balance sheet for the Richmond, as distinct from the whole group, after all.

Two more things happened that day. First, I was taken to see the Imperial Hotel, which had been part of the group. It was in much better condition than the Richmond. I was told that, during socialist times, all the surpluses from the group were put into the Imperial. And there were large subsidies from Russia, from where many of the guests came. The maintenance engineer who took me up there pointed out that 'they've got one of our chandeliers!'

The young managers of the Imperial were flushed with success, very ambitious, and very interested in some kind of partnership arrangement with me. In terms of philosophy – Karlovy Vary has to be a spa, this end of town should retain its quiet wooded character and not become some kind of cross between Las Vegas and Disneyland – we were fully agreed.

I was also taken to see the town architect. I wanted to know if there was any kind of strategy about development. He was rather new in the job and talked of the Richmond as 'the pearl of Karlovy Vary'. But as for development strategy, there was none. I wrote to friends:

There are elections for mayor in November. I honestly believe that if I stood I would have a good chance. The ticket would be that I'm the only person around who neither gives nor takes bribes. People long for this and a hint was dropped that I should try. It's all right, don't worry, I won't!

Back in London the Bayswater Institute's Chairman, John Marks, was taking a great interest in all this. He lectured me about accepting the idea of having money, learning to spend it, treating myself to things I was not used to. Being wealthy requires training, and my training had all been in the other direction. Besides, from the point of view of money it was simply too late. There had been times in my life when an injection of money would have made a big difference, but not now. What would make a difference to my peace of mind was some kind of cushion for the Bayswater Institute from the economic stringency with which I had learned to live for so long. He changed tack. 'All right, then. But don't put money into the Institute, you don't know what will happen to that. Put it into something that can, if necessary, make grants to the Institute.' That seemed good advice, and I set about creating a charitable foundation, giving it Luis's name.

When Mr Kaszirer heard that there was to be a five-week gap between the restitution decision and the handover, he went berserk. He ranted and raved at me on the phone from Israel, screaming abuse, accusing my lawyer of taking bribes to make sure that I wouldn't get it, accusing Ing Mikeš of all kinds of corruption. It happened that John Marks was with me when this call came and he listened in astonishment as I stood, with the telephone held at arm's length, while this screaming poured from it. Somebody on the other end of the line seemed to be trying to calm him, but without success. I began to think I could not sell the Richmond to someone so irrational, no matter what foolish promise I had made.

Turbulent as these things were, they did not take up a lot of time, my job was still running the Bayswater Institute. Harold had said, 'You have to choose between your past and your life's work, you can't deal with both.' The trouble was, I couldn't give up either.

A weekend in Karlovy Vary

The next trip was in early December. There were contracts to clarify, and there were Christmas parties. The tradition in the hotel was to hold a rather formal reception for local business people and other dignitaries, and to hold a Christmas party for staff, after which the hotel closed for several weeks for cleaning and repairs (the *saison* being now considerably lengthened).

I have never kept a diary. But sometimes, when things go crazy, I write them down in order to bring some order to the chaos and keep my head in one piece. That is what I did during that weekend in December 1994:

Wednesday 7th in London

A rush to get the documents for the Alois Klein Foundation ready. The handover contract between the State Company and me seems to be agreed (I haven't even seen it). Ing Mikeš, Director of the State Co., has said that he wants it ratified in court, by a judge, to protect himself against possible accusations of having accepted bribes from me. This seems entirely reasonable. We thought it would happen in the New Year. The longer the delay, the better for me ...

Yesterday Dr Hrdina suddenly sent a fax to say that the court hearing is set for next Tuesday, Dec. 12th ... Always great drama ...

Just to help things along, last night Jeremy Rosen phoned, ostensibly out of friendship, in reality to 'warn' me (again). Mr Kaszirer is totally convinced that Mikeš has bribed Hrdina to make sure I lose it. If we make a six-month rental agreement, is the latest version of this, I will never get it back because of tenancy protection laws ...

Thursday 8th

Fly to Prague. Věra Koubská meets me at the airport with hotel car, tears of joy and flowers. She is clearly delighted to see me again, so are the others when we get there, and I am instantly hooked again. In the car she says, 'Another half-hour and we'll be home' and it is the weirdest feeling.

The ostensible reason for this visit is two parties. On Friday evening there will be a reception in the Richmond for Karlovy Vary business people such as Mattoni and Becherovka, and two Deputy Ministers are expected. Hrdina and a colleague will come, Hrdina will bring the rental agreement (and a German translation, I hope. All Walter says when he phones is 'Don't sign anything!') But mainly, I think, he wants to come because he and his colleague particularly like the band which is coming from Prague and which plays old R.A. Dvorsky numbers. I have brought with me one of the albums which R.A. Dvorsky gave me as a ten-year-old when we were leaving. The second party is the staff Christmas and closing-down-for-the-winter party on Monday. In between should be a fairly quiet weekend: working with Hrdina on Saturday morning and, I hope, seeing Claire Wallace on Saturday afternoon to talk about getting research started on the shift from centrally planned to market economy. I brought some boxes of chocolates but forgot Mrs Pudová, which is upsetting. The trades union Chairman is delighted with the photographs. There are very few guests left, intensely curious about me and then they pluck up courage to come and ask me questions and finally to wish me 'strong nerves'. It is very understanding of them.

Friday 9th

What really buckled my knees yesterday was that the two women managers (Koubská and Ševčíková) had made themselves hair appointments for today and they made one for me too. I am one of the girls and, protesting, I get frog-marched to the hairdresser and come out with every single hair standing up, stiff with glue.

Joanna faxes a draft of an application to the NHS R and D programme she has been working on. I play with it a bit and phone her and we agree the final version on the phone. This is the mix that seems so bizarre.

Hrdina phones to say all the computers in his office have crashed because of cranes working on a building site next door. He has lost the rental agreement and will have to set it up again. He'll have to miss the party and come on Monday morning – we'll have about two hours before the staff party (at which Ing Mikeš has to make all sorts of announcements) to go through the handover contract and the rental agreement and agree them with Mikeš. Don't know if he will have had time to get it translated. Also he is afraid that the Minister (Mikeš's boss) may not agree to rental agreement because the Ministry wants these things finished and out of the way. Could Mr K. be right? No! I know Hrdina wants to hear this band! And we'll presumably be alone in the hotel all Monday evening. He will stay overnight because of the court hearing Tuesday, my flight back is also Tuesday, I offer to stay but am not needed. Am I paying for all these hours?

Getting ready for the reception, at the last minute I decide not to wear ear-rings. British understatement, and I don't want to look 'rich'. Yesterday I asked Věra Koubská whether people resent someone coming from the outside and getting the hotel. She thought not, but what some resent is that I am thought of as 'rich'. Takes me back to schooldays when children were simply categorised as 'rich' or 'poor' and 'rich' children had to take a 'poor' child home for lunch. Agony for everybody. Difference between rich and poor in fact much greater in the UK, but people don't quite talk in these categories. Yet.

At the reception I get captured by Dr Dolina who goes on and on about Bath VI and about a Swiss hotel group he knows who are 'interested'. He wants to put me in a car almost there and then and drive to Ragaz. I don't want to get caught up in playing politics with him. Certainly Hrdina should contact them, but I don't know what people mean when they say they are 'interested in some form of partnership'. Several sets of people have expressed interest of some sort, and we make positive and encouraging noises and then they don't go on to say what they mean. I'm missing something, I know I am. And according to Fiona [the solicitor setting up the Foundation] I am probably not free to pursue such things.

The band is wonderful, but nobody dances. I've shown the band-leader my Dvorsky album, and he has introduced this VIP lady and dedicated a number to me, but still nobody is dancing. It's not supposed to be that kind of a party. I almost can't bear to hear good music and not dance. Finally I decide to play the eccentric old lady and say I'm going to force the Minister to dance with me. Somebody brings him (both of them) over to introduce us, but they start a discussion about Thatcherite economics. They congratulate me on the restitution, saying not many people have succeeded. I explain that I tried to make professional contacts four years ago without success; the country seemed to be stuffed full with second-rate Western consultants. They agree – 'We don't need consultants, we need investors.' I try to say that the restitution has come too suddenly, in my case anyway, there needs to be a process of evolution and development. This rings no bells at all – there are only structures. Ownership is in this set of hands or that set of hands, the idea of a process means nothing. Then I simply ask Minister Česka to dance with me, and the poor chap has no choice. He is very polite about it, thanking me profusely for the honour after-wards. He can't be a day over thirty. It does get the ball rolling a bit, though, because now a few other people are dancing as well. And it has its uses, because afterwards the two Ministers say to each other that it would make sense to agree to the six-month lease, the poor doddery old thing does need time to muster some capital. What will Fiona say?

Saturday 10th

In the morning I'm free because Hrdina didn't come, and write a million Christmas cards. Some of the guests at the reception came from Prague and stayed overnight but by lunchtime they are gone. It's very spooky being in the hotel alone, with just a porter. Claire was picking up a friend at the airport and then coming here, but his plane was fog-bound and they are late. We go out to dinner – he is a survey-sociologist, head of the Paul Lazarfeld Foundation in Vienna and, though we argue a bit about the use of social science, he explains that in a country as small as Austria social scientists get used whether they like it or not.

He is adviser to a former Minister of Finance who knows a lot about tourism. He explains that hotels are hardly ever run by their owners. The choice is not keep or sell, but several variants in-between, in the form of management contracts. I think this is the link which I had intuitively thought was missing. I wonder if we can write it into the Assignment? All the lawyers will be cross with me and it will cost a lot but it sounds better. If the Foundation gets a regular, index-linked income? God, what a mess.

Sunday 11th

In the morning there is a phone call from a young woman who is director of another small hotel ('Bellevue') and who wants to put a proposition. We arrange to meet at two, and I ask her to bring someone who can interpret for us.

Go for a walk, have coffee in the old Café Elephant. At two Emilie Mahovska and her colleague Richard Janca arrive. Together with two other independent business people they have formed a company and would like to rent and manage the Richmond. Sounds exactly the sort of thing Christian was talking about last night, but I don't know how to assess their quality and strength. I refer them to Hrdina who by now has been approached by four or five such groups.

Then I do some work for the Institute on research methods for production managers; try to read a biography of Mattoni in Czech and am quite pleased that I can sort of get the gist; watch television (why only German channels?); and write this, to try and preserve my sanity.

Monday 12th

Hrdina arrives about 10.00, unshaven, having been up since four, poor chap. Ing Mikeš arrives and we have two hours to sort out two contracts, the handover contract and the lease.

On the lease, they discuss insurance, taxes, bookings for the year (what to do about bookings for after June?). In the middle of this we have to go down for the festive Christmas lunch, after which M. makes quite a long summing-up-the-year speech and announces pay rises, so people are quite happy. The guests include pensioners, which doesn't mean what I thought it meant but the communists who were pensioned off in 1990.

Then the party starts, and after a bit we go back to the board room to talk contracts. There has been a bit of a suggestion that this is men's stuff and the little lady might just as well stay at the party, but I go with them. On the handover contract, the issue is what is being handed over. The building and the land (there are three small areas Alois Klein didn't own, do I want to buy them, they would make a good car park?) I don't get the contents, do I want to buy them? We all agree that it would be a waste of money to get a proper valuation and have someone come in to count the spoons, better to agree some global sum. We did, but I've forgotten it. This doesn't matter for the next six months, but six months will pass quickly.

There are also some works of art, old pieces of furniture and pictures. Since they are movable, nobody knows where they really came from and I don't want to quibble. Who wants a picture of a dead pheasant anyway. But then I ask 'What about the chandeliers?' There are beautiful chandeliers, many of them, they more or less make the place. Ing M. misunderstands the question and looks at his list to check the price (there was a valuation of some kind in 1992). Their value is between £4000 and £5000 each. I say they must be part of the original building: the Germans may have taken stuff away, they are hardly likely to have turned up with truck-loads of chandeliers and installed them. Neither are the Russians. The two men look at each other for an astonished moment and then say 'she's right!' So that's about £200,000 worth of chandeliers which get written into the contract. Then the little lady does go back to the party.

One of the cooks is a smashing dancer, and I spend the afternoon alternating between dancing with the cook and the T.U. Chairman, and haggling upstairs about chandeliers. Bizarre is too weak a word. At 4.30 Ing M. has another appointment and Dr H. joins the party. At 6.30 we go out for a meal. We have a long agenda of things to work out, but don't solve any of them. I'd better make some kind of list, though.

— End of lease 30.6.95
— Insurance – get quotes, he will phone tomorrow. He thinks it should be insured for about $11m. To justify this we have to have a valuation. I will have to pay half the premium, say 100,000 Kc. And I will have to pay for the valuation.
— Building tax (?) M. will pay but I am responsible. 1st Jan is the date that counts.
— The hotel has a new telephone switchboard – I have to buy it.
— Bath VI?
— Notice to staff would have to be given on 31.3. if problem not solved by then. I was thinking of having a party on the weekend of

March 24th. But if we have to close and give people notice that would be unbearable.

— What to do about the various people who have expressed interest, some to me, some to Hrdina, and the many people who are offering advice about valuations, venture capital, joint ventures.

— Hrdina has for a long time suggested (or rather his office has) a way of dealing with the [Czech] tax question. His colleague has still not spelled this out in writing, and he says he is going to chop him into noodles and send him to me in a parcel.

Over coffee we discuss what a muddle there will be if I die in the next few weeks. He says 'It will be worse if I do'.

When we get back, the party is still going and everybody is a couple of degrees squiffier than before (but not as roaring drunk as they would be in England). The staff are in love with me, and I like it. One of the waitresses takes my hand and strokes it with tears in her eyes, saying 'You are so wonderful because you are ordinary'. Hm.

Tuesday 13th
Hrdina and Mikeš go off to court, I get driven to the airport. Věra Koubská apologises for not coming with me, she has a stomach upset from the 'red champagne' hooch of yesterday.

Wednesday 14th
Fax from Hrdina saying there were no problems, it was all over in half an hour. The state will cease to own it on 31.12.94; on 2.1.95 he will take possession of it in my name and hand it back to the state as tenant. The chandeliers are in the contract. The fax ends, 'Your problems start now'.

A double life

Pavel Hrdina was right, from then on it became complicated. In a letter to Walter about that visit I wrote, '. . . That was the last time it was fun. There is a photo in a magazine of me dancing with the Deputy Minister for Privatisation, and I think what I'm saying to him is you can have it back now, and what he is saying is no thank you . . .'

It was quite hard to adjust to the idea of this restitution. I had not expected it to happen – at this stage of my life I didn't need it, it was Luis who should have had the restitution, and anyway it was the wrong end of town. Karlsbad seen from this angle was not really home. Home was the very ordinary quarter where we had lived, where now there was a mini-cab company on the ground floor of the apartment house. And it wasn't owning a hotel that I had been homesick for all this time, it was the forest, the smell of candles burning by a shrine among the pine trees, my father's hushed voice saying, 'Look, Hasi, there's a squirrel!' But there it was: I was the owner of the Richmond Hotel, Karlovy Vary, and where no one had been interested in a social scientist who could really make a contribution to the country's industry, the heiress to the Richmond was something else. Doors were opened, newspapers wanted interviews, a dance tune was dedicated to me. I even featured in a scandal sheet, which is quite an accolade. With property, it seems, comes respect. It was a revelation.

For nearly three years I led a double life, running the Bayswater Institute in London and coping with the Richmond affair in the Czech Republic. Three guesses which one people found more interesting. No one any longer said 'How are you?' or 'How's work?' or 'What's happening in the hospital research?' All anyone ever asked was 'How's the hotel?' Even my clients in the hospital research. And even the Institute's trustees couldn't keep their minds on the job.

Selling it was not easy. There must have been at least fifty 'expressions of interest' from individuals or groups, or initiatives on our part, which in the end came to nothing. There was the posh London estate agent whose representative in Central Europe did nothing for eighteen months except have a freebie weekend in the hotel, during which he got so drunk that the staff were still talking about it a year later. There was a trip with a hotel consultant to visit potential buyers in France and another to Switzerland. There was the would-be buyer who rang from Spain suggesting time-share arrangements for the hotel; an hour later he rang again, saying that the future in medical services lay in plastic surgery – 'Put a plastic surgeon on your staff and you'll up your profits by £200 per week.' I thought about combining the two ideas – how about plastic surgery on a time-share basis? Every second week in May you can have another tuck.

From everything that I learned about him I became determined not to sell to Mr Kaszirer, even at the risk of being sued. His plans were described as a cross between Disneyland and Las Vegas, and in any case all his various activities in Karlovy Vary seemed to be running into difficulties and in the event they all came to nothing. Whether the paper I had signed constituted a legal contract was a bit unclear, and depended on which country one was thinking of. In Belgium, it seems, it did not, because it was not witnessed by a notary. In Britain it did not, because there was no 'consideration'. So far, in any case, he has not sued me. Meanwhile he continued to inject an element of melodrama, not to say farce, into my life.

At one point Mr K was coming to London and wanted to talk to me. The only time he could manage was an early morning, and he invited me to breakfast in one of the hotels on Park Lane. Now radiotherapy had left me with some internal damage. I had a degree of incontinence, and had to be up and about for about two hours before it was safe to leave the house. So meeting someone for breakfast at 7.30 meant being up before five. I had learned by then not to get into one of these encounters on my own, and John Marks offered to come with me. Mr K always travelled with an entourage, and this time it included his son-in-law the rabbi as well as the current girlfriend. John Marks is a committed Christian, and over the orange juice and the muesli he and the rabbi got into a learned discussion about original sin. It seems that, when Adam and Eve ate the forbidden fruit, from a Judaic point of view this was an act of sin. From the Christian point of view it put them into a state of sin, from which they then had to be redeemed, and that is very different. And I was sitting there thinking, for this I got up at half-past-four in the morning?

For a time there was an American manager looking after Mr Kaszirer's affairs in Karlovy Vary. He was seconded from the Donald Trump or-ganisation and was said to be very experienced in hotel matters, having run the Taj Mahal hotel in Atlantic City, with its four thousand gaming machines. During one visit I learned that he very much wanted to see me, to convince me how respectable their operation would be. I was reluctant, I was by then determined not to sell to them, but he insisted and I suggested he should come over to the Richmond for coffee the following day.

It was my last morning that trip. The evening before I had been out to supper with Věra Koubská and three of her colleagues. We didn't talk about business, we talked about our families, and clothes, and cooking. It was the season for apricot dumplings, a great Czech speciality. You wrap an apricot in a very thin layer of paste, preferably the kind that has some curd cheese in the mix, boil the dumpling, and then slather melted butter, sugar, and cin-namon over it. There is only a short period in the year when the apricots are right for it, and the Richmond's chef had a high reputation for his apricot dumplings. In spite of a mild, calorie-related, protest on my part, the unanimous decision was that this was to be my lunch the next day, before leaving.

When Mr Kaszirer's manager came the next morning, we sat in the sunshine on the terrace while he painted a lyrical picture of the kind of holiday the hotel would offer clients under his management: there would be plane-loads of American tourists coming direct to Karlovy Vary (they would get the airport enlarged), eager for the perfect holiday. This meant husband spending the day on the golf course; wife spending the day having her hair done, her face done, her nails done, her feet done, her body massaged. In the evening they would meet up for a relaxed dinner, and then go to the gaming tables – 'and it's not just gambling, we run tournaments, with big prizes'. It seemed to me that the aim was to make sure they didn't realise they were not at home.

He clearly saw his job as a cultural and humanitarian mission. He misunderstood people's objections and had run into a lot of, to him, incomprehensible difficulties in the town. But if I was really unhappy about the Richmond being used as a casino, he said, he would use it as the 'sweetener' for their other enterprises and keep the gambling in the Richmond to a minimum. What did that mean? Well – maybe only fifteen tables and fifty machines. (On the other hand, Donald Trump's first wife was Czech, perhaps the cultural issues are not so clear-cut. One could also say that the Czechs wanted the investment but didn't want the investors.)

I said that there had been other ways of holidaying – for instance, in these surroundings people used to go for walks. 'Oh, we'll create walkways,' he said. They used to listen to music. 'Oh, we'll fly in Pavarotti!'

For some minutes I had seen, out of the corner of my eye, Věra hovering in the doorway. She sized up the situation, came stomping out onto the terrace and announced firmly, 'Your apricot dumplings are getting cold. And the chef is getting upset!' That ended the negotiation, and perhaps deprived Pavarotti of an engagement. I enjoy the idea of having defeated Donald Trump with apricot dumplings. Fly in Pavarotti, indeed.

The idea of taking it on myself was tempting. Even sober-minded English colleagues were saying, 'You've spent all these years researching and advising, here is a chance to actually do something.' I was over sixty, I had one bout of cancer behind me, I had no hotel experience, I didn't speak the language, but I was really tempted. I even went so far as to explore the possibility of borrowing half a million pounds from the bank for necessary repairs. Amazingly, it would have been possible. I had a strong sense that the people from the bank were also caught up in a romantic fantasy. But the thought of taking on such a loan and the repayment schedule made cold sense prevail.

The beauty of the building led many people to fantasise. There were Russians interested in buying, Americans, a Russo-American, Germans, Austrians, a Czech who was very, very keen but turned out to have no money, an Egyptian group whose managing director very temptingly invited

me to Egypt, Israelis, Turks, Hungarians. There were people who approached Dr Hrdina to whom he did not respond, and people to whom he did
respond but who had no money. The number of times Ing Mikeš and his
staff had to show people round embarrassed me. Altogether, the patience
and tolerance shown by the staff, by Ing Mikeš, and indeed by the Ministry,
were remarkable. The six-month lease was extended for another six months,
and another, and another, as solutions evaded us. Every time I went over, I
thanked them for their patience and kept them up to date with what was
happening. Real friendships developed during this time, and I don't think
their trust ever waned, but it was hard for everybody. They knew that when I
said, 'I don't know,' it was because I really didn't, and although they didn't
like it they continued to trust me. For my part, I said in one meeting that,
having been homesick for over fifty years, I was now cured!

There was, in the way the place was run, a directness that one had
forgotten existed. When a young receptionist made a mistake, her manage-
ress said, 'I'd really like to put you over my knee and spank your bottom!' I
wondered how Western management gurus would fit that into their theories.

The Chairman of the trade union committee tried to be tough, but found
it difficult. A little ritual developed with him every time I visited: a few
minutes after I checked into my room there would be a knock on the door
and Mr Perutka would be standing there with a beautiful bunch of flowers. I
would thank him for them, and then he would say, 'So what's going to
happen, then?'

Alongside these heart-warming relationships there were also misconcep-
tions, which it took a long time to understand and clear up. On my side, I
had not really taken in the significance and function of the building called
Bath VI. It was a rather ugly building near the hotel, had not been part of
Luis's property and didn't interest me. But for forty years it had been
organisationally linked with the Richmond, because it was part of the
company. The Richmond's patients regularly used its facilities, which were
integral to what the Richmond offered, since the Richmond's medical
facilities were not self-contained. When there was a meeting with the
Richmond trade unions, staff representatives from Bath VI were automatically part of it. And Ing Mikeš had to get it privatised. Because of the
link with the Richmond I had priority rights to buy it, and was frequently
urged to do so, but I didn't have the capital and was in any case not
interested. There were endless plans and plots for dealing with it in which, I
realised later, I didn't show enough interest. There were also the three little
plots of land that had not belonged to Luis and which would make such a
good car park, and a couple of garages that also had not been his. By

showing no interest in any of these, I made it difficult for Ing Mikeš to finalise the privatisation. These items did not make sense except in connection with the Richmond – if I didn't buy them, who would?

On their side, it took a long time to convince them that someone coming from the West does not automatically have a lot of capital. They thought I would buy the inventory, get the central heating and wiring replaced, get eighteen new bathrooms built, purchase Bath VI or a share in it and the other items. In return, I would have their loyalty and hard work, and I am sure I would have had.

In the end the Richmond people did understand that it was not sensible for me to take it on, and in the end I understood about Bath VI and the realities of privatisation. It was quite an educational process.

One of the most difficult parts of the whole business for me was coping with all the offers of help that flooded in. It seemed to me that everyone I knew had a daughter-in-law who worked for a travel agent, a brother-in-law who was an estate agent, a sister-in-law who had once worked in a hotel. And pretty well everyone I knew was, of course, a consultant. Or, if they weren't, they wanted to be. 'I'm a very good listener,' said one, many times. 'What you need is an OD programme,' insisted another. I didn't ask in what language he was proposing to do this. The time and energy taken up in this way was at least as great as the time and energy taken up by the business of managing this transition itself.

Someone who did not urge consultancy on me was Johnny Hirsch, a friend from Karlsbad days, and he in fact turned out to be very helpful. At one point he came to Prague with me to interview potential buyers, none of whom, it turned out, had funds. Johnny wouldn't let me pay for his help, so we came to an agreement that I would pay him in potato soup. I make very good potato soup. Not long before he died he said he was putting his fees up, he wanted some ratatouille.

I told Johnny once about how I had missed meeting Pavel Hrdina at the airport in Prague. I was on my way back to London, he was flying in from somewhere, and we had arranged to meet in the coffee bar. We had sat in different coffee bars for two hours, each getting increasingly worried and cross. 'I can trump that,' said Johnny (he was a devoted bridge player). 'I once arranged to meet someone for breakfast. He had breakfast in the Savoy, and I had breakfast in the Ritz. And I can tell you, breakfast in the Ritz is better than breakfast in the Savoy.'

So I demanded to be taken to have breakfast at the Ritz. It was fun, and we started to meet for breakfast in the posh hotels of London about every six weeks and came to consider ourselves to be experts. The only time we disagreed was in the Dorchester, which I thought passed the marmalade test while he didn't.

The eventual buyer was a Czech, and everyone was glad about that. There were problems with a badly chosen manager he installed at the beginning, but after that things went well. The staff like him, and the business is doing well. Pavel Hrdina says that, of the various privatisation ventures he knows, this one has been the most successful. The sales contract includes a clause permitting me to have thirty bed-nights a year, and I have made some use of that, going for long weekends with several groups of friends and once with a group of Bayswater Institute colleagues. Currently we are considering whether to have our twentieth anniversary party there.

I had realised that it was going to be a worry, but I wanted to have some fun as well. During the heady early days I asked the staff to let me know a weekend when there were not many guest bookings, and set about inviting friends to a house-party. There were not as many places as I would have liked, but twenty-five people came. Walter's daughter Margaret came from New York, Hannah Boneh, a distant cousin I had only recently discovered, came from Tel Aviv, friends came from Vienna and Prague, several former Karlsbaders came from England, friends' children, colleagues and even two clients, a cardiologist and a midwife from a hospital I had worked in, came to Karlovy Vary.

The weekend was magical, and from their comments and letters afterwards I know they all felt it. Ing Mikeš enjoyed it and was impressed and asked afterwards if I was going to do it again, but I don't think you can repeat that sort of experience. I only regretted not having more places.

People who had not known each other mingled easily. There was no structured programme, and they would wander round the town sight-seeing, run into one or two of the others and join up for coffee, separate again, and meet up in the hotel for meals. Two of the vicar's children palled up with one of Sarah and Roger's, Marie Jahoda at eighty-nine came with her daughter Lotte Bailyn and charmed the socks off people, the cardiologist said, 'If anyone has a heart attack, I'm a plumber.' Some went to Marienbad, some took the little funicular railway up the mountain, most tried the waters. Margot Garrett had herself photographed on the steps of their former house, Johnny Hirsch took his goggle-eyed daughter round his old haunts.

The only arranged bit of programme was a party on the Saturday evening, and for that I had wanted to invite some of the staff and their wives and husbands. Immediately there had been anxiety about which ones, and I said we would draw lots. We had a meeting at which we solemnly put all the staff's names on pieces of paper and I drew out twenty-five. '*Ah, demo-kratická*,' said the trade union Chairman with awe.

The staff, in turn, had a surprise present for me. There was a local dancing school, and they had arranged for some of the pupils to do demonstration dances. They had also arranged for the dancing teacher to make me start the dancing off and, of course, I danced the whole evening – with friends, with staff, with everybody.

The next morning I started to limp. Being completely out of condition I had damaged a knee, and it took months to come right. For a long time I went down stairs sideways like a crab, overweight old ladies shouldn't dance the polka. But it was worth it. For the only time in my life I had managed to bring the different parts of my life together – old friends from Karlsbad, young friends from the street where I live now, colleagues, clients, a trustee of the Institute, staff from the Richmond, even two real relatives. And they all got on together as if there was no problem in having disparate aspects. I remember thinking this is as near as I am likely to get to being happy, I could die now.

Well, I didn't die and it is not the end of the story, but this seems quite a good place to stop. Just one more thing:

About the time the hotel was eventually sold, a new spring was discovered near the entrance. It was on a piece of meadowland belonging to the town, not on Richmond land. But the new owners wanted to make a big feature of it and have a structure built round it, presumably to draw visitors to that end of town. They approached me to ask for a contribution to the cost and said they would like to call it after my uncle – 'Just think, it will stand between Beethoven and Goethe!' Then, a few months later, I was invited to the formal opening. A white ribbon was cut, flowers were presented, the new director made a speech, I made a speech, the mayor made a speech, a priest made a speech and blessed the water. A film star posed (the opening had been timed to coincide with the Karlovy Vary film festival), television cameras whirred, a brass band played, and I tried not to think about Clochemerle.

So there it is now, a little white pavilion with Luis's name on it, sheltering a small spring of water that is supposed to be good for male potency, although its small trickle is not a good advertisement. Standing, as the new director had said, between the statues of Beethoven and Goethe.

And the Bayswater Institute regularly has Czech participants on its Working Conference, funded by the Alois Klein Foundation.

Appendix 1

From a box of letters

I had in mind to translate some of the letters and postcards from the relatives who stayed behind when we came to England, my father's in Prague and my mother's in Pilsen. The early letters still came direct to us in England, the later ones came via M and Mme Devaud in Switzerland once war had started. However, these are letters from people who know the recipients and are known so well that they allude to things that a different reader cannot know about. I, too, don't always understand the allusions. They also often disguise the names of people and addresses, to defeat the censor; there would have to be a running commentary with the translation. My grandmother's letters are so coded, and so peppered with abbreviations and nicknames, that I often don't understand what she is saying. Some of the code I have managed to decipher. When they say they have visited Beate, it means that they have been to a consulate, either the American or the English; for some reason one didn't say 'British' at that time. When they ask after the Devauds' brothers and sisters, they mean us. So here, instead, is some of the general gist and flavour:

The letters are on tissue-thin airmail paper, in tiny handwriting so that a lot can be crammed onto one sheet (airmail was expensive), with several people contributing to each one. Along with the exchange of ordinary news between people who are used to being in touch with each other almost daily, most of the relatives' early correspondence is about their efforts to get out, and it swings between optimism and despair. The smallest piece of news that brings encouragement leads to wild happiness, sometimes they seem to be almost packing to leave, and then there is another disappointment. The position about affidavits to America I have described – Beate tells somebody that according to the official criteria they would have to wait eight years, and somebody else 'many years'. For England you need a permit, there is much talk of powers of attorney, references, guarantees, would it help if this or that person provided these? What can Fanni do at this end to help?

The most consistently unhappy situation is that of Richard and his wife and little Stefan, appearing in the letters like a regular chorus – everything seems to go wrong for them, every effort meets with defeat, Richard is looking so thin and worried.

There is also much reporting of what is happening with other people, their families, their health, the news they have from those who have left, their efforts to get out. But where to? There is talk of Belgrade, of Chile, of Bolivia, Bombay ... Mrs L. and her daughter are going to Shanghai, they already have the boat tickets ... The Quakers help, no one else does.

The relatives are very hungry for news from us. What is everyday living in England like, they can't imagine it? And, of course, there is talk of their immediate situation. Money is running out, will their pensions be valid? Complicated arrangements with Pepp and Luis are suggested. My father's relatives – Fritz and Ida, Marie, Friedl and his wife (also called Ida but generally referred to as Gois) are all living together. Only Viktor lives separately, he walks for hours every day for exercise and comes to eat with them. They have moved into different lodgings (twice, I think). The latest lodgings are 'where it's steep, ten minutes from beautiful trees'. They are unfurnished, various friends will lend furniture, it is very crowded. There are 'Kosttage', days when you arrange to eat with somebody else. But luckily the heating is good and the spirit cooking stove Luis got for them works well. It is very cold, clothes left behind by people who have left and couldn't take everything with them are being made over. And 'did the moths get into your winter coat?'

Nevertheless, humour often breaks through. My grandmother confesses to a long-held ambition to be the pastry cook in Luis's hotel. She says she could demonstrate her skills even better now, making delicious pastries without butter or sugar or eggs. Viktor, the farmer, who is not used to having time on his hands, writes a sketch about the negotiations at the gate of heaven, at a far-distant future date of 1955, when his brothers and sisters and their wives and husbands try to persuade St. Peter, who has the broadest Egerländer accent, to let them in. It allows him to let his hair down and dissect their various characters and foibles, and is very funny. One of them doesn't even make it as far as the gate. He laughs about Marie, who has apparently fallen in love with someone, the silly old hen. To his divorced wife in Austria he writes about the farm, what needs doing and what he plans for it. To us he writes about how good she is.

Fritz, the doctor, also wishes he could work. He doctors among relations and friends, and also for us. Luis and Fanni and my parents write to him about their symptoms and he writes back with advice. My mother has

problems with her teeth. Her sister Trude writes, 'That dentist from Marienbad is good, but whatever you do don't play bridge with him before your
treatment, you will lose all confidence in him.'

Every now and then they interrupt and refer to me, and these references
are always proud and loving, and often humorous. They enjoy my letters,
though Ida says my handwriting is even messier than it was at home. She
tells me to keep careful count of how many lunches she owes me. Fritz
teases me, and sometimes calls me Lysol; he cites me, when very small,
saying 'I shan't get married, I don't like all the arguing'; he apologises to my
mother, 'Don't be angry, but I am having a lot of success with her essay
about her mother's hands.' Marie, who is mainly preoccupied with whether
post has arrived from her son Pepi in America, says, 'If you stand her in
front of Mont Blanc she'll find her way.' Even Viktor writes, 'The only thing
in all this mess that is dear and lovely and gives any pleasure is Lisl;
everything else is rubbish.'

This is quite surprising because we hadn't had much contact, and there is
a clue in it to something else: I, and the fact that I was safe, seemed to
symbolise for this older generation that there was a future. All my life I have
been warmed and sustained by the knowledge of all this love, yet at the same
time it brought with it an awful burden of responsibility.

My cousin Peter, on the other hand, is the same age as me and is not
sentimental. At eleven he ticks me off for not writing enough, and adds, 'But
I'm writing to you for your birthday just to show that I am not like you.' At
around twelve or thirteen, some letters are embellished with little drawings
that make plays on words. At fourteen he is no longer in school but is
working as a mechanic in a workshop. And his need is for a real, concrete
future, not the symbol of one. In 1942 my grandmother writes that a letter of
mine reduced him to tears. I must have written about school because she
says that they were not tears of longing, but rather tears of envy: I will
probably be able to go to university, and he won't. And sure enough, further
down the page he himself writes, 'I envy you dreadfully'; nevertheless adding
a lot of kisses to the message.

Once the war has started the letters continue via Switzerland, but the
anxious discussions of ways to escape fall away because now it is hopeless.
Luis and Fanni worry that the relatives back home will hear about air raids
and be worried for us. The stamps change from President Masaryk's face to
Hitler's.

Gradually the relatives resort more to postcards, because censorship of
letters creates long delays. And because the destination is Switzerland they

are able to send occasional formal postcards even after they are deported to Terezín; once they are in Terezín, only postcards are allowed.

The last postcard from Switzerland is dated 6.4.44. Written by Helène and Marcel Devaud themselves, it says that they have heard from Ida, her husband, and Viktor. Irma's mother (my grandmother) has visited them, they are well and send their love.

Appendix 2

Grandfather Wilhelm's notebook

This is the family tree from grandfather Wilhelm's notebook, the result of his researches. There are in fact two notebooks, one longer than the other. He must have started on the task twice. The spelling of names varies a little and it is clear that, in the longer of the notebooks that brings the family tree up to date, he made occasional efforts to save energy. Double letters, as in Hermann or Fanni, are sometimes reduced to one, the long German i, which is written ie as in Marie, is sometimes shortened, and I have the impression that towards the end of this long effort he was getting tired. I give here the longer notebook, supplementing it only where there is some extra information in the shorter one:

My paternal great-grandparents:
Veit or Feischl Klein, born Udritsch 1746, died 8.10.1811
Sara Klein, nee Maier born B.Neustadt 1748, died 1813
Their children:
1. Abraham Klein in Udritsch 1781 – 14.7.1844
    his wife Franziska, nee Weiss
2. Isaak Klein in Udritsch 1784 – 4.11.1854
    his wife Rachel, nee Weisman
3. Jakob Klein in Udritsch 1786 – 11.6.1851
    his wife Theresia, nee Simon-Abeles Waltsch ([died] aged 77)
4. Rachel Klein married Kandler 1764 – 1.1.1852
5. Blümele Klein married Hirschl in Kisch
Family of Abraham and Franziska Klein
These were childless and adopted their nephew Moses Hirsch, born in Kisch.

Family of Isak and Rachel Klein, née Weisman
Children: David[26]
Lazar (Ludwig)[27]
Jittl, Judita, married Benj. Klein
Veronika, married Markus Kandler
Libele
Blümele, married David Richter
Josef Klein, railway official.
The above named David and Lazar were actually stepsons of Isaak Klein and children of Isaak Klein and children of Rachel Klein's first husband, who was also called Klein and who was a cousin of Isaak. He was robbed and murdered in Flöhau, where he was staying overnight in an inn; this may have happened on 2.10.1800.

Family of my grandparents:
Jakob and Therese Klein, in Udritsch
1. Rebeka or Elke, married Kohn Krasch, born 10.2.1801
2. Moses Klein born in [?house no.] 56, 15.4.1805 – [? died in no.] 33, 20.4.1880
3. David Klein, born in [?house no.] 19, 27.7.1807
4. Benjamin Klein [?house no.] 19, 29.2.1809
5. Veit or Feischl Klein [?house no.] 19, 10.4.1812 – 1853
6. Wolf Klein [?house no.] 60, 4.2.1817

Family of Rachel Klein, married Kandler, and of Veit Kandler in Udritsch
Children:
1. Markus Kandler
2. Feile Kandler
3. Marjem Kandler died 22.2.1865

---

[26] The first-named David emigrated to America in the year 1845–46 with the youngest sister of my deceased mother, called Hanni.
[27] The second, Lazar/Ludwig, studied about 80 years ago at the politechnik in Prague under the Director, Professor von Gerstner. Prof. v. Gerstner was invited at that time – 1833 – by the Russian government to build the first railway in Russia, Petersburg-Sarskoje Selo. Gerstner accepted the invitation and travelled with his best pupil, that was David [sic. But isn't this a mistake, wasn't it Ludwig?] to Russia, where they stayed for three years until the completion of the railway.
Shortly afterwards Gerstner was invited to America to build railways. He travelled with his wife and again with his pupil Ludwig Klein to America, where he devoted himself to building railways.
After three years in America, Prof. Gerstner became ill and died there. On his deathbed he begged his pupil not to abandon his wife but to accompany her back to Europe. L.K. not only kept his word, but later married the widow.
L.K. went on to build railways in various German lands, especially Würtemberg, and was appointed senior surveyor/architect to the Würtemberg court.

Family of Blümele, married Hirsch, and of Samuel or Schmule Hirsch:
Moses Hirsch, whose wife Nettl nee Weiss
Benjamin Feischl, whose wife Bine nee Beck

The shorter notebook ends here. The longer one continues:

Rachel, married A. Hirsch, Petersburg
Libele, married Rafael Beck, Königs[illegible]
Frummet, married Hermann in Kisch
Family Moses Hirsch
Fani, married Weinfeld, 4.9.[1]840
Samuel born 1.7.[1]842
Mina, married Stein 23.6.[1]844
Adolf born 6.8.[1]846
Mali 1.10 [1]850
Family of Libele Beck & Rafael Beck
Bine, married Feischl Hirsch
Babeth, married Dr Neuberg
Fani, married Dr Löbl, Podersam
Family of Elke, married Kohn, father's sister, and of Jachim Kohn, Krasch
Children:
Sara, married Bergmann, Nelschetin [?]
Springl, who emigrated to America
Wolf Leb Kohn, whose son Jac. Kohn is here
Family of my parents, Moses Klein, born 15.4.1805 and Amalie Klein, daughter of Salamon and Sara Löbl. died 27 June 1890
Children: Sofie born 14.2.1835
Fani born 20.3.1837
Katti born 4.6.1839
Wilhelm born 9.11.1841
Johanna born 20.7.1844
Mina born 6.1.1847
Charlotte born 15.9.1849
Elisabeth born 9.7.1853

Good heavens, grandfather was a boy with seven sisters! And the names are suddenly less Jewish and more Germanic. And Elisabeth is later referred to as Lisel.

Family of my uncle Benjamin and Jittl Klein, Udritsch
Filip born 3. 3.1842
Fani   "   1. 9.1843
Adolf   "   7. 4.1845
Klara   "   21.10.1846
Lisel   "   2. 5.1849
Siegfried " 11.12.1849 [is this a mistake?]
Family of my uncle Wolf and aunt [illegible] Klein, née Hermann
Children:
Eduard born 5.12.1849
Karoline   "   8. 4.1852
Jacob   "   21.11.1853
Theresia   "   6. 7.1864
The son Eduard emigrated in 1865 to America.
The son Jacob was doctor in Miess and died there after not many years.
Family of my sister Sofi born 14.2.1835, died 1884
Sussman Kohorn
Sofi
Children:
1) Salamon
4) Sigmund
2) Resi (married Lowinsohn)
3) Ignaz
6) Ida, married
5) Josef
7) Anna, married
8) Heinrich
Family of my sister Fani
Joachim and Fani Hirsch, Passnau
 . . .

These last two sections are clearly unfinished. He must have put the children of Sussman and Sofi Kohorn in the wrong order, but with pen and ink this was difficult to change. The numbers are added afterwards in pencil.

Family of my sister Katti
Josef and Katti Löwenbach
Children: Rosa
Julius

Sigfrid
Sigmund
Wilhelm
Milian
Hermine

Family of Wilhelm and Karoline Klein née Kohn
born 9.11.1841   born May 1845
[aunt Fanni's shaky   died 31 May 1885
handwriting adds:
died 29.6.1918]
Children:

born in Steeben	Josef born 5 Aug 1866 Sigfrid " 8 Dec 1867 Viktor " 10 July 1869 Alois " 19 April 1871
born in Udritsch	Fani " 22 March 1873 Scheni [Jenny] " 23 Febr 1875 Ludwig " 2 Febr 1877 Emil " 26 Dec 1878 Mari " 18 Oct 1880 Ida " 1 Nov 1882

Family of my sister Mina
Markus & Mina Goldman
Children: Emil
Scheni [Jenny]
Ema
Martha
Sigfrid
Ernst
Hellen

Family of my sister Lisel
Josef & Lisel Goldman
Fani
Julius
Berta
Ida
Hedwig
Theres
Sofie
Lina

Family of my sister Lotti
Hermann & Lotti Zentner
Schenni
Ernst
Hermine
Paul

So these, the last three groups, are my father's cousins. The names explain a lot of the people who were around when I was small. Some married each other, which makes it more complicated. Some of them and their descendants also emigrated, to Sweden and England. In London I knew Rosa Goldmann, the widow of Julius, and Hermine Moser (née Zentner).

My grandmother on my father's side
Theresia, daughter of Simon Abeles, [from] Walsch, married Jacob Klein
Children as shown above
Her siblings:
Gutman Abeles from Walsch
Sara Abeles, married Löbl, Luck
Family of Gutman A.
David A. died March 1911, aged 103 years
Rubin A.
Resel married Hermann Libiz
Geitsche married Friedlander, Luck
The names of my great-grandparents on my mother's side are not known to me.
Their family:
Maier Löbl
Salamon Löbl, Luditz. My grandfather
Emanuel Löbl, Duppau...Podersam
Family of Salamon Löbl and wife Sara Löbl née Simon Abeles, [from] Walsch
Children:
1. Elke, married Gutman Leiner
2. Josef, emigrated to America
3. Nachma
4. Amalia (Malke), married Moses Klein
5. Theresia Esther married Mendl Goldman
6. Hanni 1846 & 1847 to America

7. Abraham to America
8. Wolf drowned in the Luditz stream
Family of my great-uncle Maier Löbl
...

Family of my great-uncle Emanuel Löbl
Children:
David Löbl
Doctor Löbl, Podersam
Doctor Löbl, Michel[illegible]
Family of my aunt Elke, married Lerner
Gutman Lerner, Elke Lerner
Children:
Maier Lerner 1854 to America
Mansche
Jachim [?] America
David Saaz
Family of my uncle Josef Löbl
Daughter to America
Family of my mother Amalie Klein
See above
Family of my aunt Esterl, married Goldmann
Mendl Goldmann, Esterl Goldmann
Children: Wilhelm
Marcus born 1842
Josef

Grandfather then goes on to do the same for his wife's family:

Parents, grandparents and relatives of the late Karoline Klein, née Kohn
Grandfather on her father's side
Nathan Kohn, Steeben
Children:
1. Leb Kohn, Kinelleschen
2. Simon Kohn, Tuep[pelsgruen, nr. Karlsbad
3. Samuel Kohn, New Orleans
4. Seligmann Kohn
5. Lea Kohn, married [?New Orleans]
6. Joachim Kohn, Paris

7. Fani Kohn, married [a different handwriting has added 'New Orleans']
8. Herman Kohn, Steeben born 6 June 1805
9. Josef Kohn, Steeben

Family of Leb Kohn, Kinelleschen

Children: Isak
Sara
Jacob
Gabriel
Adam
Israel
Abraham
Eva

Family of Simon Kohn

Children: Eva Beneikt [Benedikt?}
Karl Kohn
Sofie, married Kohn
Bertha Schwalb
Hanni Glaser
Emil Kohn
Jetti Kantor
Nathan Kohn

Family of Samuel Kohn

. . .

. . .

Family of Seligmann Kohn

Children: Emma
Eva Hoffer
Fanni
Eduard Kohn
Wilhelm Kohn

Family of Lea Kohn

Fani
Leopold
Fanni
Resi
Carolin
Mari
Juli

Family of Joachim Kohn, Paris
Arthur Kohn
Gustav Kohn
Amalia, married Heine
Family of Fanni, nee Kohn
Simon
Natan
Hanni
Liebert
Sibille
Family of Josef and wife Sofie Kohn
Emilie
Family of Herman Kohn and wife Mari Kohn née Stein
Natan
Resi, married Lauscher
Fanni, married Fischer
Sigmund
Karoline, married Klein
Rudolf
Natan went to America in 1851 and was accompanied as far as Hamburg on foot by the Steebner grandfather
Sigmund [went to America] in 1856
Rudolf [went to America] in 1865
Sigmund studied for several years at the University of Philadelphia. At the outbreak of the war to abolish slavery he volunteered for the army of the Northern states, but unfortunately lost his life in the second year of the war in one of the battles, at the age of twenty-one years.
Family of Resi
Joachim Lauscher, Resi Lauscher
Josef
Moritz
Bertha
Anna
Karl
Siegfried
Fani
Ida
Julius

Parents, grandparents and relatives of the late mother Karoline Klein née Kohn, on her mother's side

Grandparents

Moritz or Mosche Stein, Schönhof

Resi Stein, née ?

Their children:

Josef Stein

Sara, married Glaser, Dunkelsberg

Fani, married Kohn, Deutsch Rust

Amalie, married Landsman, Prague

Lisi, married Löbl, Litschkau

(grandmother) Marie, married Kohn, Steeben [someone has pencilled in 1812-1877]

Joachim Stein in Schönhof was the brother of the above Mosche Stein, therefore uncle of the Steebner grandmother.

His children:

Natan Stein

Leopold Stein

Mari Stein [someone has pencilled in 1812-1877. One of these notes must be a mistake, probably because two cousins had the same name]

Appendix 3

Extract from *My Life in Industry* by George Clift

On the 17th March 1900, when I was a young fatherless lad of thirteen, I was taken by my mother to see the C.I. Volunteers off to the South African war. Going through Long Lane on our return my mother saw a notice in the window of a small shop advertising 'BOY WANTED'. Much against my will, I was taken in to apply for the job and was interviewed by Mr G.T. When I pointed out to him that I was too small to reach the hand-press he showed me, he replied that if I stood on a box I would be able to manage very well. The outcome of this interview was that I started work there and then. I soon discovered that the staff of the firm consisted of the two governors, Mr E.L. and Mr G.T., their young brother Mr H.A. Boutle, George Hodson – 'Bill', George Gardener – 'Bill', C. Ellery – driver. The reason the two Georges were nicknamed 'Bill' was to avoid confusion with Mr G.T ...

On Summer evenings the two Bills and myself hired bicycles for 3d an hour and went careering up and down Southwark Street. This pastime gave us the feeling of great importance; later we bought our own bikes. I gave the princely sum of three pence for mine and, although I paid so little, it was quite a presentable machine. In 1901, on the day of King Edward's coronation, we all cycled to Keston Ponds. We were returning home that night when, whilst speeding down Masons Hill, Bromley, my chain came off, throwing me into a very prickly hedge and that was the end of my three-penny bike.

In preparation for the coronation of King Edward VII we undertook the manufacture of street ornaments. These were tinplate Crowns painted gold and fitted to the top of poles in the West End of London ...

By 1904 we had outgrown our premises and the business was moved to Weston Street. It was there that we installed our first power press and power driven seaming machines. With these machines available we were able to develop our range of bottles from 1-pint to 2-gallons and our levers from

1/2-pint to 9 1/4″ × 4″. These tins were double seamed and fully soldered. For the first time, we engaged women to do soldering. The first two women thus employed were Mrs McNally and Mrs Thompson. By the way, they both came to us from Riley Road ... It is interesting to remember that our first two power machine operators were sisters named Hall. They were shortly joined by the two Whitnell sisters.... .

Shortly after our move to Weston Street, the late Mr Oliver joined the Firm. Mr Oliver was quite the old time gentleman with his top hat, morning coat and striped trousers. It was Mr Oliver who first introduced the idea of mass production to the Company. As far back as 1908 he argued that if orders of sufficient size could be obtained production could be carried out at speeds and prices far below anything that had been accomplished to date. With this end in view, he went into consultation with Jenson & Nicholson and obtained their co-operation. They regrouped their orders to enable us to pass large batches of individual sizes through the shop at a time. I fear that the high-speed production that we know today was still far off when Mr Oliver died in 1912.

Now and again the Company purchased extra machinery to meet the increased demands for our products. We had three hand presses, two guillotines, a hand swage, a set of circular cutters and a collection of hand tools, such as beak irons and grooving mandrels. Our soldering irons, which were heated in coke stoves, were fitted with 2 1/2-lb copper bits. We cut these bits from round bars and forged them ourselves. The solder was bought in 1/2-cwt bags and I used to be sent across London Bridge to collect it, carrying it back to the Firm on my shoulder and finding it getting heavier with every step. The delivery of our first piercing die created quite a stir. Mr E.L. and Mr G.T., full of excitement, set it between them. After positioning the base, Mr G.T. told Mr E.L to pull the handle home, quite forgetting that his thumb was still between the tools. This was one of the many occasions that the air turned blue ...

With the passing years the business continued to expand in volume and range of cans produced. We bought the tools to manufacture the complete range of ink tins from one to twenty-eight pounds; these we supplied to Ault & Wiborg and Winstons. Vanner & Prest were buyers of large numbers of hand-made pint bottles, the tops of which had to be cut individually on circular cutters, formed up on a funnel stake and curled and sized with a hand-press tool. With the exception of 6″, slip cover lids were hand-made. The 6″ were formed up in a hand-press. Another example of our widening range of products was the manufacture of copper incubator tanks. We were also making a few of the smaller paint tins.

Two or three deliveries each day by our horse-drawn van were all that were necessary to clear the work. Our premises were situated below a private residence and the stable was at the back. I had the job of holding the horse's tail down while he was led through the passage on his way to and from the stable ...

Like the Company, I was lucky enough to continue to make progress, and I was later promoted to Head Foreman. As such, I held the keys of the Factory, besides which my address was registered at the Police Station so that the Police could call me in case of fire or burglary. Once, when the night was freezing, the Police called for me at 2.00 a.m. and asked me to go to the Factory. I quickly dressed and made my way to the Factory. There I found a Policeman looking through the peep-hole in the main gate. He said that there were lights on in the Factory. A little excited, I looked through the hole and saw the moonlight reflecting on a pile of tinplate. I had another look at the Policeman and saw that he was drunk. You can guess I told him a few home truths before I stuck him down in the gateway and returned home to bed ...

The two senior Boutle brothers became interested in motoring around 1909. Mr G.T. returning home one night saw for the first time a motor cycle with a kind of bath-chair towed behind it. The owner was standing by cursing the machine which had broken down. Mr G.T. was so interested in the machine that he made an offer for it which the disgruntled owner was pleased to accept, paid the money and pushed it home. When he had repaired the fault he took his best girl for a ride around the block. Returning to his starting point he looked round and found the chair empty. It afterwards transpired that she had been tipped out at the first corner that they had rounded.

George Hodson, now a widower, surprised us all in 1916 by marrying Miss Morris from the office ...

In the 1914–1918 war air-raids were few, but during one raid a dud ack-ack shell came through the roof and landed on the floor. One of the workers, believing it to be a bomb, picked it up and took it into the office. Much to the consternation of Mr G.T., he put it into the safe....

Mr G. Hodson designed the Matchless Motor Cycle tank soon after the 1914–18 war, and he organised a department to manufacture them. We were always highly complimented by Collier Brothers on the quality of this tank. Of all the thousands we produced we never had a faulty one returned to us, although we repaired hundreds of faulty tanks which had been made by our competitors.

The war left us with large stocks of 5 1/8″ blanks which had been cut from biscuit tin tops, and in order to dispose of them, a whistling kettle was designed and marketed by Woolworths for sixpence ...

In 1922 the German mark collapsed in relation to the pound sterling. Mr E.L. and Mr G.T. bought thousands of these marks on the supposition that they would recover their value. When it became obvious that they were fast becoming valueless outside Germany, Mr G.T. packed all the marks into suitcases, rushed to Germany with them and bought a collection of German machines from Karges Hamer & Schuler. These included groovers, flangers, double seamers, and a very fine six throw power press which is still in operation today. ...

In 1928, T.F. Boutle & Company became a Limited Company and the following year the family business was merged with The Metal Box & Printing Industries ...

The advent of World War II in 1939 again created an upheaval in our regular routine. We very quickly got going on an anti-tank mine. This was really a shortened form of paint can with a detonator fitted in the bottom. We made this in two diameters, first of all 6″ and later 8″. Altogether we made about six million of these during the war. We also made approximately eighty-two thousand No.77 grenades a week for several years. These two main contracts were supplemented by grease tins, camouflage paint tins, smoke generators and cylinders for containing flares. Several of these contracts necessitated us having C.I.A. Inspectors on our premises. The less said about these people the better for all concerned ...

Thinking back to the names of our employees during the first World War and earlier, I find it noticeable how many of their children and grandchildren we still have in our employ. This must tell the story of good employers and local employees. Take 1919 for instance, we had Snells, Witnels, Halls, Ervins, Pocknells, Laws, Crisps, Windmills and Northwoods working for us. All of these names are still on our books and the people are direct descendants of our old work people. Many people whose names have changed through marriage can also be traced.